Media Policy for the 21st Century in the United States and Western Europe

THE HAMPTON PRESS COMMUNICATION SERIES
New Media: Policy and Social Research Issues
Ron Rice, supervisory editor

Media Policy for the 21st Century in the United States and Western Europe

Yaron Katz

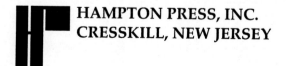

HAMPTON PRESS, INC.
CRESSKILL, NEW JERSEY

Printed in the United States of America

Library of Congress Cataloging-in-Publication Data

Katz, Yaron.
    Media policy for the 21st century in the United States and Western
    Europe / Yaron Katz.
        p. cm. -- (The Hampton Press Communication Series)
    Includes bibliographical references and index.
    ISBN 1-57273-518-X -- ISBN 1-57273-519-8
        1. Mass media policy. 2. Globalization. 3. Mass media and technology.
    4. Local mass media. I. Title: Media policy for the twenty-first century in the
    United States and Western Europe. II. Title. III. Series

    P95.8.K38 2004
    302.23--dc22
                                                            2004040649

Hampton Press, Inc.
23 Broadway
Cresskill, NJ 07626

Contents

02-16-06um

List of Tables

About the Author

Yaron Katz has been involved in media policy for many years, both professionally and academically. His family founded Israel's first cable TV system in the late 1960s, and he successfully led the system in the late 1980s and early 1990s to the highest penetration rate worldwide. He was then an entrepreneur in establishing Israel's modern cable TV system and a leader in the establishment of satellite services in Israel. He has since been advising in various issues of media services and telecommunications projects, including to the Israeli government. He received his PhD in Mass Communications at Loughborough University in the United Kingdom in 1994. He is a lecturer in Communications at Bar-Ilan University in Israel and has been considered to be among its outstanding lecturers. He is the author of *It's A Seller's Market—Mass Media and the Marketing of Politicians* (1999). More details can be found at www.katzmediapolicy.com.

Introduction

The purpose of this book is simple: to analyze global changes in media policy. The research examines the changing course of media policy and markets by exploring the effects of global developments that have become dominant in the media and telecommunications sectors. The focus is on the social, cultural, technological, political, and commercial implications that dominate the new structure of media policy, as they have come into existence at the global level and make an impact on local policies in each country.

The book is divided into two parts. The first part examines the course of development of media policy—a process that has impacted the formation of global media policy. The second part examines the impact of global media policy on local policies and markets, a process that leads to a transformation from cultural perceptions to commercialization and globalization. The reader should be advised that the book provides a comprehensive discussion of media policy and at the same time chapters can be read independently of each other. Certain concepts, mainly in the introduction and summary of each chapter, are repeated to help the reader who might be skipping around.

Past, present, and future developments are the fundamental aspects of the process of global change and must be included in the foci of the analysis. The main argument made here is that the course of development of media policy and markets has been distinctive. It started with local policies influenced by public service perceptions in broadcasting. Although new media technologies of cable and satellite enabled the transmission of multiple channels, including locally originated and public, educational, governmental, and entertainment services, media policies have limited the development of cable systems by restricting their use to the relay of over-the-air broadcast channels. Since the late 20th century, following the adoption of new media policies and technologies, cross-national differences have diminished. The change of perspective in public broadcasting turned into a global process. Media policy has been transformed into a uniform structure with the impact of new media and telecommunications services felt simultaneously around the world. Media policies have become global, creating a new structure.

The impact of new technology and cultural processes can be seen in the change of perspective from the "old structure" to the "new structure" of broadcasting. In the old structure, each technology and medium had different goals and policy and the development of cultural perceptions dominated media policy and markets. In the new structure, all new media and telecommunications services are interlinked and an integrated policy is required to deal with technological and policy changes.

This structure dominates the current state of development, in which television systems and media markets are undergoing far-reaching and profound changes with the emergence of technological innovations and deregulatory policies. Globalization, deregulation, privatization, and convergence have been dominating all media systems, with the integration of broadcast, new media, and telecommunications policies.

The evolving construction of national broadcast and telecom systems demonstrates the trajectory of media policies. It leads to the conclusion that all countries are heading in the same direction of adopting the common goal of free market approach—according to which global policy objectives dominate the development of media systems and markets around the world.

In order to understand this framework, it is important to describe some major processes, which have established the foundations of media policy for the 21st century. These include the development of new media technologies, the impact of these innovations in the digital age, and the consequent triumph of globalization and technological advancement.

THE DEVELOPMENT OF NEW MEDIA TECHNOLOGIES

For several decades, national organizations with limited channel capacity dominated broadcasting markets. These channels transmitted off-air (terrestrial) services, and the development of other technologies was restricted. Initial changes in media policy were made possible with the advent of new media technologies of cable and satellite that provided multichannel services—the most important development in the television sector after the inception of television and the addition of color transmissions in the last century.

The development of new media technologies has gone through distinctive phases. The initial development was restricted for many years and then had substantial differences according to policies initiated at the local level in each country. It was the adoption of technological initiatives and the domination of free market perceptions that triggered policy and technological changes—leading to the current structure of global media policy.

The development of cable and satellite has gone through three separate periods, which approximate the three-stage course of media policy discussed in this book.

The First Period: CATV Systems

In the initial period, during the early years of broadcasting, cable systems had the sole goal of providing better reception of terrestrial television signals in their areas of operation, and commercial use of the satellite technology was restricted by national governments. The first cable systems were developed in the United States in the late 1940s and in the 1950s, as Community Antenna Television (CATV). They relayed established broadcasting transmissions, and their function was simply to bring television signals into communities where off-air reception was either impossible or very bad, due to mountains or distance. They had developed in similar form in Europe, although restrictions on the development of systems did not allow the expansion of cable beyond an insignificant role in serving small communities.

The development of cable and satellite was limited because of policies that favored and protected broadcast television. This caution can be explained as a reaction to the ability of the cable TV technology to provide multiple channels and the resulting fear, on the part of governments and public authorities, that their ability to regulate the airwaves would be undermined in case of local competition. In the 1950s and 1960s, cable systems began to import additional programming from neighboring regions or countries. But although additional signals could be retransmitted from neighboring areas or countries, the relatively limited structure of cable systems (limited number of channels) provided only better reception of the available off-air channels and did not change significantly until the 1970s.

The Second Period: Open-Skies Policy

The second period is that of cable and satellite. The development of the satellite industry began only after permission for commercial operation was given in the United States as part of an open-skies policy. In this period, low-powered communications satellites provided new broadcasting entrepreneurs with the means of access to an expanding cable market. The satellite industry operated first domestically in America and later in Europe, and about a decade after the first commercial operation it started to operate internationally.

This process also pertains to the development of cable systems, and it can be said that since then the development of cable and satellite has gone through basically the same course. Cable systems flourished in the United States in the 1970s and in Europe in the 1980s, with the advent of technological advancement and the start of commercial use of satellites.

The combination of cable and satellite transformed the broadcasting sector. In this structure, satellites provided additional programming to the services available through terrestrial broadcasting, that could be transmitted through cable systems. The programming produced and packaged for distribution solely to cable subscribers provided the basis for an independent and competitive television service. This state of cable and satellite dominated new media developments until the 1990s, when the initial cooperation between these technologies turned into direct competition.

The impact of the satellite technology was intensified by improvements in transmission and reception equipment, as a new generation of high-powered Direct Broadcast Satellites (DBS) started to provide unmediated reception by relatively small domestic dishes. This trend is demonstrated by the commercial advent of cable and satellite services, as the footprints of new satellites place the means for programming to provide services on a global scale. Satellite transmissions reach beyond national frontiers and create large international broadcasting markets, enabling domestic satellites to compete with the services offered by cable systems.

The Third Period: The Digital Age

In the third period of new media development, digitalization has prevailed. This phase applies to the current state of the cable and satellite technologies, in which multiple television channels and services are available and television programming is only one of the services on offer. The cable industry, which led the development of new media until the 1990s, is lagging behind the satellite industry in terms of digitalization and adoption of advanced services. This gives satellites technological and marketing advantages, although it can be assumed that all media and telecommunications services would operate in the same competitive environment with the completion of the transformation into digital technology.

This structure is going to dominate the 21st century. Competition is accelerating among all media and telecommunications services, and new media policy is catching on around the world. Future developments involve competition of all media and telecommunications services, including broadcast television, telephone companies, wireless communications, and the Internet. With digitalization leading the technological development of these services, competition of all delivery systems is underway in a growing number of countries—dominated by the integration of media and telecommunications policies.

THE DIGITAL REVOLUTION

Following the availability of multichannel services, media policy has changed considerably—from concentrating on public policy to free-market competition. The structure of global media policy, dominated by digital technology, is making an impact on media policies and markets and changing the way local societies use media and telecommunications services. The 21st century is dominated by competition of all media and telecommunications technologies and transformation into digital technology. Digital television is still in its infancy and its overall penetration level remains relatively low, but the market for digital television is expected to expand around the world and become the leading technology service.

The launch of digital transmissions is predicted to transform the media and telecommunications markets by providing increased channel capacity and improved picture and sound quality. Digital television brings two main advantages: the quantity of the services that can be delivered to the home and the technical quality of these services. The digital age is expected to create additional social changes, because in the new development of digital technology, television programming is only one of the many advanced services with interactive potential on offer.

The research in this book advocates that the digital revolution is not purely a technological and global phenomenon, and the role of regulators in establishing new media policy is critical. The seemingly boundless opportunities presented by the digital revolution would never have been realized had it not been for the influence of leading regulatory institutions—global agencies and national governments.

The history of new media shows that technological advancement and political decisions have influenced the general course of development of media policy and set the stage for the current period, which is directed by market forces. Today new media technologies are in direct competition, and digital services are becoming available in all formats. The global trend is based on a new order of market freedom that leads to a predominate position of global media policy.

The new digital age is breaking down further traditional barriers between media and telecommunications technologies and policies and creating a new global environment of competition. The broadcasting and telecommunications sectors are undergoing dramatic structural changes with the digitalization of cable, satellite, and terrestrial services and the launch of advanced telecommunications services.

In examining this course of change, it is undoubtedly clear that the impact of new technologies on the development of media policies has been dramatic. The change of American policy, involving deregulation, privatization, open skies, and convergence, made its impact on the development of other media markets, too. The process was similarly started in Europe and spread globally, creating a global course of change in media policy and markets that affects all advanced countries.

The global transition was gradual. The large number of channels that proliferated in the United States with the adoption of open-skies policy for cable and satellite in the early 1970's, and the technological advancement that followed the change of regulatory environment, have revolutionized media and broadcasting policies and services. The introduction of additional channels, mainly pay TV services, changed the basic approach of cable systems from a system that retransmits broadcasting channels to a sophisticated industry operating for profit. Pay TV services offered a second tier of programming and increased the extent of services available on cable systems. The additional charge added to the basic service allowed systems more available money and gave them more opportunities to transmit more programs and new channels.

In contrast, until the late 1980s this development was not duplicated in any European country because of a complex of issues that involved cultural values and technological advancement. These included regulatory issues, language barriers, market size, debate on advertising revenues from new services, and the overall cultural perception that identified new media development. With the growth of deregulation and commercial broadcasting in Europe, however, the development of cable and satellite distribution services has been inevitable.

The competition between terrestrial television and new technologies has been further intensified with the introduction of digital technology, which should become dominant in the new global media scene. At the start of the digital age, the broadcast industry is the most powerful media force in all national media markets. In Europe, public and commercial national broadcasters dominate, with low cable and satellite penetration. In America, although most of the population is connected to cable or satellite services, two-thirds of the eight hours of television the average household watches each day is dedicated to national networks. The advantages of broadcast networks put them in good position in the digital age, too, with large audiences and traditional habits, lots of money, great promotional abilities, libraries of programming, and decades of experience in attracting and keeping big audiences.

Terrestrial broadcasting companies are entering new fields, including digital television, interactive applications, and Internet operations. They have the ability to promote their interactive services and Web sites with unlimited amounts of advertising on television, benefiting from their high ratings and the persuasiveness of traditional television programming (where advertising comes not from the network's inventory of 30-seconds commercials, but within the programming itself). The strategy of broadcasters for the digital age is to combine Internet and broadband services. They are building broad portals to present a unified view of television programming and Internet sites, creating a medium full of endless entertainment and information, including search engines with interactive features such as news, e-mail, electronic commerce (e-commerce), and television commerce (t-commerce).[1]

In addition to broadcast television, the development of cable and satellite has been phenomenal around the world. The rapid growth of American cable, following deregulatory moves, proved an important catalyst in provoking new thinking regarding the regulatory regime that governed European cable. Following the example from across the Atlantic, during the 1980s satellite transmissions were permitted in Europe. This changed European cable services considerably, and led to both their increased commercialization and globalization. The addition of the technologies of cable and satellite meant changes in the role and status of public broadcasting, resulting in a multiplication of channels and the erosion of the relative autonomy of broadcasting policy.

The exploitation of cable and satellite left traditional public broadcasting organizations vulnerable and gave new media better opportunities in the marketplace by exposing broadcasting outlets to stiffer competition for audience and revenues. The development of new media in the United States and Europe has been an example for other countries to follow; it created a global trend of technological advancement and orientation of free market. This process demonstrates that the development of new media and advanced technologies is now guided by global media policy, despite local differences between countries.

Advanced systems have the capability to carry hundreds of television channels and offer interactive services, with the result that the traditional dominating position of terrestrial broadcasters is now under threat. The direct competition of new media services with traditional services of terrestrial broadcasting has been propelled by a combination of digital technologies. Although programming remains their core business, additional revenue will come from advanced services of interactive television, high-speed Internet access, and local telephone services. The new competitive structure means wide-ranging competition for the provision of all advanced services. Other competitors are telephone companies, which are permitted to supply multichannel television services and high-speed Internet access, and wireless communications providing mobile telephone and interactive and data services.

GLOBALIZATION AND TECHNOLOGICAL ADVANCEMENT

The growth of new technologies has been phenomenal, creating a global market and changing the rules under which local media markets operate. Globalization and technological advancement dominate the development of media policy in the new competitive environment.

The concept of globalization refers to the transmission of television signals across cultures and continents, involving commercial and transnational proliferation of information, entertainment, and advertising. In terms of technological advancement, it was the spread of satellite technology that granted television broadcasting the ability to become global, bypassing national governments and ignoring social, cultural, political, and geographical boundaries. In terms of public policy, globalization emerged because global policies and markets have become the leading forces that determine the phase of advancement at the local level in each country. The result of the transformation of media policy and markets is that regulatory institutions and cultural trends with global impact have become more important than local institutions and cultures in determining future developments in the media and telecommunications sectors.

Global competition is going to dominate the new structure of media policy for the 21st century. The nature of the services available through each delivery system would determine the nature of competition between media and telecommunications services, involving all media, new media, telecommunications, and information technologies. Following the course of development of media systems and the triumph of global media policy, local policies have become influenced by the combination of key developments of globalization and technological advancement—convergence, deregulation, privatization, commercialization, and digitalization. These factors constitute the main aspects of public policy in all countries in the new era of global media.

The global impact on local societies is a major focus of this research. Although there can be no argument that globalization offers a vast increase in the number of channels available, together with options for a wide range of advanced services provided on a global scale, the globalization of media policy and markets has made substantial impact on local media systems as well.

The new structure of media policy is being accomplished with the growing influence of digitalization, which can already be considered as the most significant factor in the development of media policy and markets at the global level in the foreseeable future. Deregulation policies provide the evidence that commercialization and privatization are the governing perceptions in the development of media policy and markets, leading to open-skies policy, multiservice and multichannel environment at the global level. Convergence of policy and technologies means that all media and telecommunications services are in competition, as technological advancement and policy changes provide the mechanism for a truly competitive structure dominated by global media policy.

Based on this development course, it can be said that new media and telecommunications developments in the United States and Europe have set the stage for global markets. Multichannel services and advanced services are growing rapidly with a relatively high penetration in a growing number of countries.

New technologies flourish in the United States. The country's major cable networks dominate the American market. There exist over 10,850 cable systems in America with 69 million subscribers. The existing resource services 97 percent of homes and businesses and is connected to over 68 percent of the residences. The United States enjoys the greatest number of cable channels. Most offer basic programming, some are pay-TV transmissions, and a few are pay-per-view services.

Advertising is another aspect of the commercial exploitation of the cable and satellite industries that demonstrates the changing attitudes toward new media technologies and services.

American cable offers a proliferating range of nationally distributed nonstop channels aimed at niche markets including: news, sports, youth, blacks, Hispanics, the religious, health, films, culture, business, music, children, family, and entertainment—in addition to a number of local, community, educational, ethnic, public access, and leased channels. It has been cable's capacity to substantially increase the number of available channels that has attracted the attention of the public and provided the basis for the active promotion and development of cable systems.[2]

In Europe there are different levels of cable developments. There are heavily cabled countries, such as Holland, Belgium, and Switzerland and a near-cabled country such as Germany, and in contrast countries with little cable, such as the United Kingdom to very little cable, such as France, Spain, and Italy, as well as other smaller countries. It was the advent of cable and satellite broadcasting that significantly changed European media policies and markets. The success of cable services from private operators and the arrival of direct broadcast satellite technology at affordable prices to both operators and customers have allowed niche programming to be beamed to new markets.

The satellite industry is also growing swiftly, and direct broadcast satellite is considered the leading digital platform today. The satellite industry has major advantages in the heightened competition. Firstly, digital satellite services are able to provide the most channels with the greatest ease to customers. They already offer hundreds of channels and plan to launch new satellites to provide even more channels. Secondly, digital satellite services provide better picture and sound quality and various interactive television and high-speed Internet access. Thirdly, the great number of channels available and the technological capabilities allow digital satellite services to offer local and narrowcasting channels, compete in larger markets, and approach various segments in different societies. And fourthly, the development of digital satellite technology is increasing the importance of competition between different delivery systems and leading to the establishment of global television networks and global transmissions provided simultaneously to different continents.

In Europe, pan-European services are available through direct broadcast satellites, with private operators providing multiple channel services. This technological innovation started in 1989 and offered for the first time direct competition to the services offered by cable systems. Digital satellite services started in late 1998 in Britain, offering 200 channels. The current situation for new media in Europe is that the spread of satellite services and the diffusion of cable systems are growing rapidly. This is because digital technologies increase the number of channels and services on offer while attracting a growing number of customers across the continent.[3]

Digital satellite services are exploding in the United States too, and have had a phenomenal growth experience since 1994. The new small satellite dish is the fastest growing consumer electronic product in American history, with an estimated number of 18 million subscribers. A new 18-inch digital satellite dish is sold every 12 seconds, with an average daily subscriber growth of 7,200 for the satellite industry.[4]

According to the FCC annual report on competition in the multichannel marketplace, satellite is growing nearly two and a half times the cable subscriber growth rate. In a survey conducted by the American Consumer Satisfaction Index (ACSI) in the first quarter of 2002, DirecTV reached 70 percent satisfaction and EchoStar 68 percent, while the numbers of cable were lower. Time Warner Cable received 61 percent, both Comcast and AT&T Broadband reached 56 percent, and Charter received 53 percent.[5]

The development of new media illustrates the growing globalization and commercialization of media policies. Profound changes in technology and culture have produced a commercial race to dominate the television screens around the world, with structural and commercial changes in television broadcasting generating a wider choice of channels and increased competition. Global rather than national markets have become the focus of attention of regulators, market forces, and broadcasters, with transnational advertiser-supported channels transmitting via satellites.

The result of these developments is that new media and advanced technology have evolved dramatically around the world. In this sense it is possible to say that globalization and technological advancement have influenced media policy worldwide. Like all other developments in the fields of broadcasting and telecommunications, this also began following deregulatory moves in America, and came into play in Europe—a process that resulted in new media becoming a large industry around the world. New developments of advanced technologies are now spreading to other parts of the world, including Asia, Latin America, Australia, and Africa, making media policy and markets global phenomenon.

The conclusion that can be drawn based on this analysis is that globalization provides evidence that all advanced countries are expected to experience the same pattern. The future may be uncertain, but the outcome of developments to date is clear. The global structure of media policies has established a media sector headed by large and powerful companies that are well aware of the wider potential of new media and telecommunications, with European policy following the course of development established by the American experience. The new structure is spreading globally, leading to the implementation of global media policy.

THE STRUCTURE OF THE BOOK

The book is divided into two parts. The first part examines the process that has led to the development of global media policy. The second part analyzes the consequent changes in the nature of media policies that have developed following their formation into a global structure. The primary interest in this discussion is the impact of commercialization and globalization trends on changes in new media and telecommunications policy and markets.

The first part of the book (Chapters 1-4) concentrates on the stages of media policy, the role of governments in this process, the globalization of media policies, and the technologies of the 21st century. This examination includes an analysis of the development of media policy as part of a global process of technological and commercial change. It includes an investigation of the main aspects of the global policy process and analyzes key developments in new media policy.

The first chapter covers the three-stage development course of media policy—the transformation from early perceptions of national broadcasting into new media policy and then into the current process of global media policy. In theoretical terms the research argues that the major change from media policy to new media policy and then to global media policy has evolved in three distinct phases.

In the first stage, early perceptions advocated for a national distinctive of broadcasting as part of the old media of terrestrial transmissions. Later, new media polices were formulated with different goals in each country, combining between old media and new media technologies of cable and satellite. Later still, media policies became global, creating a uniform global media policy. This structure dominates the current stage of media policy for the 21st century.

The argument made in this chapter is that media policy of all countries falls, or should fall, within the limits of the model of the three-stage development course of media policy. This demonstrates that the direction of change is a global process. Although each country has taken a different route and acted at a different speed, the end result is that all countries are heading in the direction of the ultimate structure of global media policy.

The new structure of media policy is examined throughout the first part of the book. Global media policy includes three main processes that are common to all countries: the first is deregulation and privatization policies, the second is convergence of media and telecommunications policies, and the third is competition of all media and telecommunications services. These aspects are examined in the following chapters: Chapter 2 examines the role of governments, Chapter 3 examines the globalization of media policy, and Chapter 4 examines the technologies of the 21st century.

The second chapter examines the diminishing role of regulators in media policy. The focus is placed on the role of governments in the transition in cable policy in the three largest media countries of Europe (Britain, France, and Germany). The comparative analysis examined offers the opportunity to asses the argument that public policies passed through essentially the same stages of development, even though the role of regulators has differed. The research demonstrates that the involvement of governments in determining the course of development of cable systems has comprised three main stages, which follow the three-stage development course of media policy explored in the first chapter.

In the first stage, governments tried to ignore cable and prevent the establishment of cable infrastructure. This policy was consistent with early perceptions that considered cable as a technology secondary to broadcast television. The second stage is identified with the promotion of cable by public authorities. In this stage, governments regulated the technology in order to promote a national cable policy and encourage the overall development of the broadcasting media. In the third stage, although at different speeds and perceptions, governments deregulated cable by giving permission to market forces to dominate its development and abandoning the social and cultural goals that had dominated cable policy. The changes in media policy led to a diminished role of governments, which supplements the free market approach. This course of development has been characterized by the introduction of market-led and global expansion of cable and satellite, and brought the consequent formation of a global trend of market domination at the global policy level.

The contrasting experiences of the countries discussed in this chapter and the different ways that media policy has subsequently developed on the part of public authorities can be attributed to the interplay of a series of factors. They include differences in social and cultural perceptions of media policy, in the political culture, in the regulatory environment, and in the relative power of central and local governments. These factors are particularly relevant to new media policy and can reflect on the overall transition into global media policy dominated by leading regulatory institutions with global impact. The new role of governments in the digital age is restricted to advancing competition among a variety of technologies and services, with competition as an alternative to regulation

The third chapter investigates globalization by underlying the transition of new media policy from cultural values to commercialization. The examination explores the process that has become common around the world—the convergence of new media policies. The transition in media policy is examined according to the main perceptions adopted in the largest media countries in Europe (Britain, France, and Germany), as part of a global process that is implemented within the limits of the commercialization of national media systems.

In all three countries, early policies were influenced by cultural values, although they differed in the social and political perception and in the political culture. Then, following technological development and market change, policies changed, reinforced by new approaches toward new media development and based on free market perceptions. This led to the next stage of development, the convergence and globalization of new media policies. The consequent changes in the nature of media policies mean that technological development has prevailed over cultural differences and policy convergence and globalization have become dominant.

The fourth chapter describes the technologies that are expected to dominate the 21st century. The new structure of media policy means that all technologies are permitted to compete for the delivery of all services, and as a result traditional dominating positions are changing in the digital age. New technologies include digital terrestrial television, broadband cable and satellite, telephone, wireless communications, and the Internet.

Under the new structure, all technologies will operate differently in the 21st century. Terrestrial broadcasters are in transition from the traditional analog transmission system into digital technology, which allows multiple programming and other advanced services. Broadband cable and digital satellite services provide, in addition to programming, advanced services of interactive television, high-speed Internet access and local telephone services. Telephone companies are now permitted to supply high-speed Internet access and multichannel television services in addition to traditional telephone services, and wireless communications is providing mobile telephone, interactive services and high-speed Internet access. Other competitors are Internet Service Providers (ISP) and Advanced Interactive Multimedia (AIM) content providers offering interactive television applications.

The second part of the book (Chapters 5-8) examines key issues in the social, cultural, technological, and commercial implications of global media policy. The investigation explores the impact of global trends on changes in local media policies and markets while looking at the global linkage between culture and technology and the consequent development of global media markets.

The fifth chapter examines the attempts to create the information society, which stands at the heart of global policy. The research explores the course of social adoption of information technology, which has become an overriding issue of social policy following advances in new technologies and the vast increase in the social use of media, telecommunications, and information services.

The argument made here is that the prospects for information technology have followed the same patterns of the three-stage development course of media policy discussed in this book. In the first two stages, public authorities and commercial entrepreneurs explored certain applications of community and interactive services, although these experiments proved unsuccessful in terms of public response and cost effectiveness. In the third stage, new technologies with digital capabilities have created renewed public interest in the relationship between telecommunications and localism.

The examination goes further to explore the social aspects of the new structure of media policy—a process likely to lead to the formation of the information society. Following advances in information technology, the chapter assesses the potential of and prospects for digital technology. In doing so, it investigates the impact of digitalization on local societies in the era of global media policy—a trend that dominates new media and telecommunications developments.

The sixth chapter explores the globalization of media markets—a process that followed the globalization of new media policy. It is argued that the globalization of new media technologies and culture created global media markets where common policy values and cultural character dictate the commercial flow of information and entertainment. This trend demonstrates the transition in the nature of competition in media markets with the addition of new media technologies.

The research in this chapter analyzes the changes that have brought new forms of competition and led to the creation of new media markets dominated by global and commercial forces. This transformation includes changes from cultural perceptions to commercialization and globalization and from a perception of new media as part of a social and cultural project to a new structure of global media culture.

Initially media policy and markets concentrated on social and cultural goals, creating a social and cultural project. This structure had been dominated by requirements for community and public access transmissions, imposition of "Must Carry" rules and establishment of pilot projects to test future social adoption of new media. Then new perceptions of free speech and free flow of information, coupled with technological development and policy changes, led to the creation of global media culture. This structure, which comprises global economy, global culture, and global politics, is leading the development of media systems for the 21st century. It identifies broadcasting systems around the world to a degree of common values and content of television programming while creating a global process under which the domination of global media networks is determinant.

The development of new media markets operating globally and using advanced technology and global communications networks is leading to the new generation of information services. The information society is a distinct product of globalization and technological advancement, and information is now delivered through global networks. The spread of communications networks has brought about the growth of multinational media conglomerates that dominate movies, television, information, and music worldwide. Global operations form global links aimed to control the next technological revolution that will serve the information society—the global information superhighway.

Chapter 7 examines commercialization in the digital age. It establishes a theoretical focus of the commercialization of local markets—a process that can be considered as an obvious result of the new era of global media. While combining the new trend of global media policy and the development of media commercialization, the inevitable linkage between culture and technology creates a new social order. Under this structure, the cultural aspects of media commercialization mediate between local forces and global trends by setting out local dimensions of the globalization of culture and technology. The result is that despite global impact on national media policies, the cultural role of media commercialization is provoking sociocultural perspectives in seeking to understand the effects of economic and technological changes in each country.

The global change from cultural values to commercialization has created a more or less uniform media policy, which can be identified with certain broad trends that demonstrate the way commercialization in the digital age can be examined. These are: the mediating role of media commercialization, commercialization policy, the new public television, new media markets, Americanization, protecting local culture, the social role of advertising, and the linkage between culture and technology. These categories are effective in all countries, and as a whole constitute a global process of commercialization of local media markets.

The entirety of this process suggests that although commercialization has been adopted at a different path in each country, it was the promotion of new technologies that accelerated the globalization of media policy and markets in the digital age.

The last chapter offers a conclusive approach by attempting to forecast the future structure of media policy for the 21st century. Four main trends are explored: a global structure of media policy, competition as alternative to regulation, changes in local markets, and the technologies of the future.

The main argument made in this chapter is that the new structure of media policy dominates developments at the global level. It is making an impact on all countries, which have witnessed the restructuring of the media and broadcasting sectors away from public service obligations toward greater dependence on market forces. In this structure, commercial opportunities have prevailed and commercialization became alternative to regulation. Despite the globalization of policy and markets, however, local policies differ in response to the challenges imposed by new media technologies and the success new competitive markets. Although the future structure may be unknown, forecasts can be made based on the way global media policy has developed. The current phase of development is based on commercial competition and digital service, and is certainly going to change the way we live and communicate in the digital age.

1

The Three-Stage Development Course of Media Policy

Media policy has changed considerably in recent decades, following technological development of new media services and change of perception in favor of wider competition. The main course of development has been a shift from the perception of new media technologies as having a secondary role to broadcast television to a definition of them as a global and market-led industry, dominated by commercial and competitive forces.

The changes evident at the global level of policy demonstrate that despite important initial differences in approach between countries, new media developments have gone through essentially the same phases of progress, although at different speeds.

The process includes three distinct stages:

1. In the first stage, early perceptions of the "old structure of broadcasting" influenced by public service principles dominated media policy.

2. In the second stage, a free market approach was adopted, encouraging competition of the old media of terrestrial broadcasting and new media technologies.
3. In the third stage, a global structure of media policy dominated by deregulation and convergence was adopted around the world.

The transformation in technological development and policy-making has four major social results. Firstly, differences in the structure of new media and advanced technologies have diminished following their commercialization and globalization. Secondly, market forces have taken center stage, displacing social and cultural policies initiated by governments and creating policy objectives common to all advanced nations. Thirdly, the new competitive structure environment has been influenced by deregulation, privatization, and convergence policies, which made the difference at the global level. And fourthly, the end result of these changes is globalization of media policy. New policy objectives have become dominant and are moving into a new global policy for television services and programming in the 21st century.

In the current stage, which leads to the formation of global media policy, the extent of regulation is determined at the global level. Because traditional policies cannot cope with the technological reality, changes are inevitable, involving the transformation of technology and politics. Under the new structure, media policy has become dominated by competition of all technologies, new media, and telecommunications services.

This chapter aims to demonstrate that the growth of media policy is a global process that applies to all countries, despite variations in development and speed. It is argued that despite differences among countries, reflecting different policy styles with special characteristics, common to the development of all media systems has been the growing recognition of the inevitability of deregulation, privatization, and convergence policies. This course demonstrates the intercircle of the trajectory of the development of broadcasting systems and the tremendous changes in the role of new media in society. The new structure discussed in this book can reflect on the overall transition of the broadcast media into a market-led industry, where commercial considerations have prevailed over public service perceptions, and the arriving of new elements of globalization.

In theoretical terms, the model of the three-stage development course of media policy put forward can be divided according to the following distinct periods:

1. First Stage of Media Policy: The "Old Structure" of Broadcasting

In the early period, which started in the 1940s and continued until the 1970s and 1980s, public service objectives dominated public policies as part of the "old structure" of broadcasting. This structure was at the heart of public perceptions of the cultural role of broadcasting systems in all countries. There was a resemblance between policy objectives of public broadcasting service in Europe and dominance of broadcast television in America.

Although policy varied, from the American free-market approach for broadcast television to the public service perception that dominated European broadcasting, a major characteristic was the role of television networks with a national character. These networks were operated by private initiators in America and by public service organizations in Europe. Because they had been the most powerful forces in broadcasting, the development of other means of broadcasting provided by new media technologies was limited or restricted by public policy.

2. Second Stage of Media Policy: New Media Policies

In the second stage, which started in America in the 1970s and in Europe in the 1980s, new media policies had been formulated. Deregulation of media systems demonstrates the change of media policy, as cable systems developed with programming that began to be produced and packaged for distribution solely to cable subscribers. The provision of new services was later helped by the availability of low-powered satellite systems that provided transmissions directly to cable systems.

This trend represents a transition in the conception that dominated media policies, following the permission for new media technologies to operate alongside the old structure of terrestrial broadcasting. It was the combination of technological development and deregulation policies, helped by changes in the political climate and adoption of market-oriented policy, that provided the basis for independent and competitive television service of new media technologies.

3. Third Stage of Media Policy: Global Media Policy

In the third stage, media policies have become global, as the transformation into digital technology progresses. Following technological development and deregulation policies in the United States and the large media countries of Europe, this tendency is now dominated by global policy objectives. The global adoption demonstrates the recognition that new media can compete with national broadcasting services rather than serving as an obstacle to an advanced media system. Technological developments and social transformations have created a new concept of global media policy that dominates new media and telecommunications policy.

The concept of global media policy means that uniform and global policy thinking prevail, with the impact of new media and telecommunications services spreading simultaneously around the world. Following deregulation and privatization (policy changes at the local level) and globalization (adoption of open-skies policy), convergence of policy and competition of all media and telecommunications services dominate the new structure, with global rather than local objectives that make-up media policy.

1.1 THE "OLD STRUCTURE" OF BROADCASTING

In the first stage of development, media policies centered on broadcast television and advocated a national structure of broadcasting. This period is considered the "old structure" of broadcasting, in which prominence was given to the quality of programming that only well-established broadcasting organizations with a national character could guarantee.

Within the general model of development of media policies discussed in this chapter, a rich variety of national styles of regulation existed, reflecting differences of historical experience and regulatory culture. Despite common characteristics between countries, the nature of public expectations from broadcasting during the early period of development varied considerably. American obligations were minimal, voluntary, and related only to the allocation and supervision of broadcasting licenses, with no control over content and the type of programming. In contrast, in Europe detailed and obligatory regulation of licensing, structure, content and the type of programming characterized public broadcasting systems.

The distinction between American and European broadcasting policy was evident in the role of public broadcasting and the overall impact of this perception on the development of media policy. Whereas in the United States its impact had always been marginal in favor of commercial domination, in Europe there was a strong commitment among broadcasters to public service broadcasting. This resolution applied to the handful of institutional arrangements for licensing and monitoring the activities of broadcasting and restricted the development of private and commercial outlets, including advanced technologies.

Within this structure, other means of broadcasting were restricted. Cable systems developed only as Community Antenna Television systems (CATV). Initially the systems operated at the local level to provide better reception of terrestrial television signals in their areas of operation and later they began to import additional programming from neighboring regions or countries. Satellite services were unavailable. Initially they were not technically possible and later they were restricted to government control and not permitted for commercial use.

The "Old Structure" in the United States

Examining the development of American media policy and the role of public authorities during this stage, it is evident that the Federal Communications Commission (FCC) was the most influential force in broadcasting. The FCC was created by the Communications Act of 1934 to regulate interstate and foreign communications by wire and radio in the public interest and was assigned additional regulatory jurisdiction under the Communication Satellite Act of 1962. The scope of the FCC's regulation includes radio and television broadcasting; telephone, telegraph, and cable operation; two-way radio and radio operators; and satellite communication.

The foremost and principal idea that American media policy rests upon is freedom of speech and freedom of the press. This commitment stems from the First Amendment, which underwrites the idea that no government—federal or local—has the authority to interfere with the right of the media to deliver whatever information they wish.

The First Amendment to the United States Constitution reads that Congress shall make no law abridging the freedom of speech or of the press. The amendment is the earliest and most important statement of the relationship between the government and the mass media, and its protection of free speech is addressed solely to government threats to abridge that right. Because it is part of the Constitution, all other laws and government policies must be consistent with it, or otherwise they are deemed to be unconstitutional and consequently illegal.[1]

Under these circumstances, and because no control over content is permitted in accordance with the First Amendment, the ability of the FCC to guide the development of the broadcast media is limited to regulating technological and structural aspects. During this early period of development, the "old structure" of broadcasting was apparent in that the policy initiated by the FCC was intended to protect the interests of national broadcasters by promoting a national public service network and limiting cable to a supplementary service. As a result, the broadcast media were dominated by terrestrial television, and the development of new technologies was limited.

The policy adopted was designed to create an alternative to the commercial television system, in the form of public television. The new broadcasting outlets were proposed to be noncommercial and deliver educational and cultural programming to the public—programming that was generally not available on commercial television stations.

The operation of public television is divided into two main periods: between 1952 and 1967, and since 1967. In the first period, it operated through educational stations as part of the concept of noncommercial broadcasting encouraged by the FCC. The issue of educational television rose up during the FCC freeze on new television stations' licenses, between 1948 and 1952, when educators made strong presentations to the FCC. In 1952, the FCC first set aside 25 channels for educational television stations, and in 1958 educational stations were located in 31 communities. These stations represented large cities and university centers, and even reached entire states.

The growth of the noncommercial educational television industry was phenomenal. In 1964 there were about 100 stations, and this number grew to 125 by 1966. But despite the enthusiasm of educators, the stations neither fulfilled their purpose of serving the public nor made enough profit to stay in business. Lack of funds was the biggest problem that educational stations faced. They needed money to operate and had difficulties in raising funds. Although in 1962 Congress passed the Educational Television Facilities Act, which provided $32 million over a five-year period to develop state system of educational broadcasting, this budget was not enough.

In the second period of public television, which started in 1967, noncommercial television was implemented through public broadcasting stations. These stations are known today as public broadcasting channels—noncommercial services that operate alongside the commercial stations available in America.

A change of policy was inevitable, because the budget of educational stations was not enough. In 1967 the report of the Carnegie Commission for Educational Television appeared, which recommended the establishment of a public broadcasting system, distinct from Educational Television. The report concluded that a well-financed and well-directed educational television system had to be brought into being in order to serve the full needs of the American public. They recommended that the new structure of noncommercial television had to be substantially larger and far more effective than the one that had existed in the form of educational stations.

The Public Broadcasting Act, which followed the report, formulated a nonprofit corporation—the Corporation for Public Broadcasting

(CPB)—to be in charge of encouraging the growth of educational television and to draft a national policy that would make noncommercial transmissions available across the United States. The act allocated additional funding to public broadcasting stations and started a new era for noncommercial television.

Resulting from this change in policy, in 1970 the CPB formed the Public Broadcasting Service (PBS)—a public organization owned and operated by member television stations. This organization, which matched the perception of noncommercial television, became the primary distribution system for programs serving public broadcasting stations. Its main contribution to the impending success of non-commercial television was to provide services and programming for national distribution from its member stations and from independent producers and suppliers of programming.

The founding missions of PBS established by the Carnegie Commission program were to provide a voice for groups in the community that may otherwise be unheard, serve as a forum for controversy and debate, and broadcast programs that help to depict America whole, in all its diversity. But PBS was always considered as subsidiary to commercial broadcasting, and its impact has been constantly diminished since the 1970s.[2]

As can be seen from the development of public television, the FCC was keen to promote a noncommercial television service. The same objectives that directed the Commission in encouraging noncommercial television applied to the development of cable systems. During this period of media policy, the FCC saw its function as guarding the revenues of both local and national terrestrial broadcasters and public broadcasters. The problem for a national character of broadcasting was, in the view of the FCC, in the form of direct competition from cable systems offering programming and advertisements from stations in nearby cities.

According to this policy thinking, cable was restricted to carrying signals of local origin. Given the initial small-town role of cable systems and the complexity of the work in trying to establish a nationwide terrestrial television service, the FCC promoted the newly established noncommercial public broadcasting service and prohibited commercial development of cable systems. Based on their plans for public broadcasting, it was easier to link cable to potentially harmful auxiliary services rather than to consider this technology as a possible solution to television's problems.

During this stage, cable TV systems served as CATV (Community Antenna Television systems) with the aim of providing better reception of terrestrial television signals in their areas of operation. They relayed established broadcasting transmissions and their function was simply to bring television signals into communities where off-air reception was either impossible or very bad, due to mountains or distance. Limiting use to the relay of off-air channels prohibited the commercial exploitation of systems. There was little program origination on most systems, and movies, sports events, and other special programs were generally unavailable. Although in the 1950s and 1960s additional signals from adjacent areas were retransmitted, until the 1970s the essential economics of the cable industry changed very little, as a typical cable system essentially still resembled the pioneer CATV systems.[3]

The Old Structure in Europe

In Europe, the old structure of broadcasting was more distinctive because almost all commercial operation was prohibited. The most prominent character was that public authorities controlled broadcasting and the development of private broadcasting channels was generally restricted through limiting regulatory agencies operated by public authorities.

The traditional method of regulating the broadcasting sector was by government ownership or by licensed monopolies. Regulatory measures were designed to ensure diversity, fairness, and minority interests that only public service organizations operated by public authorities and not subject to commercial considerations could guarantee.

According to the public service policy, which dominated the old structure of broadcasting until the 1980s, broadcasting was aimed at serving the public good and was independent of economic and political interests. Although there were many variations according to national priorities and traditions, the generally accepted version was one that tried in the public interest to advance the quality of service and deplored the notion of diversity and a national political or cultural interest.

The public service system was based on four main elements:

1. Cultural programming policy that represented diverse tastes, interests, subcultures, and different regions and minority languages.
2. Public accountability was achieved mainly through regulatory bodies and parliaments that had ultimate control over broadcasting. These bodies were responsible to maintain universal service, diversity, editorial independence; social responsibility and accountability; and cultural quality and identity in the transmissions of the public service organizations.
3. Public service broadcasting was a monopoly that occupied a politically sensitive position and responded to the typical concerns of the elite and the political system.

4. The method of finance was license fees, and broadcasting was noncommercial in nature—designed to shield program making from the need to make profit.

The old structure included both extreme and revised models of public service. The extreme version, which dominated in the first years of broadcasting, was restricted to limited channels and programming choice and enforced requirements for educational and other demanding programming. It defined broadcasting as a common valued resource that a democratic government should organize for the collective welfare of its citizens to ensure that they are properly informed and educated as well as entertained.

According to this structure, the role of public broadcasting was to educate, enlighten, and help make better citizens, as well as to entertain. It was legally obligated to represent the interest of all parts of society, including minorities, and provide a universal service—yet still be noncommercial. The reason for this restriction was that the idea of public service broadcasting, which developed as a result of the perceived impact of economic institutions, should not be dependent on commercial consideration.

The revised model, which came into existence in the 1960s and 1970s, permitted limited competition and a limited amount of entertainment programming to be transmitted within the strict structure of cultural content of broadcasting organizations. Limited advertising was also permitted in some countries, although the advertising element was carefully regulated so that public broadcasting organizations could maintain their noncommercial nature. The new approach was adopted all over Western Europe, whereas across Eastern Europe the strict model of public service broadcasting remained common throughout the first and well into the second stage of media policy.

A typical feature of the new structure was that despite the changed nature of public broadcasting, the main goals did not change across Europe, and even the limited commercialization permitted was restricted to public control and dominated by government's direction. This means that although the original objectives of public broadcasting had been redefined and the means to accomplish these objectives had been revised, the basic arrangements of the broadcasting media remained unchanged.

The revised structure had a mixed system of public service, accountable to the people through Parliament and private enterprise. The broadcasting authorities worked according to terms and conditions put forward through Parliament, but otherwise had editorial and managerial independence in their provision of television and radio services.

Legislation was often the result of a lengthy period of extra-Parliamentary activity, as well as parliamentary discussion and decision. A distinctive character of this structure was that the will of the Parliament and other public authorities had been most crucial to the development of broadcasting.[4]

The general attitude that identified the old structure of broadcasting was decisive in the development of new media too. The technologies of cable and satellite were restricted by national governments as policymakers defined these technologies as having a secondary role to broadcast television.

CATV systems were installed only in specific places, mainly in remote areas, serving small communities, and provided only better reception of off-air transmissions. The systems were limited to serving small communities, as their primary functions were to improve reception and to bring in channels that subscribers could not receive locally. No commercial or program orientation was permitted. This policy was common across all of Europe. It was meant to prevent the establishment of cable infrastructure in order to protect the national television services—thus, to maintain the monopolistic public service nature of broadcasting. The exploitation of satellite services was not permitted as governments maintained public supervision on the development of the technology and prohibited any commercial or private use.[5]

The policy adopted in Europe demonstrates the decisive role of public authorities. New media development was not encouraged because governments ignored it so that new technology would not compete with public service television distributed through terrestrial broadcasting. Although the initiative to advance the broadcasting media was left in the hands of governments, there was little incentive to install large cable systems given that most European television homes could receive the public broadcasting channels, and attempts to advance cable developments were easily blocked.

Although countries differed in the extent of the public supervision they represented a strong commitment to explore cultural objectives by determining the nature of the development of broadcasting outlets. The importance of national policies was that major aspects of development, mainly the cultural, commercial, technological, and programming nature of public channels and cable infrastructure, had been determined according to the policy dynamics initiated by public authorities in each country. The impact of national policies on the structure and actual development of broadcasting systems was decisive as a result of this policy.

This structure dominated throughout the first stage. It was not until the early 1980s, following policy changes, that European governments chose to encourage the development of cable systems in an attempt to exploit social and cultural as well as economic and technological objectives.[6]

1.2 NEW MEDIA POLICIES

The second stage of media policy is identified with technological development and powerful ideological social and political pressures that changed public policies and set the stage for new media policies thereafter. Policy changes followed the imperative impact of new technologies of cable and satellite, which have provided opportunities for the evasion of established broadcasting regulation and the establishment of market oriented principles. The United States was the leader in adopting new media policy in the early 1970s, and the largest media countries of Europe (Britain, France, and Germany) followed suit about a decade later. It was only after new policies had been established in these countries, that other countries also adopted the same policy objectives.

In the United States, this structure combined old media of terrestrial broadcasting and new media of cable and satellite. The prosperity of new media began after cable systems started to import additional programming from neighboring regions. Later programming began to be produced and packaged for distribution solely to cable subscribers, providing the basis for independent and competitive television service. Deregulation and the distribution of programming via satellite helped additional development. The new technological means created a second source of revenues to cover the high costs of production through direct consumer payment. In this competitive environment, which provided a diverse program marketplace in which consumers have a high degree of sovereignty, the favorable status of terrestrial broadcasting was no longer guaranteed.

In Europe, the change of media policy included greater reliance on market forces and greater belief in the future economic growth. New policies were initiated through the adoption of new technologies and within a mixed structure, which included three main principles:

1. Mixed sources of revenue (advertising and license fees).
2. Mixed goals (some determined by governments and politicians, some by professionals, some by interest groups, and some by the audience).
3. Diverse supports within each society: the political elite, the cultural elite, public authorities, the press, and the audience.[7]

New Media Policy in the United States

The shift in the development of new media started in America in 1972, when the FCC deregulated cable at the national level and announced an open-skies policy for cable and satellite. The Cable Television Report and Order relaxed the FCC ruling and allowed cable operators to import all distant signals, but still imposed restrictions on the contents of pay TV channels, limiting movies, sports events, and series programming. The open-skies policy related to commercial operation of satellites by authorizing privately operated satellite systems.

The permission for new media to operate alongside the terrestrial television network represented considerable change in perspective of the future development of American broadcast media. It was the recognition that public broadcasting ranked as a great disappointment—lacking viewers and funding—that brought policy changes in favor of a commercial approach.

The lack of adequate funding for public television stations created a problem with respect to the quality of the programs and demonstrated the unclear and indecisive mission of the noncommercial network. The low budget of the stations made it difficult for them to compete with commercial outlets or retain the services of competent and experienced program personal. In addition, federal support for public broadcasting stations had the effect of reinforcing the three networks' dominance, and it became evident that PBS stations did not enjoy the success of their commercial competitor network.[8]

The change of policy is evident in that initially the satellite technology developed according to the perception that it would be best provided by governments through treaties between countries. At the dawn of the satellite age it was assumed that a global satellite network would be too big an undertaking for any one government or private enterprise. Satellite services were operated internationally by Intelsat—an international organization established by several national telephone companies, in Europe by Eutelsat—the European satellite organization, and in the United States by Comsat—a special quasi-governmental cooperation responsible for the operation of satellite services.

Other than these operations no commercial or private use was permitted. In contrast, the new open-skies policy endorsed by the FCC permitted the import of distant transmissions and gave permission to private companies to launch commercial satellites. The logic behind the change of policy was that private competition would create a more dynamic satellite industry than could the government.

Following these regulatory changes, the satellite industry developed swiftly, privately operated and providing new services that attracted program suppliers and customers. The new era of technological advancement started in the spring of 1975, when RCA launched a commercial communication satellite, Satcom 1. In September of this year Home Box Office rented a transponder, and for a fee started beaming movies to any cable system operator willing to set up a receiving dish antenna.[9]

The development of the satellite technology transformed the cable industry considerably, changing the history of broadcasting in the United States and starting a new era for new media around the world. Since the mid-1970s, the cable industry has experienced a dramatic expansion, as a direct result of satellite-transmitted channels.

The availability of new channels with satellite programming, for which subscribers could pay extra, created a revolution in the cable industry, with the result that earth receiving stations proliferated at cable systems across the United States. The growth of cable was spurred by a sharp reduction in costs and by a rapid acceleration in the number and variety of satellite services. By offering new nationwide channels aimed exclusively at cable audiences, satellite services made it financially viable for cable systems to offer program packages that would attract new subscribers.

One lesson that can be learned is that the rapid growth of American cable was helped by the deregulation of the industry. Many of the rules have been dropped or relaxed under FCC and Congress deregulation policy, which gave cable operators the right to import distant signals.

Changes throughout the 1970s were tremendous. Following the deregulation of the cable and satellite industries in 1972, in just a single year—between 1975 and 1976—more steps were taken to provide cable with the economic resources and impetus to leap ahead than had occurred in the whole of its first stage of existence. The most important step was the elimination of the "leapfrogging rules," which had had prevented cable systems from taking in stations if there was an independent station in the Top 25 market nearer to it that could be carried.

Additional deregulation was implemented in the 1980s. In 1980, the FCC dropped other restrictions, after determining that the Congress Copyright Act of 1976, which made cable systems liable for copyright payment, obviated the need for complex rules. By 1981, all remaining restrictions on importing out-of-region distant signals were eliminated. Since then, cable operators have been free to carry an unlimited number of channels. The following year, the FCC deregulated the domestic communication satellite industry, too. Instead of the need to operate as common carriers, leasing services at rates approved by the FCC, satellite owners were allowed to lease or sell satellite transmission facilities. As a result the number of satellites and satellite services (including the number and variety of cable basic and pay TV channels) have grown rapidly.

These deregulation moves have been part of the broader process of deregulation of cable and the telecommunications sectors in general. In 1984, Congress adopted a comprehensive Cable Act, establishing a national regulatory policy for cable and providing guidelines for federal, state, and local authorities. It represented the first major revision of the Communications Act of 1934 and provided the first successful legislative effort to create a national cable policy.

In creating the act, Congress relieved the cable industry of many regulatory burdens, allowing it to compete more effectively with other forms of new electronic media. The act constituted a mixture of regulatory and deregulatory components, which although they generally limited state and local governments' regulation, also permitted some state regulations previously preempted by the FCC. Local authorities were given the right to demand certain kinds of facilities and hardware, but no control over content. Although the act supported the liberation of cable from local regulatory bodies, the defacto extent of local governmental authority to regulate cable by means of the franchising process remained uncertain.[10]

The conclusion for American new policy structure is that the combination of technological advancement and regulatory responses to this preference changed the broadcasting system. Deregulation provided the cable industry with the means to develop into a fully commercial competitor to broadcast television. With the adoption of new media policy objectives, American cable developed in a dynamic regulatory and competitive environment. The surviving rules have been minimal, permitting cable systems wide latitude in both design and operation. Since the mid-1970s cable systems and services have grown at such a rate and in an atmosphere of such optimism, that the impact has been felt around the world. Between 1975 and 1981 the total number of cable subscribers in the United States doubled, and then jumped again by more than 50 percent by 1985. Cable's penetration rate reached 50 percent of American households in 1988—40 years after the first CATV system was established, and then reached more than two thirds of the households by mid-1990s.[11]

New Media Policy in Europe

As can be seen from the foregoing discussion, until the late 1980s, compared to other countries, American regulation appeared minimal. The growth of the American cable system was felt around the world, mainly in Europe, and new media technologies became dominant in European media policy too. Most importantly was the adoption of new media policies in the leading countries (Britain, France and Germany). The traditional bases of broadcasting regulation had been unable to cope with the impact of new technology and policy change, and new policy alternatives had been established with the adoption of new media policies.

In the early 1980s, the three countries permitted the addition of new media technologies of cable and satellite and private channels. Later in the 1980s commercial channels were licensed across Europe. The weight of argument shifted rapidly in favor of free market principles and changes in the old structure of public service broadcasting. Deregulation and privatization policies were implemented based on commercialization and new media developments.

Examination of the process that occurred in Europe demonstrates that deregulation and privatization were the trigger for the change of media policy. The adoption of new policies reflected the overall question of public service and commercial aspects of broadcasting, because of the changing role of television broadcasting. The new perspectives meant that ideological changes that followed the swift development of new media policies resulted in growing enthusiasm for privatization.

A major characteristic was that the regulatory responses to the technological and social developments increasingly questioned the rationale for close public regulation of broadcasting and advocated a new deregulated media market, dominated by new media technologies and commercial broadcasting services. The commercial attitudes of the free market approach considered new media technologies as more economically significant, and brought open-market competition into broadcasting, with little room left for extensive content regulations or restrictions on market entry.

The resulting new structure represented a shift in the nature of public broadcasting and new media technology. Whereas in the first stage national broadcasting represented a uniform state-run broadcasting system, the commitment to a balanced range of programming that reflected the entire scope of public opinion did not change in the second stage. It was, however, the nature of policy that had changed, with new policy objectives that became dominant and common in the new scene.

This process of change had been revised in comparison to earlier policies, but it was still contrary to the policy trajectory that prevailed in the United States. Unlike in America, where private operators had been given the freedom to exploit new media developments, in Europe broadcasting was within national jurisdiction. In this situation, national governments had to establish the legal framework to allow private commercial broadcasting and new media developments.

The change of direction meant that media policy combined the old structure of broadcasting and new media policy objectives based on a mixed structure of public and commercial goals. When private stations were first licensed, it was generally understood that like the public channels they, too, should reflect the diversity of public opinion and not be subject to the influence of interest groups. Supervisory institutions were set up to guarantee the coexistence of public and private broadcasting. These institutions had to ensure that the private channels comply with the conditions of the licensing agreements and control any possible moves to create a cartel among the station owners.

Despite the combined new structure, however, the adoption of new media policy resulted in the relative decline of public service broadcasting and the rise of commercial forms of broadcasting. This meant that although prominence was still given to terrestrial broadcasting, the new commercial environment had an impact on the operations of public broadcasting.

The structure of public broadcasting services had changed as a result of the new policy objectives. The availability of new media services left traditional public broadcasting organizations exposed to competition for audience and revenues. The sinking revenues from advertising or the license fees and the rising cost of program material in the marketplace forced public channels to initiate structural reforms to reduce the financial pressure and continue the obligation to serve the public good. The state of public stations became difficult with the loss of viewers, identity, and political support, and resulted in the collapse of the public service nature of media policies and triumph of commercial perceptions. As a result, the license fee, a classic public service mode of funding, has been questioned, with growing interest in extending the scope of commercial forms of finance.

The restructuring of broadcasting systems resulted in the addition of private commercial stations and new technologies. Governments across Europe determined that public broadcasting corporations were no longer to be the sole providers of television programming, but had to make room for private broadcasting. This emphasized the rise of political parties committed to privatization and deregulation policies and established a new social, political and economic structure for media policy.

Under this structure, the entry of new media and telecommunications interest groups wielded as a major influence on policy in each nation. In response to these pressures, deregulation policies were implemented by a variety of governments, but the extent of deregulation in each country was also shaped by the amount of counter pressure of local forces—with the most prominent being public organizations and broadcasters.

Despite differences among countries, policies resulted in the collapse of early perceptions and the triumph of commercialization and new media. The combination of technological development, deregulation of American cable and satellite industries, and social and political transformations in Europe allowed for the immense growth of private broadcasting services in the large media countries and made its impact on other nations too.

The result of this trend was that new media policies around the world have been dominated by deregulation and privatization, coupled with technological convergence and globalization. The new policies gave new media technologies and services better opportunities in the marketplace and exposed traditional broadcasting outlets to a new environment of commercial competition for both revenues and viewers. The contribution of this transition was decisive to the establishment of a new structure of broadcasting. It was followed by deregulatory policies for the entire broadcast media, as a new commercial atmosphere started to dominate European broadcasting. The new trend can now be seen as part of the convergence of new media and telecommunications policies, which has developed during the third stage of media policy.[12]

1.3 GLOBAL MEDIA POLICY

The third stage of media policy, which extends to the current state of development, is dominated by global policy objectives common to all advanced countries. Following America and the three large media countries of Europe, commercialization spread across Europe and in other parts of the world. The result is that, in general, similar solutions to the development of new media were chosen to address similar problems and opportunities posed by global policy making and advanced technology, creating the new concept of global media policy.

The growth of new media technologies was enormous, and set the stage for further technological developments. The development of cable reflected the changing nature of the industry—from a service that merely provided better reception of off-air transmissions in the first stage of policy into a sophisticated service capable of providing multiple transmission and telecommunications services in the second stage. The further development of the satellite industry provided a transnational service that has had an impact on media policies in all countries and established a new form of commercial competition that involves different technologies and ignores distinctions between countries and societies.

Global media policy is going to dominate global communications. The new structure, to which all countries are heading, can best be examined according to competitiveness of media markets. Today all new technologies participate in the competition for the provision of advanced services on a global scale, and media policy is determined by the new global structure.

Global media policy is based on three main principles:

1. Deregulation and privatization policies: The transformation into global media policy starts with deregulation and privatization policies, which are determined at the local level in each country. These policies relate mainly to public service organizations and the start of private broadcasting and have a tremendous impact in commercializing broadcasting systems. The next step up in is adoption of open-skies policy, which means opening up local markets to global competition. Adoption of this policy endorses free market competition and allows new entrants to operate in enlarged media systems.

2. Convergence of media and telecommunications policies: Subsequent to globalization and regulatory changes, media policies face increasing pressure for convergence—the integration of media and telecommunications policy. Policy convergence enforces regulatory changes in a way that the weight of influence in determining new policy and market development is transferred from public authorities to market forces.

3. Consolidation of policy and technologies: The final stage in this structure means opening up markets for free-market competition of all services and technologies. Consolidation of policy and technologies means that the particular countries have adopted the main principles of global media policy including regulating new rules and adopting digital technology. The further implications of this structure mean increased competition between technologies that traditionally provided different services: public television organizations with commercial operators, new media technologies of cable and satellite with telecommunication services, including digital technologies, telephone companies, wireless communications, and the Internet.

Deregulation and Privatization Policies

The commercialization of public broadcasting organizations and the impact of new media have changed the rules under which public policies are determined. In evaluating the role of public and commercial broadcasting, deregulation and privatization policies provide a shift in the nature of public service and commercial broadcasting and change the course of media policy.

Deregulation is defined as removal of rules and regulations as part of a strategy for modernization of the economy. It is a political perception that aims to commercialize the media sector as part of a public policy to remove the impediments to the free play of market forces by reducing bureaucratic inefficiency and financial chicanery.[13]

The main advantage of deregulation is that it can serve all interests—governments, market forces, and the public sector:

1. On the part of the government, deregulation does not lessen government action, and may actually increase it. Government intervention is needed because the new branches of the broadcast media require public supervision and government protection within the new competitive markets.
2. On the part of market forces, deregulation means a shift in the nature of government action. The new policy requires the government to relate to new markets and allows new players to gain dominance in these markets.
3. On the part of the public, deregulation increases competition and choice. The obvious benefit is that the state oversees a marketplace of competing interests in which no single player is capable of controlling decision making. The range of competing participants requires the state to monitor the demands of all relevant interest groups.[14]

Privatization is described as all forms of public intervention that increase the size of the market sector and give entrepreneurs operating within it freedom to maneuver. In order to examine the extent of privatization in each country, a series of mechanisms that highlight the overall process of privatization has to be examined:

1. The impact of selling shares in public companies to private investors varies depending on how the shares are placed and the actual transfer from public to private ownership.
2. The impact of liberalization policies, which are designed to introduce competition into markets that were previously served solely by public enterprise, depends on the terms on which this competition is allowed to proceed.
3. The process of commercializing the public sector, which is meant to allow public broadcasters to supplement their income by taking advertising, depends on the extent of the commercial involvement in public broadcasting.
4. The regulatory environment involves the shift in the overall rational of media policies from a defense of the public interest

to promotion of corporate interests. The impact of this process depends not only on the number of rules being loosened, but also on the extent of the overall deregulation policy.[15]

The links between deregulation and privatization establish a new structure of media policy. Examination of the impact of global policy on local media policies demonstrates that it has proved to be the best solution to create an atmosphere of change and establish the actual adoption of new media technologies. The impact of new technologies on the perception of public service broadcasting forced public debate on the question of commercialization of broadcasting systems. The extent of the debate demonstrates the conflict of interests that has characterized media policy at the local level, as the process of deregulating and privatizing the broadcasting sector gathered a complex of conflicting interests of social, cultural, political, technological, and commercial nature.

The combination of deregulation and privatization policies also provides for policy changes that promote new global thinking. In the process of commercializing the media sector, the role of deregulation and privatization is aimed at countering inefficient government policy by transferring powers from the government to the free market. It is assumed that deregulation of broadcasting provides the opportunity to properly react to new technological and market developments by allowing diversity and choice in program provision while the process of privatization of media sectors has to mediate between local and global forces.

The resulting structure of public policy explores the relative impact of the different parties in each country. The role of government action and commercial interests is changing, because both parties are required to relate to new markets and new rules. From the public interest, new media development and commercial outlets offer greater possibilities to establish consumer supremacy by furthering competition in domestic and global markets. In the new structure of competitive broadcast media no single player is capable of controlling decision making and composition of competing participants is required to monitor the demands of all relevant interest groups—combining public service and commercial conceptions.

The main change had been transfer of influence from the government sector to market forces. As a result of the changes in commercialization policies and the triumph of market forces, differences between countries have diminished. The most important aspect of this process has been the adoption of the main commercial objectives of American media policy. This provided a common set of principles to which all countries adhere—thus creating a global course of change in media policies.

Within this process, the adoption of global policy objectives (or as also can be referred to as the adoption of the American version of commercialization) has resulted in complex and inconsistent developments at the level of regulatory behavior in many countries. This was first evident in Europe, where the process of commercialization resulted in bargaining and negotiation between social, cultural, political, and commercial forces.

Deregulation and privatization provide the best solution to resolve these conflicting interests, as they relate to changes in the nature of public broadcasting services and to the responses of different governments to these changes. They clearly identify changes in public and commercial perceptions, with the extent varying according to the relative impact of local and global forces in each country.

In the course of this transformation, public authorities in all countries promoted technological development and commercialization while creating a deregulatory process that encourages the introduction of commercial services. The global impact is evident because the globalization of broadcasting has led to a growing recognition of the need for wider regulatory changes. The regulatory responses to both global and local forces have endorsed a new market for broadcasting services, with deregulation policies a major factor in accounting for the privatization and commercialization of media policy.

The growing global agreement on the advantages of these polices meant that changes have become evident in all media systems. Following the structural changes in the nature of public broadcasting organizations and the addition of new media technologies, the next step was the transfer of influence from the government sector to the free market by opening broadcasting to global competition. This has been achieved through open-skies policy.

The global consensus over open-skies policy has led to regulatory and technological changes. The American open-skies policy for cable and satellite had provided an example for other countries and regulatory institutions to follow. In accordance with this policy, the European Community assumed a new prominence of media policy. This was implemented in the adoption of a broadcasting directive characterized by the birth of an effective common policy for the European Community and the exertion of elements of global media. The new policy is led by deregulation and technological advancement and is aimed at allowing competition of all new media and telecommunications services.

The new European policy objectives were determined in the 1989 Television Without Frontiers Directive, which allows the free flow of movement of television broadcasts within all member states and in whatever way they are provided—off-air, cable, or satellite transmissions. The 1993 Cable and Satellite Copyright Directive also dealt with the protection of copyright in connection with cable and satellite transmissions across the continent. This policy is aimed to encourage free flow of information by reducing the role of governments to the level of a secondary force to the policy of the European Community.[16]

The policy adopted in Europe has diminished the impact of domestic legislation in favor of global policy since the question of open-skies policy combines both aspects of integration and conflict of interests. Although policy changes and technological advancement have identified new media policies in all countries, open-skies policy has not been adopted until public supervision of broadcasting systems was reduced in favor of commercialization.

Policy changes emerged since open-skies policy started dominating the development of media markets around the world, opening the way for new technologies and further competition. As a result of this global process, media markets have grown in a dynamic regulatory and competitive environment that is making an impact on the evolution of global media policy.

The change in global media markets was enormous, too, as technological advancement and increased competition led the new policy objectives dominated by global competition of all media and telecommunications services. The combination of technological development and open-market policies changed the traditional bases of broadcasting regulation because new technologies have been transformed from a medium of scarcity to one of abundance in which the favorable status of terrestrial broadcasting could no longer be guaranteed. The accessibility of new technology, such as cable and satellite transmissions and the Internet, established a policy process subject to influence from commercial interest groups and diminished the role of national governments.

Today the concept of open-skies policy dominates all media markets. The changes that have affected broadcasting systems following the swift development of American new media technologies and the growing enthusiasm for privatization in other countries have provided opportunities for a global free market approach governed by more market-oriented principles.

Global policy had several implications on local policies. It opened up markets to new service providers, diminished the role of the government by reducing the rules that limit market competition, and benefited consumers by providing them with lower rates and better service than they experienced under the old structure of broadcasting. On the other hand, calls for further deregulation of open-skies policy have clashed with cultural forces campaigning for the continuation of the heavily regulated and nonmarket system that has identified broadcasting policies for many years.

The commercialization of the broadcast, new media, and telecommunications policies created an entirely new set of challenges for established and emerging operators. All entrants must understand the new marketplace, the technical and regulatory constraints, and the commercial and global challenges. The global promotion of the free market approach, which has become a dominant feature in the development of media policy and markets around the world, has secured the transformation of the media sector into a global and market-led industry, dominated by commercial considerations and technological advancement.

The transition in media policies and markets and the adoption of open-skies policy are providing the means for further technological advancement with global impact. Competition from new media technologies and digital transmissions has further accelerated the global impact of new media policies by promoting multiple channels and services. Deregulation and privatization policies can be considered the main factor in accounting for global adoption of new media policy. In view of the fact that traditionally media markets had been characterized by a high degree of regulation in the interest of public service criteria, the broadcast sector has become diversified, following the impact of deregulation policies, with commercial operators dominating the marketplace.

The biggest difference relates to the readiness of countries to open up to global processes. Countries that have decided that they cannot open up to the world because they cannot compete with global technology have tended to adopt local policies and have lagged in their economic and technological development. Countries that have seen new technology as an opportunity to change their course of development from the old technology to the new structure could take advantage of new technology and benefit from the global connection.

Although many countries' cultures are rooted in age-old traditions, they are turning into new technologies and broadband services as a way to boost their economies and develop their telecommunications networks. Driven by deregulation, privatization, competition, and adoption of new technology, they regard building new telecommunications infrastructure as essential for the economy to recover, because global companies are investing millions of dollars in local and international telecommunications projects. Privatization of major state-owned telecom operators is progressing around the world, making room for new players and increased global competition.

The conclusion of the globalization of media policy is that open-skies policy has in effect become dominant around the world. This process is leading to common policy objectives of free market competition according to which all countries should operate. It also enforces technological development and a new social order as part of a global media market. The result is that convergence has become evident, involving competition between all information services—broadcast television, cable TV, satellite services and telephone companies, and guided by commercial considerations.

Convergence of Media and Telecommunications Policies

With the move to digital television in all its forms, the changed structure of media policy means that policy and technological convergence are the logical results of the development of competitive markets. Deregulation and privatization policies have created changes at the mostly local level in the leading media countries, and open-skies policy opened up these markets to global competition. Further changes in the direction of global media policy combine technological and policy developments, with the consequent convergence of policy and technology.

Convergence of policy means that whereas traditionally communications services were separate, as they operated on different networks and were regulated by different laws and different regulations at the national level, now they are regulated by international organizations and operating on a global level. Convergence of technology means that digital technology allows a substantially higher capacity of traditional and new services to be delivered over the same networks and to use integrated consumer devices for television, telephony, and computing.

The globalization of media policy and markets is leading to convergence of media systems and services as part of the decline of national monopolies and public service organizations. The traditional media sector and the telecommunications sector are becoming increasingly related following the pressure of technological and economic developments. Whereas in the first stages new media and telecommunications developments had been characterized by a high degree of regulation in the interest of public-service criteria, they have now become diversified, with private service providers dominating the marketplace. The consequent convergence includes changes in the nature of public supervision in the direction of free market, changes in the nature of supervising authorities relating to global policy, and permission for competition of all technologies.

These aspects provide a clear evidence that policies around the world have been integrated, with European policymaking following American policy objectives of free market approach and a central supervisory authority for all media and telecommunications services. In this global and commercial environment, all new media and telecommunications services are in competition at the global level, with free market approach identifying public policies around the world.

The new environment of global media policy poses new challenges to the ability of governments to create national policies for media and telecommunications technologies and services. The globalization of media policy and the process of the changing structure of technology and markets have been extraordinarily powerful, with the result that changes in public policy have affected the development and use of broadcast, cable, and satellite systems around the world.

New technology has already had a dramatic impact on broadcasting, offering greater opportunities and creating new challenges for audiences and broadcasters. Viewers are able to control their own scheduling, choose from channels carrying interactive programming, and purchase goods and services via television. Computers and telephone services can offer television programming, Internet services, and interactive applications—allowing participants to link into global information networks.

Convergence is forcing policymakers to adopt the rules and policy objectives enforced by the new trend of global policy, with underlying uniform objectives that identify the current stage of media policy. The changing course is related to technological development and changes in social and cultural perceptions, which resulted in uniform policy objectives and the implementation of global media policy.

The relationship between technology and commercialization has become central to the globalization of new media and telecommunications services and policy, mainly because the impact of new technologies is shaped by the advent of liberalization and privatization. The operations of new global services have been stimulated by the desire for cultural influence and profits while creating global markets. In order to provide global services to new markets, a common policy should be effective as the move to global media policy is being driven by the new policy objectives of free competition.

The clear-cut boundaries that separated different communications markets are blurring as convergence joins both infrastructures and services. The result is that the development of new media technologies brings up the issue of the effectiveness of national media policy. The shifts in the balance of power between public and commercial perceptions and the growing impact of economic policy and commercial broadcasting have diminished the impact of political institutions. They have similarly promoted the role of industrial and commercial interests.

Convergence is leading enterprises to push into new fields. With the progress toward global policy, new media policies have been a consequence of deliberate governmental and commercial strategy, placing more weight on the development of new technologies as a major force in each nation and at the global level. The driving force behind these policy changes has been provided by the combination of technological developments and market change. The main players in the new global media sector are government and regulatory agencies, terrestrial broadcasters, cable and satellite operators, suppliers of telecommunications services, and other suppliers of equipment and programming services. Market forces that aim to capture new markets and dominate new technologies are taking the lead. The convergence of new media industries and policies has established a media sector headed by large and powerful companies that are well aware of the wider potential of digital technology.[17]

The transformation in the nature of media policies is best demonstrated by the changing role of media technologies. In the old structure of broadcasting, each medium had its own nature and style of supervision, and public authorities had different conceptions according to the service provided. Under this structure, public service organizations were responsible for public transmissions, commercial operators transmitted commercial transmissions, cable systems provided additional channels, and satellite services provided programming and channels for cable systems.

This structure also related to telecommunications and information services, as it distinguished between the media, telecommunications, and information services. Telephone companies were the sole providers of telephone and other advanced services and on-line services had been available only through computing.

The direct competition of all media and telecommunications services has been propelled by the combination of cable and satellite technologies. The adoption of technological initiatives and the domination of free market perceptions triggered policy and technological changes. Direct Broadcast Satellite (DBS) services have revolutionized media and broadcasting policies and services, as new services became available on a global scale. The footprints of new satellites provide the means for programming to reach beyond national frontiers, creating large international broadcasting markets.

The nature of competition that develops between broadcasting services, new media technologies of cable and satellite, and information technologies, can be considered the main factor in the globalization of media policy and markets. The potential of digital technology should intensify the competition between the various services and increase the globalization of policy and markets.

This process is being endorsed by political institutions with a global impact, meaning that regulators prepare laws and regulations for the digital age, in which the predominance of market forces and the access of competition of all media and telecommunications services are evident. These developments demonstrate that in the era of global policy, media policy is undergoing significant changes of restructuring of national media industries. The new global policy provides the means for convergence of technologies and competition of all media and telecommunications services. The result is that with the convergence of telecommunications and media services, policy trajectories are likely to converge rather than diverge, thus creating a global media for all media and telecommunications technologies and services.

The new policy adopted in a growing number of countries has established a new structure of technological development and changed the traditional composition of the broadcasting media. The combination of convergence and digitalization, which is dominating the global environment, developed a new dimension of competition—between terrestrial broadcasters and new media operators for the provision of digital television and telecommunications services. The transition into the digital era combines digital terrestrial, digital satellite, broadband cable, telephone companies, wireless communications, the Internet, and interactive television applications.

Today's policies concentrate on enhancing competition. Regulatory moves around the world are designed to remove competitive restrictions, aimed at intensifying competition within the market with the integration of media and telecommunications policy. Political decisions are changing the course of media policy by diminishing the role of national governments, converging media and telecommunications policies, and enhancing competition within the electronic media.

Under the new structure of media policy, regulatory institutions with global impact lead the way for policy changes. These developments have important implications for global policy, because local policies can no longer be exclusively guided by cultural considerations. The end result of convergence is that with the domination of global competition, the media and telecommunications sectors have started to pursue objectives outside the technological and economic field, leading to globalization.

Consolidation of Policy and Technologies

The final stage in the adoption of global media policy is based on consolidation of policy and technologies as part of the "free enterprise" philosophy originally embraced by the FCC and adopted in other countries. In this stage, countries around the world tend to adopt the model of global new policy in full.

The domination of deregulation, open-skies policy, and convergence means that in the new competitive scene all media and telecommunications systems are capable of carrying a variety of sophisticated services with a significant increase in the number of the channels and services available. As stated, policies today are based on the principle of competition of all media and telecommunications services and permission for all technologies to carry all services. Under this structure, telecom companies are moving toward becoming Internet and telephony providers, cable companies are moving away from traditional cable services, and satellite operators and Internet service providers make all services available. It can be predicted that sometime in the future traditional media services (broadcast television stations providing only programming services and telephone services providing only phone calls) will cease to exist.

The FCC and the European Community are leading the adoption of global media policy. In the United States, the 1992 Cable Television Consumer Protection and Competition Act guaranteed access to satellite-delivered cable programming services by alternative multichannel video providers, such as DBS operators. The main contribution of the act to advance competition in the multichannel market is by providing television stations with certain carriage rights on local market cable television systems. Additional competition has been provided by the provision for other technologies to provide cable services—telephone companies and the broadcast networks, and the start of competing DBS services transmitting direct to home transmissions. The 1996 Telecommunications Act is the first comprehensive revision of federal telecommunications law since the enactment of the Communications Act in 1934. It opened up the market entirely for competition of all technologies by removing remaining restrictions on telephone companies and other advanced services to acquire cable systems and provide programming services to cable systems.

The Telecommunications Act started a new era for media and telecommunications services. Following the passage of the law, there are no longer statutory barriers to telephone companies entering into cable. It also opened up local telephone markets for the first time and established a flexible regulatory environment and encouraged significant investments in new infrastructures and services while cable, satellite and telephone companies are entering the wireless and data services markets.

The act created a new system of broadcast television in the United States called digital television. It revolutionized the telecommunications industry by letting anyone enter any communications business and any communications business compete in any market against any other. The purpose of the act is to deregulate all communications industries and to permit the market rather than public policy to determine the course of the information superhighway and the communications system of the future. The law is roundly considered one of the most important federal laws. It has initiated the direction for the main players in the global communications market, including all media and telecommunications services: telephone companies, cable and satellite operators, broadcast stations, wireless communications, and the Internet.

This policy is being implemented in the transformation into digital technology by determining that the entire American broadcasting system would become digital. It is designed to promote further competition among programming service providers, enhance consumer choice, and assure wide access to all media and telecommunications services—in a digital environment.[18]

The recognition that digital technology is leading to the convergence of media, telecommunications, and information services has been adopted at the level of European policy too. European policy for media and telecommunications services is aimed at determining the regulatory environment to allow the development of information technologies of all kinds.

The development of digital technology differs in Europe. The United Kingdom is leading digital development with a multiple service of terrestrial, satellite, and cable technologies. The 1996 Broadcasting Act determined that licenses for six multiplex services of digital terrestrial television broadcasting should be awarded with the aim of offering a wide range of advanced options from television broadcasting to telebanking, teleshopping and the Internet. Other European countries are expected to progress in digital technology toward the same level.[19]

These policy changes lead to the conclusion that in the current stage of media policy, digital services are starting to spread commercially around the world. The commercial exploitation of digital television will deliver an almost unlimited number of channels and generate a whole range of image and text services. This process demonstrates that with global reference to multiservice competition in programming, the future of all media and telecommunications services is dependent not only on cultural perceptions, but, and even more decisively, on commercial stakes and technological development.

The European Community has followed American policy by adopting a continental rather than national policy for new media and telecommunications developments. According to the new European policy, since 1998 all telecom services, including public telephone companies, must be privatized and national markets deregulated. Since 1999, all public cable systems within the European Union must also be privatized.

This approach has been explored in the European Commission's "Green Paper on the Convergence of the Telecommunications, Media and Information Technology Sectors and the Implications for

Regulation." The paper projects the future extent of impact and change in telecommunications, media and information services and the way these services should be regulated at the European level. It stresses that restrictions should only be introduced where there is an absolute need and even then should be as light as possible. It views technological and political development and leads to a common European policy based on the convergence of media and telecommunications industries and allows competition of all advanced services as part of a global process. This policy will be pursued by the already announced European Telecommunications Review for the 21st century.[20]

The technological, commercial, and social revolution will emerge following the full conversion into digital technology and the natural adaptation of a free competitive and global environment, in which each technology is allowed to provide all services. This global revolution will provide new channels and services with better quality and wider technological options and commercial choice. Digital television will significantly increase the resolution of video signals and offer vastly improved picture quality. Pay TV and Pay-Per-View services will allow the consumer to purchase a program (a movie or a special event) through a computerized order processing center. This technology allows for the processing of a high volume of orders in a short time period, providing entertainment and information services to its subscribers. Following the completion of legal changes that are taking place around the world, these services will be offered by all media, telecommunications, and information technologies in a multiservice competitive scene.

The globalization of policy and markets, which is becoming the inevitable result of the new era of global media policy, means that policy changes are being enforced at the global level, allowing new competitors for the delivery of information and entertainment services directly to homes.

In future terms, the defacto constitution of global media policy is evident in the formation of a regulatory environment necessary to allow the introduction and development of all media, telecommunications, and information services. This course of convergence of policy and technology should lead to the union of media and telecommunications services, with further elimination of historic state and local barriers to competition in media and telecommunications technologies.[21]

SUMMARY

Media policy has developed according to three major phases examined in this book. Initially it was dominated by early perceptions of the "old structure" of broadcasting and influenced by public service principles. Then a free market approach was adopted, encouraging competition between the old media of terrestrial broadcasting and new media technologies of cable and satellite. In the current stage of development, a global structure has been adopted around the world.

This development course demonstrates a shift in public policy, from the perception of new media technologies as having a secondary role to broadcast television to a definition of them as a global and market-led industry, dominated by commercial and competitive forces. Policy changes have become global, despite important initial differences in approach between countries, creating a more or less common process for new media developments in the United States and Western Europe.

Media policy for the 21st century is dominated by globalization and the transition into digital technology. Technological developments and social transformations have created a new concept of global media policy, which dominates new media and telecommunications policies. The main objectives of this policy structure, which is going to take center stage in the third millennium, include deregulation and privatization (policy changes at the local level), globalization (adoption of open-skies policy), policy convergence (and competition of all media and telecommunications services), and consolidation as policy and technologies.

The three-stage development course of media policy examined in this chapter is explored throughout the book, according to major issues discussed in other chapters. These include the role of governments, globalization of media policy, the technologies of the 21st century, the social adoption of information technology, globalization of media markets and localism of media commercialization.

The new structure of global media policy demonstrates that competition for the provision of advanced services is developing on a global scale, with major regulatory changes in favor of market policies. Different countries have experienced different levels of policy changes although adoption of digital technologies and permission for competition of all media and telecommunications services means adoption of the main principles of global media policy, with wide-ranging competition between technologies that traditionally provided different services.

2

The Diminishing
Role of Governments

The role of governments in the development of media policy has shifted tremendously with the adoption of a market model perception. Whereas initially prominence was given to terrestrial television and new technology was restricted, deregulation policies in the United States and political changes in Europe had been the catalyst for the development of commercial perceptions. Although the end result is that the free market has prevailed, governments have played a substantial role in the development of new media policy and technologies.

The research in this chapter examines the role of governments in the development of media policy in the three largest media countries in Europe (Britain, France, and Germany). This analysis is in response to American policy, which has been a catalyst for policy changes in Europe and in other countries toward global media policy.

The chapter is mainly concerned with the changing course of cable policy—from a policy area heavily dominated by governments to a free market structure that encourages competition by all media and telecommunications services. The relevance of cable policy to research in media policy is because the technology of cable provided the first provision of additional programming to terrestrial broadcasting. Differences in the policy structure of countries illustrate the way media policy has evolved in response to this technological development.

Comparison between the development of media and cable policy shows the similarities that identify the three-stage development course of policymaking in these areas. In both policy areas, in the first two stages social and cultural aspects dominated, with high stress on the content of the programs and imposition of national cable plans. Then, in the third stage, newer regulation eliminated these rules and changed national plans, leading to the growth of the cable industry and new media services.

To place the argument in a broader context, the history outlined in this chapter illustrates an underlying similarity in the social and political development of cable systems in America and Europe. Initially, the politics of cable was dominated by public authorities, which defined the technology as having a secondary, relay role and limited its development to the diffusion of off-air transmissions. This initial stance was then displaced by deregulation and privatization policies. Although this process occurred at different speeds and was implemented through various social and political initiatives, it was technological advancement coupled with global market forces and lobbying power of domestic interest groups that shaped the general trajectory of cable policymaking in each nation.

Based on this analysis, it is argued that the general course of media policy explored in this book provides the main trends that have identified the development course of cable policy at the global level. Although it is common to all countries that the third stage of media policy is equivalent to the third stage of governments' policy for cable and new media, the course of change in cable policymaking demonstrates that the role of European governments is particularly notable. Initially European and American public policies differed in two main aspects: the basic consumption of the role of governments and the adoption of free market approach. In the course of change in European policy, differences diminished, and so has the role of governments.

On the same level of the changes in media policy, the development of cable systems in Europe has gone through three distinctive stages. Initially governments ignored cable, then they regulated the technology as part of a larger plan for the overall development of the broadcasting media, and later all governments deregulated cable, thus creating a uniform policy with the distinct domination of market forces.

In theoretical terms the research proposes that the three-stage course of media policy also applies to the role of governments. The four countries examined here represent the main trends in the involvement of governments and have had a leading role in the changing course of media policy around the world. This can be considered as a global process that led to the current state of global media policy.

The argument made here is that although policy differed from country to country, the role of governments in the development of new technology was implemented at large through three distinctive stages.

1. First Stage: Governments Ignored New Technology

In the first stage, the role of governments was decisive, as they tried to ignore multichannel services. This perception was meant to prevent the establishment of cable infrastructure in order to protect broadcast television. Common to all countries is that in this early period, despite a rich variety of national styles of regulation that existed, cable systems were considered a service secondary to terrestrial broadcasting. They were developed mainly in remote areas, serving small communities, and provided only better reception of off-air transmissions. The result of the policy initiated by governments was that the development of cable did not realize its potential or was restricted because of public regulations that ignored the technology.

2. Second Stage: National Cable Plans

In the second stage, governments became involved in cable policymaking and the technology was regulated, reflecting significant differences of historical experience and regulatory culture among countries. The adoption of free market approach for cable and satellite in the United States established an open-skies policy for the entire American broadcasting system. This policy has dominated American media policy since the 1970s, and made an impact on policy changes elsewhere, too. In the 1980s, the three largest media countries of Europe launched ambitious plans to install a national cable network as part of a public policy for the overall development of the broadcasting media.

Whereas in the United States the new policy diminished the role of public authorities in favor of market domination, in Europe the regulated era involved long-term social and cultural aspects and national technology programs. In all three European countries, the development of cable systems was regulated with the aim of restructuring the broadcasting media.

The actual cabling process demonstrated, however, that despite the decisive involvement of governments, the development and overall impact of cable in Europe was marginal. This was also in contrast to the United States, where the free market policy allowed cable to proliferate. As a general course of development, it can be concluded that although the process differed among countries, the common result of the national cable plans initiated in Europe was that the regulation of cable hindered the development of the technology and the ambitious plans proved unsuccessful.

3. Third Stage: Common Policy Objectives

In the third stage, following the failure of the plans to establish national cable policies, commercial aspects prevailed across Europe. American deregulation policy and the exploitation of American cable services made an impact on European media policies. The combination of technological advancement and political changes led to policy changes and European governments chose to enlarge the broadcasting media to the extent that new media technologies were given permission to operate on a commercial basis.

Deregulation of the cable industry aimed to explore the technical and commercial capabilities of cable systems and increase competition within broadcasting markets. The new policy led to uniform cable policy characterized by adoption of deregulatory policies and diminishing role of governments. The result was that—although at different speeds and perceptions—governments gave permission to market forces to dominate future development, abandoning the initial goals of cable's development.

The conclusion of this course of development is that a new approach of free market and global policy has become dominant in all that relates to the role of governments. This approach means that the leading role of cable, which dominated the first two stages of development, was no longer effective. The policy adopted by European governments advocates competition among all new media and telecommunications services, within a global and competitive environment dominated by new media policy in which cable is only one of the competing technologies. The changes that have affected broadcasting systems following the swift development of new media technologies and the growing enthusiasm for privatization have provided opportunities for a global approach governed by market-oriented principles and leading global authorities. This development is leading to a new structure of media policy in the 21st century, dominated by a diminished role for governments and an increased role for global regulators and market principles.

2.1 GOVERNMENTS IGNORED NEW TECHNOLOGY

In the first stage of governmental policy, the development of cable tele-vision as a multichannel service was limited because of restrictive public policies. Community Antenna Television (CATV) systems were installed only in specific places, mainly with the aim of improving the reception of television programming transmitted over-the-air. This policy was common to the United States and all three European countries examined in this research.

The United States

The most prominent policy change on the part of governments was in America. In the first three decades of American television—between the 1940s and early 1970s—the Federal Communications Commission (FCC) mainly ignored the development of cable systems and then regulated the evolving industry.

Television started in July 1944, after the FCC sanctioned com-mercial transmissions, and one year later ten stations went on the air. Cable systems started as a service to households living in remote areas where reception of off-air television broadcasts was poor. The earliest CATV systems were established in remote areas of Oregon and Pennsylvania. In Astoria, Oregon (5,000 homes), Leory Edward Parsons wired the first CATV system in 1948, with an initial subscriber list of three households. The first commercial CATV system was installed two years later in Lansford, Pennsylvania. Lansford is a small community located about 65 miles from Philadelphia, a distance too great for ade-quate television reception. Partner Valley Television Company owned the system, which enhanced the quality of television transmissions received from Philadelphia.

In the late 1950s and in the 1960s, cable operators began to pick up broadcast signals from other areas and states, and changed the basic function of cable from a service that retransmitted local broadcast sta-tions to a provider of new programming selections. But despite this development, the policy of the FCC advocated a national structure of broadcasting and encouraged the development of a public television network that would compete with the commercial network of broadcast television. The development of local cable systems had interfered with that conception and the FCC chose to ignore the development of cable systems, thereby maintaining their secondary and limited nature.

The changed attitude and policy objectives were forced upon the FCC, and in response to broadcast industry concerns the FCC expanded its jurisdiction. It became involved in cable's decision making in 1964, when CATV systems started to develop as potential competitors to major broadcast television stations. With 1,200 CATV systems serving more than one million subscribers, the FCC's conception of a proper national television system offering public broadcasting service was under threat, and a new policy had to be enforced. The FCC was also forced to regulate cable because they had exhausted attempts to persuade Congress to legislate a strict retransmission consent law and the courts rejected the contention that cable operators were unfair competitors since they did not make copyright payments for programming.

The courts had another role in this transition in policy, when the Supreme Court affirmed the FCC's jurisdiction over cable operations. They ruled that the FCC had a broad responsibility to regulate all aspects of communication, including cable, by virtue of the Communications Act of 1934. The act is the basic national legislation governing communications. It mandated the national telephone system—the first such legislation to recognize the importance of telecommunications for social and economic growth. The Supreme Court ruling forced the FCC to regulate cable. As a result of this decision, and with no cable control forthcoming from Congress or the courts, the FCC was left to take action on its own. Consequently, since 1964 all cable systems in the United States have come under the authority of the FCC.

Until the early 1970s however, cable was strictly regulated, and its development was limited. The policy was intended to promote cable as a supplementary service, and thereby to protect broadcast interests. In 1964, the FCC created the Must Carry rules, requiring cable operators to offer the signals of every broadcast station within 60 miles of their cable system upon the request of the broadcast station. In 1966, the FCC published its second major cable ruling, preventing cable operators from importing distant broadcast signals in the Top 100 markets without FCC hearing. In 1968, the FCC imposed a freeze on cable's further growth, by ruling that if a cable system was located within 35 miles of a television market, it could offer to its subscribers only those television transmissions that were available off-air.

The FCC's assertion of authority over cable brought the systems' development in larger markets to a virtual standstill. In fact, its development was even reduced—with only 5 to 9 percent of the population connected to cable systems by the start of the 1970s.[1]

Europe

The same attitude of the United States was prominent in Europe, too. All governments ignored the development of cable and did not permit any cable developments. The most evident characteristic as a result of public regulations was that cable systems did not develop. The technology of cable was identified as a service that simply boosted the quality of broadcast television signals for small communities. This image led policymakers to ignore cable because cable systems did not appear to have the potential to be a competitor or even contributor to national television systems.

Examination of the policies of the three largest media countries demonstrates that despite differences between national polices in the role of governments, initial policies had common characteristics. In reviewing this period, one can easily see that although cable was available in the United States since the late 1940s, all three countries pursued policies favoring and protecting broadcast television. This caution can be partly explained as a reaction to cable's technical ability to provide multiple channels and the resulting fear, on the part of governments and public authorities, that their ability to regulate the airwaves would be undermined.

In the first stage of development, therefore, cable did not develop in all European countries because public authorities did not encourage it. This course of development demonstrates that the distinction between America and Europe is particularly clear with regard to the role of governments. Although until the 1970s FCC regulations restrained cable growth to protect broadcast television by placing restrictions on the import of distant signals, entrepreneurs felt relatively free to invest on a market-by-market basis, responding in free-enterprise fashion to customer demands. On the other hand, European countries generally took a more centralized approach, and media services were traditionally delivered by monopolies. Cable's development was also limited, again as a result of restrictive public policies. CATV systems were installed only in specific places, mainly with the aim of improving the reception of television programming transmitted over-the-air. This policy trend, which prevailed across Europe, delayed full-scale cable installations in the first stage, while parliaments debated the social and cultural implications of cable policies.

The difference in the extent of regulatory restrictions demonstrates the tremendous impact of public policy and extremely strong role of governments in Europe. During the initial period, which continued until the 1980s, European broadcasting largely conformed to a dominant model of public service broadcasting with common values and principles of regulation. This policy meant that cable developments had also been restricted, as policy was intended to explore the social and cultural aspects rather than the commercial capabilities of broadcasting.

In France, resentment against private stations led to the nationalization of the entire broadcasting system. The government did not encourage cable and made no effort to develop it. Instead, it concentrated on more centralized projects, such as the French satellite (TDF1). The scope of cable systems was limited to the diffusion of television broadcasts normally received over-the-air. Local programming and the diffusion of original programming were both prohibited. Establishment of cable infrastructure was permitted in only two situations: to reach areas covered by a broadcast shadow; and, in border regions, to retransmit more easily all broadcasts that could be received over-the-air.

In Germany too, the expansion of commercial CATV systems was impossible, because most of the population was able to receive good signals from the public broadcast channels and the law prohibited private programs. The installation of a nationwide cable network required negotiation among the state authorities; however, no agreement was achieved.

In Britain, although the government did not directly prohibit the development of cable, the Copyright Act effectively prohibited CATV systems from making available transmissions that were not normally available over-the-air. The development was also limited because of an agreement, forced upon CATV operators by the Independent Television regional contractors, not to import the signals of other regional broadcast stations into their region. By the early 1970s, as the transmission network improved, the number of cable subscribers stopped growing and then began to decline sharply.

Regarding the first stage of public policy for cable in Europe, it is evident that public regulations restricted development. In all three European countries, the development of cable systems was delayed for many years because of the policy initiated by public authorities, with emphasis on the role of governments and monopoly status of public broadcast services. The changes that occurred in media policy in later stages, following American deregulatory policy and technological advancement, can be defined as changing logic, from the old system of public service broadcasting to a free market approach. The policy changes in the area of cable TV have followed this trend, with the abundance of the initial social and cultural perceptions of its development.[2]

2.2 NATIONAL CABLE PLANS

In the second stage, the role of governments in shaping cable policies had been even more notable. The distinction between American and European policies is evident in this stage as well, with phenomenal growth of new media in America and in contrast continued control of public authorities in Europe.

The United States

The United States was the first country to experience the whole array of services that broadcasting via satellite to cable systems can make possible. This development became prominent following the adoption of the 1972 open-skies policy, which diminished the role of public authorities and transferred domination of future developments to market forces and technological advancement. The deregulation of American cable policy allowed for an extensive growth of all media services—a direction that has dominated American media market since then. It was particularly the permission for commercial operation of satellites that changed the television sector dramatically by paving the way for a considerable growth of program networks and a conspicuous expansion in the number and diversity of programming services offered to cable subscribers. The obvious and observable result of this development was a substantial increase in number of subscribers connected to cable systems.[3]

The deregulation moves were part of the broader process to create a common policy at the national level while freeing cable from contradictory regulations. Another important aspect of American deregulation policy was the adoption of a comprehensive Cable Act in 1984. The act established a national regulatory policy for cable and provided guidelines for federal, state, and local authorities. It provided a successful legislative effort to create a national cable policy.

Until the enactment of the act, the problem for cable was that despite constitutional protection and unlike all other technologies covered by the FCC, the industry always had to deal with regulatory authorities at the local, federal, and state levels—with their respective areas of jurisdiction. Despite regulations authorized by the FCC and some degree of regulation issued by states, local governments are the primary regulatory boards for cable systems. Their powers stem chiefly from their responsibilities for granting franchises.

American legislative history has identified local franchising authorities as the primary instrument of cable regulation. Local governments have always been responsible for granting franchises in accordance with federally established sets of the technical performance standards. They typically establish the framework for franchises, select local operators, oversee systems' operations, and renew franchises. The authority of local governments to issue cable franchises and to regulate systems' operation remained exclusive even after the Cable Act was amended. It became, however, part of a planned policy, following a decade-long string of the federal deregulation actions, which constituted a national plan for cable and permitted the steady development of the technology.[4]

The changed role of public authorities was the main achievement of the legislation. In creating the Cable Act, Congress allowed cable to compete more effectively with other media technologies. In accordance with the First Amendment, local authorities were given the right to demand certain kinds of facilities and hardware, but have no control over content. The role of the FCC was reduced to monitoring the development of the broadcasting media in a manner that permits free competition.[5]

In the new structure of media policy, Congress and the FCC are the main forces in deregulating cable, but the courts have also had a role to play in the diminishing role of public authorities. In a series of judicial decisions the courts have made it clear that the First Amendment applies not only to the printed press but also to broadcasting, film, and the other mass media as well. According to this perception, cable operators are electronic publishers who enjoy a constitutionally protected right to freedom of speech. The statement of the Supreme Court guides the application of the First Amendment in relation to cable. This note states that each medium of expression, "must be assessed for the First Amendment purposes by standards suited to it." It proposes a First Amendment analysis that takes into an account the peculiar characteristics of the cable medium, including that of the local franchise.[6]

Europe

The development of the American cable system and the deregulation of the industry made an impact on European cable policy and changed the basic policy thinking in regard to new technologies. It was the satellite driven success of American cable that changed attitudes in Europe, with the result that governments concluded that their future economic welfare required the development of cable systems.

The state of cable developments at the start of the second stage was poor. Although received in many homes, European cable had little resemblance to systems in America. European systems were generally CATV or Master Antenna Television (MATV) installations that simply employed a central antenna within an apartment complex, and public policies restricted its commercial development. In the early 1980s however, following political changes and the adoption of new orientations, all three largest media countries of Europe launched national ambitious plans to cable their nations.

When comparing the policy of the largest media countries of Europe, differences are apparent because of the deep involvement of governments and the employment of public service perceptions alongside technological and economic development of a national cable network.

The transition in public policy was evident in all three countries, which sought the speedy establishment of cable, although their perceptions differed. All three governments saw cable as part of a long-term policy plan, and it became a focus of political debates on the nature and impact of new media policies. The development of cable systems explored an attempt to utilize social and cultural aspects of the technology, and the debates circled around public and commercial aspects in broadcasting and the extent of involvement by public authorities.

Although social and cultural aspects had identified broadcasting and cable policies as far as regulation was involved, the different perceptions of governments resulted in almost opposite tendencies. Britain deregulated its cable industry with limited degree of public supervision by adopting a policy of light regulation and private funding. French policy increased state control on the broadcasting and telecommunications industries by supporting cable systems with public funds with a modicum of regulatory controls. Germany decided in favor of a policy that combined the desire for the speedy establishment of a nationwide network with public support by adopting a policy that granted the Deutsche Bundespost powers and funds to cable the whole country.

This course of new media developments leads to major conclusions about the role of European governments.

Firstly, the policies initiated have to be seen as part of a broader process headed by national industries and economically engaged branches of government, which saw the development of a national cable network as part of a long-term plan involving social and cultural aspects. Common to these initial developments is their implementation as government policy intended to ensure economic and technological benefits from the development of an advanced cable network.

Secondly, as part of the national cabling plans, although to a different extent, the three governments chose to limit the commercial potential of cable by preventing the technology from competing with terrestrial broadcasting channels and by establishing plans for national cable infrastructures with long-term social and cultural goals. The restrictions on commercial exploitation demonstrate the substantial role in the development of cable technology, which had been one of the most compelling aspects of cable policy.

Thirdly, a similar trend is evident in cable policies, despite differences in implementation. The cable plans emphasized not only the structure of the systems and the political supervision, but perhaps even to a greater extent, the programming and cultural conception. In Britain, France, and Germany the national governments chose to encourage a new private sector alongside the old. In Britain the process was initially advanced by cable franchises, in France it was a mixed order of cable and terrestrial broadcasting, and in Germany the addition of private operators was the result of policy changes that were achieved through cable and satellite technologies.

Britain

The most distinctive aspect of British cable policy was that a mixed structure of commercial and social perceptions prevailed. The role of the government was mainly in terms of formulating an appropriate and deregulated legal environment and development—based on the public demand for entertainment but supervised by the Cable Authority.

The Conservative government, which took office in 1979, put information technology at the center of public policy initiatives. In an atmosphere of changing roles and responsibilities, the Information Technology Advisory Panel (ITAP) was formed. The panel shared the government's view on the liberalization of telecommunications. Their report discussed the economics of cable, the industrial potential, and the broadcast and regulatory implications. It suggested that a major cable drive would have major industrial benefits, provide a wider selection of services and new type of television programming, such as community and pay TV channels, and advertising would benefit from easy access to target audiences. The report gave an authoritative push to the procable lobby in Britain and proposed a model of government-industry relations that gave prominence to the private sector and free enterprise.

The government responded quickly to the report by designating 1982 as Information Technology Year and setting up the Hunt Committee. The aim of the committee was to explore the practical implications of the government's wish to secure the industrial benefits that cable technology could offer. It also aimed to consider an expansion of cable systems that would permit them to carry a wide range of entertainment and other services and at the same time be consistent with the public interest.

The conclusions of the Hunt Report were incorporated in the White Paper of 1983 and the Cable and Broadcasting Act of 1984, which laid down the objectives according to which cable in Britain was going to be developed. The new law determined that cable would be privately financed and market-led and regulation would be light as possible and flexible, so that it could be adapted to changes in technology. In terms of the technology required, the law determined that any technology, including any kind of cables, could be installed. Regarding programming, it stipulated that cable systems would be developed without any restrictions on the number of channels, the programs transmitted, and the charges made to the subscribers.

The role of the British government was significant despite the market-led policy it initiated. Conservative administrations have pursued a policy of liberalizing the rules under which cable operated with the intention of letting the market dictate developments. In order to create such an environment, however, public policy set out its detailed conclusions on the broadcasting, technological, and telecommunication implications of cable systems. This explains the policy of successive Conservative governments, which was to develop new media and telecommunications to counter the decline in traditional industries. In the broader definition, the government aimed at the development of information technologies, although they were reluctant to privilege any particular system. The goal was to promote all possible applications of information technology for the national economic advantage, on the basis of private capital and market demand.

France

Social and cultural perceptions had been the most significant objective dominating French broadcasting and cable policies. Throughout this period of government policy, these perceptions had been decisive, with emphasis on several key issues: the nature and quality of programming, the development of advanced technology, and the extreme role of public authorities.

The roots of a national cable plan can be seen in the election campaign of 1981. The Socialist party, which advocated for adoption of advanced technology, promised video-communications development and broadcasting reforms. This new policy was given substance in 1982, immediately after their victory, when the new administration presented a comprehensive Broadcasting Act and Cable Plan.

The role of the government in the formulation of the new policy was particularly decisive. Before 1981, in the first stage of the government's involvement in cable's development, the policy consisted mainly of avoiding the development of local means of expression. The established political tradition of centralized control of broadcasting enabled the government to restrict television programming, and the technical potential of cable to provide additional services clashed with these goals. The government blocked the development of cable as long as it could. But international trade and economic concerns generated interest in a major governmental push toward the development of new telecommunications technologies and industries, and the new Socialist government attempted to establish a nationwide cable infrastructure with local and interactive potential. This marked the start of the second stage of cable's development in France.

The new legislation abolished the state's monopoly on the distribution of television and programs by decentralizing programming and freeing it from political influence. Although it was government recognition of the right to operate a television station that was the trigger for policy changes, the new policy was aimed at advancing an interactive video-communications network as part of a long-term plan with social and cultural goals.

The technology of cable had an important role to play within the new policy. The Cable Plan was an ambitious enthusiastic proposal for the development of a broadband network, capable of providing interactive services. The role of public authorities was decisive in this project: half of the nation's homes were to be cabled by the year 2000, with most of the financing coming from the government. The national Postal and Telecommunications Authority (PTT) was authorized to cable the nation with fiber optic links.

The plan aimed at constructing the most advanced infrastructure and providing a wide variety of interactive services. Each cable network was designed to provide basic services, and a number of optional functions such as addressable channels, video services and home security monitoring. The long-term plans were even more ambitious: future interactive cable services were scheduled to include sound and full motion video service and various pay TV and pay-per-view services, and French cable systems were intended to evolve toward an Integrated Services Digital Network (ISDN).[7]

Germany

In Germany too, like France and Britain, cable developments were limited until the 1980s. Also in common with these countries, attitudes changed following political changes. After the coming to power of the Conservative Federal Government in 1982, a strong push for the independent access to broadcasting was adopted, and the approach to cable changed.

The social and political aspects of the transition in policy were complex, however. The role of public authorities was particularly decisive. Resulting from the agreement achieved after the Second World War, broadcasting is under the authority of the German states, whereas all other telecommunications aspects, including broadcasting facilities, are the responsibility of the PTT (Bundespost—the national mail, telegraph, and telecommunications authority). This situation delayed the establishment of cable systems in the first phase of public policy, as the country confronted conflicting issues of broadcasting and new media policy.

The permission for private programming followed a 1981 decision by the Supreme Court, which made no essential distinction between broadcasting and new media. The court gave permission to the Bundespost and to local states to start private programming. The decision had two major decisions. The first was that cable had to face the supervision of the broadcasting councils in the German states, and the second, and more significant one, was the introduction of a reformed framework, allowing a plurality of programming representing the range of opinions inherent in German society.

The new wave in German media development, which began following the Supreme Court decision, accelerated in 1982 when the new Federal government introduced a new media concept. The new policy was based on the swift exploitation of cable systems throughout the country and was aimed at encouraging a variety of programming services.

The primary reasons for the change in German media policy were political in nature. The involvement of the central government and a strong push for independent access to broadcasting changed the approach to the adoption of new technologies. The Conservative administration wanted cable and satellite to compete with the public broadcasters, and introducing cable was the perfect solution to the shortage of over-the-air frequencies and the control of the states over the transmissions received within their boundaries. The role of the central government was particularly decisive, as it had been the most influential force in the development of a national cable plan. By creating local means of distribution for new media services, the government could ensure the eventual acceptance of the states as part of a national cable plan. As a result, in the coming years German states began to introduce legislation for cable and private broadcasting systems.

After a long negotiation between the state governments four pilot projects started in 1984. Their main goal was to test the user acceptance of new programs and to provide answers to difficulties that may occur. The projects marked the entrance of private industry into the delivery of television programming in Germany. Cable developments first took place under the cable projects, and only after they were properly evaluated did states make decisions for program provisions.

The national cable plan endorsed by the central government was a huge project with long-term social and cultural aspects. In 1985, the plan aimed to cable one-and-a-half million households per year, with an overall target of bringing 80 percent of the German population within reach of cable by the end of the 20th century. The German Bundespost initiated its plan to eventually install cable throughout the country, even though the project was expected to take decades to complete.[8]

2.3 COMMON POLICY OBJECTIVES

The third stage of involvement of governments in Europe started between the mid and late 1980s and still dominates cable and new media developments in the policy for the 21st century. It is identified foremost with the abundance of the public perceptions and the adoption of commercial and competitive perceptions.

With the start of this period, it was evident that the first two stages proved unsuccessful in terms of public policy. The early periods demonstrated that despite the plans initiated by the three governments, their implementation proved unsuccessful in all that relates to public reaction, and the long-term objectives failed the initial test of the market. It was only after these perceptions had been accepted, that market-led policy could be adopted for cable in all three European countries, and deregulation policies and the diminishing role of governments started to dominate cable and new media policies.

The transformation in the role of governments—from a regulated cable system with public goals into a deregulated industry dominated by commercial perceptions—is particularly decisive. The reasons for change included pressure by economic interests to allow commercial exploitation and public demand for adoption of new technologies and new programming services. The response of European governments was to decide that market-oriented principles should govern new policy for broadcasting and new media.

The most obvious characteristic of the changes in cable policies is that governments are no longer involved in cable developments and market forces dictate the nature of development. This caused the collapse of the public objectives that dominated governmental involvement in favor of market-led policies and commercial domination. Cable policies become dominated by deregulation, with minimal involvement of governments, based on the American example of deregulation policies.

The new structure resulted in adoption of advanced programming services, increase in the number of terrestrial channels, and exploitation of the potential technical advancement of cable and satellite to provide additional channels.

The profound changes in the broadcasting and telecommunications sectors can be demonstrated by the way that policy perceptions changed. During the first and second stages, the central issue was the extent of government involvement; in the third stage the central issue involves commercial aspects—the ability of the market to finance new commercial channels. Broadcast, satellite, or cable operators transmit the available services, and the debate concerns the extent of additional development of commercial outlets and the role of governments in these developments. Another issue for debate is the way to enforce technological competition between these services.

Britain

The new era of British media administrates increased market-led policy. Britain deregulated its cable industry, with permission for foreign involvement and investment in cable (which ended up being dominated by American telephone companies). The role of the government is particularly important in this transition, because it stated its position of letting the market dictate the nature of cable's development in the Broadcasting Act of 1990. The consistent commitment to development within the private sector but without financial assistance from the government, which identified the national cable plan of the early 1980s, has continued since then, coupled with further deregulation of the cable industry in the 1990s.

The main policy changes have been permission for foreign control over the cable systems and elimination of other rules that prevented the development of the industry. These changes resulted in a new atmosphere of liberalization: the involvement of American companies was encouraged by the adoption of commercial perceptions, based on the unregulated media policy of the United States. All other restrictions have also been dropped, including the supply of information services, allowing cable operators to determine the nature of economic and programming policies and technical development. New licenses issued by public authorities (initially by the Cable Authority, and since 1991 by the Independent Television Commission—ITC—that replaced the Cable Authority) offered investors an unregulated environment. In another significant provision cable operators were permitted to offer telephone services, and today cable telephony constitutes a substantial source of income and a boost to cable TV subscriptions.

This policy confirmed the minimal involvement of the government, with market domination of information and entertainment services. The gradual expansion of cable systems and the addition of satellite and cable channels (including digital services) pose an increased challenge to broadcast television, with the role of the government confined to maintaining competition within the market. This policy continued to dominate throughout the 1990s and has been intensified in the 21st century.

France

In examining the transition in European cable and new media policies, it is evident that France was the first country to abandon the original cable plan. Despite political changes of socialist and conservative governments, a continual swing to commercialization has dominated the third stage of government policy for cable. In this stage French cable policy followed the trend of reduced involvement by public authorities. New licenses to operate cable systems have become more attractive following the decision to permit involvement by commercial operators and to decline the requirement for data services.

The main course of change had been the realization that the hoped-for cultural revolution of the Cable Plan did not realize its potential, and that the reliance on cable as a dominant technology proved unsuccessful in terms of public reaction and political arrangements. By the mid-1980s it became evident that cable did not succeed in developing beyond the original nature that identified the technology as a service that served only small communities and had a role secondary to broadcast television. In addition to the growing impact of commercial broadcasting and the decline of public service broadcasting channels in Europe, the unsuccessful plans to explore the cultural and political aspects of the cable policy meant the collapse of the ideas that identified this regulated era. This led to policy changes and the inevitable adoption of new approaches by the national government.

Following the change in policy, French cable has been established based on commercial perspectives, operated by private operators. The transition in public policy demonstrates that although the industrial dimension remains substantial, commercial perceptions have prevailed over social and cultural requirements and the role of the government has diminished to a point that market forces dictate the nature of development—leading to common European policy.

Germany

Germany saw exploitation of cable and satellite since the 1980s—the fastest growth in Europe during this period. This was mainly due to the policy initiated by public authorities. The main interest of the national government was to increase commercial competition and to weaken the public broadcasting system. This policy dominated early periods, too, although the new policy was inspired by public support for additional terrestrial transmissions and the establishment of a national cable infrastructure provided the means for cable's development.

The transition from social and cultural perceptions to commercial domination is particularly noteworthy in Germany. During the second stage of cable policy, socialist and conservative states debated social and commercial aspects in broadcasting. In contrast, in the third stage this debate has been concluded in favor of commercial perceptions, with the transition dominated by the diminishing role of public authorities in the development of cable systems and services. By the late 1980s all states had issued laws permitting commercial broadcasting of all types— terrestrial, satellite, or cable—and the media sector had become competitive and dominated by commercial rather than social perceptions.

The changes included deregulation policies, lifting of restrictions on private and commercial transmissions, and the start of commercial competition to the public broadcasting system. The involvement of the central government remained influential, because the PTT continued to be involved in the development of cable infrastructure, but the liberalized programming policy enabled the market to develop commercially. The growth of German cable demonstrates that the combination of the establishment of cable infrastructure and commercial exploitation provided the means for the development of cable and satellite programming services.

Following the diminishing involvement of local governments and the Federal administration, the main characteristic of public policy is that German cable and satellite services operate according to commercial considerations, in an unregulated environment that permits competition for programming and technical advancement.[9]

Common Policy for Europe

The changes in media policy in the three largest media countries established a common policy for Europe. The new policy influenced the rest of the continent, across the five main separate parts of Europe. The first part is Scandinavia, which is often considered as a unit, and media policy has been influenced by an old tradition for cultural and political affiliation with the Nordic countries. The second part includes Latin countries such as Spain and Italy, which are among Europe's largest and most heavily populated countries, but have seen late developments of new media technologies. The third part is made of small but highly cabled countries such as Belgium, Holland, and Switzerland. The fourth includes the emerging European countries such as Greece, Turkey, and Portugal. The fifth part consists of Eastern European countries, which have rapidly adopted policy reforms and new media technologies since the breakdown of communism and the political changes that have occurred in the Eastern block since 1989. All these countries have seen rapid development of new media in the 1990s and into the 21st century.

Three major trends have influenced the adoption of common policy objectives:

1. The combination of American experience of cable's development and the unsuccessful results of the European national cable plans. The impetus in the direction of deregulation began in the United States, and it took Europe about a decade to follow suit—establishing a global process of change toward which all countries are heading. American cable developed rapidly since the 1970s, whereas the large media countries in Europe delayed cable developments until the second half of the 1980s. The new policy objectives, which were based on letting the market dictate new media developments, set the stage for unregulated cable policy. To achieve this goal, a mix of deregulation and reregulation moves identified governments' policy, aimed primarily at increasing competition within the market.

    Policy changes in Europe were the result of political changes and the adoption of new orientations, with lesser involvement of governments in media policy in general and in cable policy in particular. It is obvious in that respect, that despite the general model of public service broadcasting that had prominence before the 1980s, new media policies have become dominant. Whereas until the exploitation of cable there were common perceptions of the technology as having a role secondary to broadcasting, attitudes changed following the growth of American cable and satellite services and policy changes in Europe. European recognition that new technologies have become available, coupled with political changes provided opportunities for policy changes.

This technological, commercial, and political combination led to deregulation policies—based on American deregulation. As a result of the consolidation of policies in the third stage of media policy, the development of American and European cable has evolved around essentially the same policy trends as deregulatory moves and new media policies have progressively increased the role of market forces in shaping cable expansion and future progress.

Three major conclusions as to the role of governments can be drawn from this course. The first is that despite differences between countries, the general model of development outlined suggests that changes in media perceptions and policies have occurred in all the countries examined, even though local policy differences have been substantial. The second is that attempts to impose public policy on cable's development, through public authorities or policy requirements, have proved unsuccessful as far as public reaction. The third conclusion, that sums up the entire process of change in cable policy-making, is the diminishing role of governments occurred throughout Europe.

2. A departure from the previous emphasis on the social and cultural role of cable and adoption of new market orientations with the adoption of objectives common to European and American cable policy was that distinctions between countries have diminished, as financial interest groups and regulatory institutions with global impact dominated the rise of cable technology cable policy.

The diminishing role of governments is a result of the growing belief that private industry operating a technology-based service is better suited to serving the public interest than are elected lawmakers and government agencies. The new role of governments is to encourage industries to set their own standards and to become involved only when market forces cannot provide the means for free speech and free competition. This is when, for example, arrangements between service providers are distorted by self-interest of giant players or when a single entity controls both a transmission medium and the information that flows through it.

The prospects of public policy in all three largest media countries have established the same conclusion: cable policies have become increasingly interlinked, as the course of change of media policy integrated with changes in cable policy. Despite differences in implementation between countries, the end-result is similar: all governments have deregulated cable, thus creating a uniform policy, with the distinct domination of market forces in new media policymaking and structure.

When examining the parallels between the development of cable policies, it is imperative to look at the outcome of this process. The most notable characteristic has been the major change from a service with long-term political, social, and cultural objectives into a market-led industry dominated by commercial determinism. Another distinctive characteristic is the role of governments in shaping cable policies. It was not until the social and cultural goals of the cable policies had started to diminish that policies changed following the impact of technological advancement, financial interest groups, and market forces.

The reduced impact of governments led by policies initiated in the three countries progressed toward a policy structure common to all European countries. Policy changes have been the result of shifts in the traditional concept of broadcasting regulation and in social and political perceptions of cable's possible role in each country, and have reflected the over-all process of change in cable and new media policies in Europe.

Early perceptions of the role of regulators and governments—which consisted of deep involvement and strict public supervision—have been a principal force in promoting policy changes. Changes included two main areas: firstly, in favor of commercial rather than public policy for cable; and secondly, in favor of market-led and competitive policy for the overall broadcasting sector. As this chapter demonstrates, changes in media policy in general and in the field of cable in particular have been inevitable. They have occurred as a reaction to competition and commercialization trends at the global and local levels of policy.

The changed attitudes have to be seen as part of a broader process of globalization of media policies. In particular, they have been the result of shifts in the traditional concept of broadcasting regulation and in social, cultural, and political perceptions of cable's possible role in each country and its potential impact on different societies. In all of the countries that this chapter discusses, deregulation paved the way for commercial development. This course has developed within the transformation of the media sector from a politically inspired regulation system to a liberalizing deregulation process aimed to balance the public and the private sectors.

3. Governments have realized the need to base regulation on competitive service models rather than technology-specific solutions. Another cause for change was governments realization that the ambitious cable plans had not succeeded, but had raised public expenditures and prevented national industries from competing in global markets. This factor emphasized that the impact of cable should be measured by the attractiveness of its services and not by the extent of government's involvement or the ability to exert social and cultural goals.

Examining the role of governments and the extent of their involvement in new media development, it is evident that the traditional bases of broadcasting regulation have been unable to cope with this change. The technologies of cable and satellite have triggered new approaches, and this has led to a growing recognition of the inevitability of wider regulatory changes that would establish the preferred structure of the newly established broadcasting media. The results of this policy change have been the erosion of established broadcasting regulation and the creation of additional broadcasting services. With regard to cable policy, common to all countries is the long-term policy trend of diminishing the role of governments while providing increased competition between cable and other technologies.

The immense growth of technological innovations in the cable industry has similarly demonstrated that public ownership does not guarantee the achievement of social and cultural goals, and the contrast between such goals and deregulation policies made older regulation obsolete. The emergence of new media and telecommunications technologies created difficulties for national governments wishing to act independently in new media regulation.

The course of development of cable policies laid out in this chapter demonstrates the differences in the policymaking of governments as they have become apparent in the different stages of media policy. In examining the three-stage development course of media policy, it is evident that this course can also be illustrated by the transition in cable policies. Although the technology of cable offered multiple transmission services, until the third stage of governments' policy the large media nations of Europe chose to limit cable development by restricting its commercial capabilities. It was the combination of deregulation of American cable, commercial reforms in broadcasting policies, and the availability of satellite transmissions, that increased the attractiveness of new media in Europe.

The course of development has become evident with the adoption of open-skies policy. The influence of commercialization and the increased number of the channels available created global media markets and promoted new aspects of global policy. This trend has been intensified by the liberalization of telecommunications policy, because the forces promoting the globalization of telecommunications policy and markets are less supportive of the relevance of national boundaries and jurisdictions.

As a result of this process, leading institutions and commercial forces with a global approach have assumed a new prominence while promoting new applications of digital technology and new forms of advanced technology. The new objectives of media policy deal with the protection of free competition as part of a global process. This trend should be reinforced by additional deregulation at the global level of policy, aimed at allowing competition of all new media and telecommunications services. This leads to the postregulated era of global media policy that identifies the current stage of development.

2.4 FROM REGULATION TO COMPETITION

The convergence of broadcasting and telecommunications toward a single multimedia market dominated by multinational companies has changed the role of governments as regulatory barriers to entry in both telecommunications and broadcasting markets have been falling, and are likely to continue to do so as a result of the triumph of global companies.

The development of multichannel services and the anticipated use of digital technology have essentially increased the role of the free market and removed the necessity for tighter regulation. The historical regulatory separation of broadcasting and telecommunications issues has become blurred with the convergence of different technologies, and a merger of multiple regulation and regulation authorities is required. In the past, shortage of effective spectrum created perceived barriers to entry to broadcasting and telecommunications services, and prior structural regulation was instituted to prevent abuse of monopoly power. Today the cross-entry of broadcasting and telecommunications firms into each other's markets raises significant questions on the ability of governments to regulate multiple service providers.

Telecommunications markets around the world have been liberalized. The main regulatory efforts have been the Telecommunications Act in Britain, and the judgment that split American Bell company into seven "Baby Bells" and AT&T (in 1984), the Telecommunications Act (1996) in the United States, and the liberalization of the basic voice telephony in the European Union since January 1998.

Broadcasting markets have also been liberalized, led by the United States and the European Commission. The main deregulatory efforts in the United States have been the 1984 Cable Act and the 1996 Telecommunications Act. In Europe these include the Television Without Frontiers directive issued by the European Union in 1989 and deregulation in different countries.

Three key factors have contributed to the considerable role of global policy:

1. The policy of the European Community to enforce common European policy and global standards.
2. Privatization of all major technologies in Europe—broadcast television, telecom services, commercial satellite services, and cable systems.
3. American and European policy of advancing competition among different technologies, rather than relying on cable as a leading technology.

The remaining major new tasks of governments are to establish the criteria for:

1. Competition rules, including rate and basic service regulations.
2. Franchising conditions, including cross-ownership rules.
3. Programming standards, including local programming rules, discriminatory levels against foreign programmers and taxation provisions to add domestic program production.

Three major regulatory superpowers have been established: the American FCC, the European Union, and the British ITC. These organizations have adopted the policy of letting the market dictate developments, as the role of regulatory institutions is limited to maintaining the conditions for competition. The changes in the role of regulators affect all media policies around the world, as defined by the FCC strategic plan for the 21st century: "the inexorable movement from regulation to competition."

1. The Federal Communications Commission (FCC)

The primary regulatory body in communications in the United States is the Federal Communications Commission. The FCC includes five commissioners, appointed by the Senate for a term of five years, with the President appointing one as chair.

The objectives of the FCC have changed through the years according to technology and policy changes. Historically, the two fundamental objectives were to ensure that local programmers had control over what was broadcast in their area and that all areas of the country had access to television services. Then the FCC deregulated the cable and satellite industries, allowing open competition in broadcasting, although regulation remained dominant. In recent years it has been moving from regulation to competition.

The Commission is now in an active process of changing its role and function aimed at reaching competition by creating fair rules and equal opportunity for newcomers. The 1992 Cable Television Consumer Protection and Competition Act guaranteed access to satellite-delivered cable programming services by alternative multichannel video providers, such as DBS operators. The act determined that cable programming must be made available to competitors, that cable companies must negotiate with local broadcasters before carrying their signals but cannot refuse to carry those signals, and that the FCC must determine "reasonable" rates for basic service.[10]

The main contribution of the act—to advance competition in the multichannel market—is achieved by providing television stations with certain carriage rights on local market cable television systems. This provision is known as Must Carry Rules, which allow a broadcaster to require a cable operator to carry a local station in a tier of service provided to every subscriber without degrading the television station's signal. Congress adopted these rules to ensure the availability of free over-the-air television, the benefits derived from local origination of programming from television stations, and the continued distribution of unique, noncommercial, and educational programming services.

Retransmission consent rules prohibit cable operators and other multichannel video programming distributors from retransmitting the signal of a commercial station without its prior consent, unless the station has chosen Must Carry. Congress found that cable systems obtain "great benefits from local broadcast signals" in the form of subscription and increased audience for cable programming services. According to these rules, a cable operator who wants to retransmit a station's signal obtains a retransmission consent agreement. Every three years commercial television stations must select between pursuing their mandatory carriage rights or their retransmission consent rights.

The act determined that cable operators are required to carry certain television broadcast signals. Local noncommercial channels have mandatory carriage rights as part of the Must Carry rules. Commercial stations that are local to the cable system elect either to require the system to carry the station on a Must Carry mandatory basis or to require that the system negotiate for a retransmission consent agreement to be carried for payment or other compensation. Cable operators must also obtain retransmission consent for the carriage of distant commercial broadcast stations.

Additional competition has been provided by the provision for other technologies to provide cable services—telephone companies and the broadcast networks, and the start of competing DBS services transmitting direct to home transmissions. The 1996 Telecommunications Act is the first comprehensive revision of federal telecommunications law since the enactment of the Communications Act in 1934. It opened up the market entirely for competition of all technologies by removing remaining restrictions on telephone companies and other advanced services to acquire cable systems and provide programming services to cable systems.

The law started a new era for media and telecommunications services, abolishing all statutory barriers to telephone companies entering into cable. It also opened up local telephone markets for the first time, established a flexible regulatory environment, and encouraged significant investments in new infrastructures and services while cable, satellite, and telephone companies were entering the wireless and data services markets.

The act stipulated that public obligations of broadcasters be extended to the digital environment by directing Congress to issue licenses for digital television for incumbent television broadcasters. The licenses permit the temporary use of an additional channel and are conditional upon the return of one channel at the end of the transition period. In 1997, the FCC adopted rules for digital television service. The Fifth Report and Order lays the groundwork for the introduction of digital television, with the FCC's deadline for recapture of the analogue spectrum in 2006. During the transition period, most stations offer some programs in the high-definition format during prime-time transmissions and broadcast in the standard digital definition the rest of day.

According to former FCC Chairman William Kennard the massive deregulation of technology imposed by the Telecommunications Act encourages the rise of the Internet, wireless and digital television. Because cable is the dominant multichannel video provider in most markets in the United States, the FCC is trying to create more competition to the incumbent cable industry. One successful trend line is that since the mid-1990s two out of three new multichannel video subscribers are going to the satellite industry, and the FCC is seeking additional competition. The spread of broadband technologies will open up ways for people to get a lot more content without relying exclusively on their cable company. According to this policy, in the next generation of technology all of the content of multichannel video providers can also be made available to people through the Internet.[11]

Another incentive for competition is the permission for satellite providers to compete with local cable monopolies. Under licensing laws enacted in 1988, satellite companies could not carry local stations but they could carry network affiliates from other parts of the country. These laws intended to increase the programming available in rural and small markets and limited the competitiveness of satellite services, as satellite subscribers also needed an off-air antenna or cable service to receive their local news, sports, and weather. Although cable companies traditionally held monopolies in their local markets, Congress deregulated cable rates in the 1996 Telecommunications Act because a new generation of inexpensive satellite television delivery services became available to customers. The DBS service was considered a sufficient competitor to cable, although satellite providers were still prohibited from carrying local channels. Although the First Amendment prohibits monopoly status in programming, no real competition had come from satellite operators because of their inability to carry local channels. The 1999 Satellite Television Home Viewers Act (Satellite Bill) enabled DBS companies to compete equally with cable systems. The act guaranteed provision of satellite delivery to local stations in rural areas and retransmission of local television content to satellite subscribers in the broadcast footprint of terrestrial television stations. A DBS provider can now simply take a local signal and rebroadcast it, although a formal agreement with the terrestrial broadcaster is required after six months.

The cable companies supported the Satellite Bill on the assumption that an agreed procompetitive legislation was far more desirable than a return to tighter regulation of their rates. The cable industry is looking to enter a new era of competition in markets of local phone services and high-speed Internet access, and a free market approach has served their interests.

The regulatory process during the 1990s started a new era of competition for advanced services and established the new role of the FCC in creating fair rules for competition. In a strategic plan for the 21st century delivered to Congress,[12] Chairman Kennard noted that "the FCC is meeting the challenge of reinventing itself to keep pace with the rapidly changing communications industry landscape. We've developed a well-thought-out plan that reflects input from customer groups, industry, state and local governments, the academic community, and FCC employees. It will allow the FCC to enter the century able to respond fully and quickly to emerging technologies and the inexorable movement from regulation to competition. The Commission look forward to a constructive dialogue with Congress and a continuing dialogue with all our stakeholders to ensure that this plan is inclusive, and address the needs of the American people."

The plan recognizes that it is necessary to restructure the way the FCC is organized to reflect changes in the regulatory landscape. It envisions that by 2005 American communications markets will be characterized predominantly by vigorous competition and will greatly reduce the need for direct regulation. The FCC will be very different in both structure and mission, and as a result must wisely manage the transition from an industry regulator to a market facilitator.

The FCC's primary goals for the 21st century are:

1. Promote competition in communications, protect consumers, and support access for every American to existing and advanced telecommunications services.
2. Refocus its efforts from managing monopolies to addressing issues that will not be solved by the market.
3. Create a model agency for the digital age.
4. Promote competition in all communications markets.
5. Promote opportunities for all Americans to benefit from the communications revolution.
6. Manage the airwaves (electromagnetic spectrum) in the public interest.
7. Focus on consumer protection and ensure that consumers are empowered and treated fairly as they navigate the new world of communications.

The changes in the FCC's role are related to the means and mix of resources that are necessary to achieve the goals in an environment marked by greater competition and convergence. In technology terms, the plan notes that the advent of Internet-based and other new technology-driven communications services will erode the traditional regulatory distinctions between sectors of the communications industry.

2. The European Union

For many years the future of European media has followed American developments, although they lagged about a decade. Today the role of global forces offers Europe the same future as the American present. Under this structure, media and new technologies industries operate in a free market dominated by global forces and a handful of huge conglomerates. The missions of European regulators in advancing competition among a variety of technologies and services concentrate on three main fields: the breakdown of national monopolies, the coming up of multichannel technologies and services, and the convergence of various media.

The core of European policy is to encourage competition, new technologies and services, and new entrants in the marketplace. According to Jean Frannois Pons, Deputy Director General of the European Commission, the application of European competition policy in the telecommunications and media markets has become the main policy issue that the Commission has dealt with in these fields.

Unlike the United States, European regulatory environment has been established through individual national regulatory agencies and government policies, and has created different platforms for the development of digital television with no dominant concept for media policy. The European television market was first opened up in the 1980s, as state broadcasting monopolies crumbled and commercial channels sprang up. The market began in earnest in the 1990s, as the commercial shakeout of European media resulted in an industry made up of dozens of struggling private and commercial channels.

The legislation effort of the European Commission began in the mid-1980s and included the liberalization of four major sectors: cable, satellite, infrastructure and telecommunications. The Commission has a responsibility to ensure that member states implement the legislation properly and to act against states whose implementation has been late or inadequate. The Commission aims to open new markets for competition through liberalization. It has close relationships with national regulatory and national competition authorities in the member states and acts only when competition is not properly implemented or new entrants are being discriminated against.[13]

Europe is the world's largest media market and since the unification of Europe, major decisions have affected the development of broadcast and telecommunications services. European-wide regulation implemented through the European Union aims to coordinate national standards and policies and to create a common market in a fragmented area with multiple systems of regulation.

Uniform European policy objectives, led by deregulation, technological advancement and increased competition, have been a catalyst for the adoption of a common European policy in which the role of governments has become secondary to the policy of the European Community, and market forces have gained prominence.

The EC has been placing increasing importance on cultural issues, as the Television Without Frontiers directive requires member states to reserve a majority of their television transmission time for European programming. The directive forms the basis of European

Community legislation and policy in the media sector, as part of the effort of the Union to forge a single European market. It was enacted in 1989 and came into force in October 1991. Although some areas are left open to local policy, the directive was aimed to unify member states legislation and establish a uniform European media policy. Under the regulations, any television station that is licensed by one country need not apply for further licenses from other members of the community. At the same time, the content of the programs being broadcast within any country are subject to the laws of that country regarding content, and one cannot broadcast within a country what that country considers pornography even if the license has been obtained from somewhere else. Countries were given five years to bring their national legislation in line with these regulations.

Political decisions by the European Commission have also influenced the development of a European cable industry and its access to telecommunications services. In October 1995 the EC issued a directive liberalizing European cable and allowing data and telephony services to be provided over cable networks. The economics of cable has changed since then, with the creation of pan-European cable operators capable of providing both television and telecommunications services. Consolidation is essential to compete in a global environment with national telecom companies, and only large entities are capable of attracting the necessary financing for investment and acquiring the expertise to develop new services. But competition was not effective enough, because even the larger cable operators were still very small compared to national telecom monopolies. The reason was that in many European countries when the national telecom service was privatized, it was left with ownership of the cable industry as well, effectively removing one key source of competition. In June 1999 the European Commission mandated that European PTTs must split their cable television operations into separate companies. The decision has been mostly effective with the two largest state-run telecom companies and state-sponsored cable markets—France and Germany—dominated by France Telecom and Deutsche Telekom, which are now forced to sell off their cable operations. It is expected that the advantages of cable in delivering broadband capacity and the coming of new competitive entrants would increase the number of European broadband-ready households.

Similar European-wide regulation was agreed upon with telecommunications services. The 1987 Green Paper led to the liberalization of telecoms in Europe. In July 1993 the European Union decided to let state-owned telephone companies retain their monopolies only until 1998. In January 1998 the basic telephony service in the European Community was officially liberalized.[14]

European-wide legislation has also been dedicated to cross-ownership and convergence policy issues. The European Commission first published the Bangemann Report on the Information Society in 1994. The report dealt with the convergence of information technology, communications technology, and consumer electronics, together with the corresponding services, content, and networks, driven forward by digital technology. In 1997 it issued a Green Paper on the Convergence of the Telecommunications, Media and Information Technology Sectors, and the Implications for Regulators. The Green Paper deals with the provision of infrastructure services, content, and the conditions for access to that content (via television, computer, or telephone networks) in the 21st century.

Results of the public consultation demonstrate that a European communications policy has been adopted. The next logical move should be the formation of a European-wide Federal Communications Commission, adapting the American model of the FCC as converged regulator. In line with this policy, the 1999 Review calls for a European policy. The wide-ranging review on the entire regulatory framework for the media and telecommunications fields, adopted by the European Commission, covers all laws and directives, with the aim of keeping regulation to the minimum necessary to meet policy objectives. The Review emphasizes that the wide variety of licensing schemes across Europe causes difficulties for pan-European operators, especially in the satellite sector, and calls for pan-European licensing. It recommends that Europe should minimize the need for specific licenses and rely on general authorizations that do not require explicit authorization by a regulator before the operator starts to provide services.

Despite common regulatory issues, however, establishing common cultural policy is difficult, because European communications represent a contrast between unity and diversity. In addition to the efforts of the European Community and the formation of the European voting block at ITU meetings, which have given the impression of a united European community in the areas of broadcasting and telecommunications, cultural issues are still divided and legislation in these areas remains local.[15]

In view of the changing technological and market structure arising from the convergence process, European regulators are investigating whether local regulations and cultural differences are barriers to competition and the development of new services and applications. New technologies such as satellite and the Internet are essentially multinational and global services and common global policy are required to maintain their operations around the world. The American free market competition model has emerged in the European Union media policy, as policy of the EU aims to liberalize the media and telecommunications markets, leaving its new roles to ensure that member states implement the legislation properly and that new entrants are not discriminated against.[16] EC Commissioner Martin Bangemann has stated that he wants "to protect the Internet with an international framework of principles, guidelines and rules for global communications in the 21st century, to be embodied in an international charter."[17] According to this policy, The European Union is changing European laws in other fields too. It set January 2002 as the deadline for member states to adopt the e-Commerce directive, which exempts Internet Service Providers and network facility providers from liability for the content of messages they have no control over. The EU's package of new electronic communications directives includes a framework for all regulation and standards for how countries can authorize networks and services. The package gives member states until July 24, 2003 to change their telecom laws into electronic communications laws.

3. The Independent Television Commission (ITC)

The role of the United Kingdom in the communications revolution has been fundamental. Britain has been a leader in the adoption of new technology and advancing competition into the market. Its market-led policy advocates for a free market approach, with competition of all available technologies and a minimal role for regulators.

Britain almost completely deregulated the media and telecommunications industries, and was one of the first countries in the world where both cable and telephone service could be delivered. Following major political and regulatory decisions, media services have gained access to telecommunications services and telephone companies have gained access to media services. It is now a leader in the transformation to digital technology.

The United Kingdom currently implements a dual regulatory approach for media policy. The Independent Television Commission (ITC) is the statutory body responsible for licensing and regulating all commercial television. The Office of the Telecommunications Regulator (Oftel) has responsibility for the regulation of telecommunications services.

Other fields of media policy are also regulated differently. Public television is under the authority of the BBC, content is supervised by the Broadcasting Standards Commission, and competition policy is addressed by the Office of Fair-Trading (OFT) and the Competition Commission (formally the Monopolies and Mergers Commission–MMC).

Perhaps the most important player has been the Independent Television Commission, with major regulatory changes that diminish its role, although in practice they are aimed at encouraging competition and diversity. The ITC was set up under the Broadcasting Act of 1990. It is a public body responsible for licensing and regulating commercial television companies to broadcast in and from the United Kingdom—whether the services are received by conventional set-top or rooftop aerials, cable, or satellite. The licenses vary according to the type of service, but set conditions on matters such as standards of programs and advertising. The ITC also monitors broadcasters' output to ensure that they meet those standards.

The commercial services under the jurisdiction of the ITC are: Channel 3 (ITV), Channel 4, Channel 5, public teletext, and a range of cable, local delivery, and satellite services. They do not include public broadcasting services, including the BBC. Commercial digital services are also regulated by the ITC. Regulation for services provided by satellite and cable is different from that of terrestrial services. There is no legal requirement that every cable or satellite channel should carry the mix of information, education and entertainment shown on commercial channels, and as a result there is a wide range of established channels offering news, films, music, children's programs, and much else.

Media and telecommunications policies are constantly changing in Britain. The main regulatory changes in recent years have been the Broadcasting Act of 1996, the Telecommunications Act of 1997, and the Competition Act of 1998, which formed the Competition Commission. Following the massive deregulation of the media and telecommunications sectors, policy is about to converge further. The government's recent communication's White Paper calls for the creation of one body that will oversee the regulation of all commercial television and telecommunications. The legislation will create a single superregulator to control television and telecommunications, one of Britain's most powerful regulators, merging the ITC, Oftel, the Broadcasting Standards Commission, and the BBC. The new body represents the new system of regulation for the 21st century, as the boundaries between media, telecommunications, and the Internet blur.

The role of regulators has been a catalyst for commercial operation and the expansion of new technologies. Market entry and new developments have been encouraged across all areas of media and telecommunications—including the transition to digital technology and changes in the operations of cable and satellite.

A new policy toward the digitalization of the entire broadcasting system was perused in Britain, which was the first European country to launch digital television services of terrestrial, satellite, and interactive cable combined. The 1996 Broadcasting Act determined that the ITC could award licenses for six multiplex services of digital terrestrial television broadcasting. These should offer a wide range of advanced options from television broadcasting to telebanking, teleshopping, and the Internet. In addition to terrestrial services, other technologies should also be offering combined digital services of satellite, cable and telephone.

The policy is meant to relax restrictions on new entrants and services, including new digital platforms, and encourage competition among various service providers using the same technology (such as cable) or competing technologies (such as cable, satellite, terrestrial broadcasting, or telephony), rather than giving exclusive monopoly to one service provider (such as cable franchises).

Changes in cable policy have been substantial too. One of the main results of the new policy is that the traditional franchising policy has been changed to encourage competition within the cable programming and services industries. The ITC licenses the use of cable systems for the purpose of delivering television services to viewers' homes. Initially, in the mid-1980s franchised cable systems had been granted after a competitive process that gave exclusive rights for the licensee to provide multichannel television for a period of 15 years. This policy has been changed, however, to favor competition, and from January 2001 cable areas have become nonexclusive. The new policy further advocates for, and in practice, a market-free competition in the cable market. Under this policy, operators other than the existing franchise holder may seek licenses and competition can start within cabled areas. Other restrictions on cable operators have also been relaxed to encourage competition, such as minimum carriage agreements that channels can impose on operators and channel bundling. Almost all restrictions have now been eliminated, and cable operators are free to offer all possible services, including narrowly focused program packages including high-speed Internet and telephony.

SUMMARY

The role of governments in shaping media policy has changed considerably, as market forces replaced cultural policies initiated by governments. The transition represents a departure from the previous emphasis on the social and cultural role of media policy and the adoption of new market orientations. Governments have realized the need to base regulation on competitive service models rather than technology-specific solutions.

The involvement of governments has diminished tremendously throughout the three-stage development course. In the first stage, their role was decisive, as they tried to ignore new technologies of cable and satellite and favored the old structure of broadcast television. In the second stage, they became involved in cable policymaking and launched national plans to develop new technologies. In the third stage, common policy objectives have prevailed, dominated by market forces and policy convergence. The current stage of development is leading to a new structure of media policy for the 21st century—with a diminished role of governments and increased role of global regulators and market principles.

The role of governments has been mostly significant in the development of new media policy and technologies. The evolution of common policy objectives was derived from the combination of American experience of new media developments and the unsuccessful results of the European national cable plans. The reasons for change included pressure by economic interests to allow commercial exploitation and public demand for adoption of new technologies and provision for new programming services. The response of European governments was to decide that market-oriented principles should govern new policy for broadcasting and new media. This policy resulted in the privatization of all major technologies—broadcast television, telecom services, commercial satellite services, and cable systems, and led to a policy of advancing competition among different technologies rather than relying on cable as a leading technology.

Media policy in the digital age is directed by global regulatory authorities, including the American Federal Communications Commission (FCC), the European Union, and the British Independent Television Commission (ITC), which became dominant in creating an open market for new media and telecommunications development. Today's policies can be considered as the postregulatory age dominated by a global market for new media and telecommunications sectors.

3

The Globalization
of Media Policy

Media policy has changed considerably with the impact of cultural perceptions and technological developments. Whereas early policies had been influenced by cultural values, policy changes have become evident with the growing impact of technological advancement. Following the adoption of new media policies in Europe, with the aim of deregulation and influenced by the American experience, media and telecommunications issues have increasingly become global rather than national domains.

In the transformation of culture and commercialization, the globalization of media policies has been predominant, involving new technology and politics. The consequent technological convergence of media systems reflects the impact of policy changes in the global arena—the transition from viewing broadcasting systems as having mainly social and cultural goals to deregulation and privatization policies that combine broadcast, new media, and telecommunications developments.

The issue of technology and cultural identity involves media policy to a degree that global trend and policy objectives can be identified. In all countries the national broadcasting and telecommunications monopolies have been reduced and the media market has been opened for commercial producers and financiers. The trading of broadcasting and telecommunications services has achieved a significant status in the political arena, and deregulation has become the key policy orientation. The new mix of information resources that make up global media policy, involving broadcasting, new media and telecommunications, has had an impact on deregulation issues around the world by changing the political culture and the ability of policymakers to explore cultural objectives.

As a result of this process, broadcasting and new media policies have become commercialized and transnational, led by the availability of new technologies and the efforts to develop global markets. This can be designated as the transition from cultural values to commercialization and globalization—a trend that involves new media technologies, deregulation, privatization and convergence.

This chapter illustrates how new media policies have been shaped by commercialization and globalization, as market forces took center stage, displacing cultural perceptions that dominated the policies initiated by governments. As described in Chapter 1, policy changes from cultural values to technological convergence led to a uniform global policy of liberalization. As discussed in Chapter 2, the role of leading global authorities in reshaping broadcasting and telecommunications markets can be seen in the transformation into a new global regulatory and policy environment that has created an open market for new media and telecommunications development. Policy convergence has been intensified by a series of deregulation and liberalization laws, setting the stage for the postregulatory environment and a global market for new media and telecommunications sectors.

The research in this chapter concentrates on the policy dynamics that have been apparent in the three largest media countries of Europe—Britain, France, and Germany. These countries represent the most influential nations in European broadcast history. They have also experienced the full course of the transition of media policy—from cultural values to commercialization and globalization. The argument put forward is that the process that occurred in these countries has created a more or less uniform policy change that can be identified according to the three stages of the general model discussed in this book. The third and current stage can be identified with certain broad trends that are common to all countries and institute the globalization of media policy through open-skies policy.

The globalization of media policy includes three major stages:

1. Cultural Values in Broadcasting

The policies of the European countries examined in this research have initially been dominated by cultural values, as part of national broadcasting and telecommunications objectives designed to monitor the development of new technologies. Within this process, differences in social and political perceptions and in the political culture of countries were evident. These differences had dominated the development of media policy in Europe—on the basis of cultural values unique to each country.

2. Commercialization and Globalization

Since the mid-1980s, the development of European media has evolved around essentially the same trends, as deregulatory moves and new media policies have progressively increased the role of market forces in shaping technological expansion. The process represents a departure from the previous emphasis on the role of culture and social and political perceptions. It began following deregulatory moves in the United States, came into play in the largest media countries of Europe, and then spread into other countries. This resulted in cable and satellite becoming a large industry in the United States and a growing service in Europe, and the privatization of media and telecommunications services around the world. The conclusion of this process is that national distinctions between new media policies have diminished and new media technologies have become dominated by domestic and global financial interest groups. The most distinct aspect of this stage is that media policy has become commercial and global.

3. Multichannel Competition

The new structure of media policy means that new media services have become widespread around the world. Multichannel competition is leading the transformation, with new programming services, advanced applications, and a free market approach adopted by all advanced countries. Although the domination of cable and satellite is the most prominent, because these technologies have traditionally provided multichannel services, new technologies—telecom and digital terrestrial operators—are entering the new competitive structure.

In examining the global revolution in media policy, it can be seen that following the convergence of new media and telecommunications policies in the United States, European policy changes set the stage for a global and unregulated market in which all media and telecommunications services are in competition. In the current structure of policy convergence, new media, which initially represented cultural policies initiated by governments, are in competition with other information services, guided by commercial and global rather than cultural and local considerations.

3.1 CULTURAL VALUES IN BROADCASTING

This section concentrates on early perceptions of the cultural role of media policy, which have dominated all countries in the first stage of development of the broadcasting media. In examining this stage, two basic assumptions are made. The first is that all countries discussed in this chapter—the United States and three largest media countries of Europe—initially concentrated on cable and satellite as a means to exploit cultural goals. The second is that although this general policy was common to these countries, the distinction between broadcasting policies is evident in the extent of their social and political perception and political culture.

The distinction between countries is particularly clear in the sense that the United States was the first country to adopt an open-skies policy (in 1972) and encourage domination of market forces in the development of media policy. It was only about a decade later that European media policies changed. The new plans had, however, included only a limited version of commercialization—combining cultural values in broadcasting.[1]

Differences in Social and Political Perceptions

European media policies developed in the 1980s with the encouragement of national governments, which saw the establishment of new media infrastructure as a national priority. The different ways that media policies have developed are related primarily to variations in social and political perceptions of a cable systems' development in each country. Whereas Britain promoted a policy emphasizing the role of the financial community in determining the extent of technological advancement, in France the notion of interactive services took priority over restrictive definitions of commercial services. Germany supported cable's development, but emphasized the entertainment aspects.

Britain

In Britain, cultural issues in the development of cable infrastructure were seen as part of a national plan to advance information technology, although the role of the government was confined to creating an atmosphere for the financial community conducive to investment in cable systems and services. Within this policy, which combined cultural and commercial perceptions, it was determined that franchises should be awarded within franchise areas. But in considering the way that franchise areas would be chosen, the government arrived at what can best be described as a negotiated compromise. This compromise can also be considered as a commercial policy influenced by social and political perceptions.

Recognizing that private companies should take the initiative, based on their analysis of market demand, it was decided to allow the initiators to propose areas for cabling rather than for the Cable Authority to divide the country into specific franchise areas. The Hunt Committee's proposal, that operators be required to take on less economically profitable areas in return for the most lucrative franchises, was toned down because of the economic problems of constructing new cable systems. This was according to the perception of market-led policy, although the Cable Authority on its part was given the power to modify proposals at the margins, so that peripheral areas of less economic appeal could be incorporated into franchise bids.

France

In contrast to the commercial policy adopted in Britain, France concentrated on social and cultural aspects and the government was the key player in framing regulatory policy for cable. The policy had a clear industrial purpose and was incorporated into a wider vision of changing France's society and culture. The Socialist government saw interactive cable as a means to increase participation and social and cultural exchange. Accordingly, cable was not seen as a commercial service and was subject to an extensive system of regulations.

The Cable Plan authorized the national Postal and Telecommunications Authority (PTT) to cable the nation. Most of the finance for this huge effort was to come from the state, via the PTT, which constructed and owned cable networks with revenues generated from information services offered over cable systems scheduled to become a substantial source of funding. Local authorities were given a key role in the cabling plan. They were expected to take the initiative in seeking to cable their areas and negotiating with the PTT on the process of building local cable networks. They were also responsible for the commercial operation of local television stations and establishment of local cable companies that would be responsible for head-ends and programming. Commercial involvement was limited. Private entrepreneurs were given permission to hold only minority interests in the companies that had to advance part of the cable installation costs to the PTT, paying back the rest over a period of years.

Germany

The situation in Germany was different from that of Britain and France because of the complex legal structure of broadcasting and the different social and cultural views of cable development among the states. These obstacles created a problem with the coexistence between private entertainment cable and public broadcasting institutions. The states under Conservative control were in favor of a free market approach and of allowing private television and cable. Four states were Socialist and were in principle against adopting cable and satellite channels. The imposition of rules on private programmers and the unfavorable financial structure of cable systems made many private companies and local councils hesitate before committing themselves to the expensive process of laying cables. In this complex situation, a consensus was required on the social and cultural aspects of cable development. There was however a long-running battle with regard to television between the claims of the states to regulatory privileges and the liberal interpretation of the constitutional right to a free flow of information. The arguments surrounding cable and satellite channels have to be seen as an expression of this conflict.

The states discussed for a long time a compromise agreement that would allow satellite transmissions up-linked in one state to be received universally across the whole of Germany. Meanwhile the Deutsche Bundespost (DBP) installed cable infrastructure with the aim of supporting commercial competition and weakening the public broadcasting system. Only with the advent of cable have some states given private broadcasters permission to transmit. Initial developments were conducted under the pilot projects, and only when these experiments were properly evaluated were further decisions taken on additional program provision.[2]

Differences in the Political Culture

The contrasting initial results of cable developments were related to differences in the political culture. The different regulatory environments

created differences in approaches toward cable and new media development, which related to the relative power of governments. Whereas
Britain adopted a policy of light regulation and private funding, France
supported cable systems with public funds and a modicum of regulatory controls, and Germany adopted a policy that granted the Deutsche
Bundespost power and funds to cable the country.[3]

Common to both French and German policies was the fact that
the government decided to supervise the planning and building of cable
systems and to support them financially. In Contrast, Britain was influenced by the American experience and adopted a market-led approach.
Common to Britain and Germany, however, was that both nations highlighted the distribution side of cable and the public desire for more television entertainment services, whereas French policy was primarily
aimed at building up interactive services.

Britain

In Britain, the political culture and regulatory environment advocated a
market-led policy with a mixed structure of commercial domination and
public supervision. According to the government's view, the Cable
Authority had to react to problems as they happened rather than to
impose extensive regulatory requirements in advance. The most noteworthy characteristic of new media policy was that despite a new positive climate for cable defined by the White Paper and Broadcasting Act,
the Conservative government was unwilling to play an active part in the
development of cable systems. Instead, it specified that all initiatives
would be privately funded, with the pace of developments determined
by the market.

In framing its long-term strategy the government sought to create a favorable environment for cable's commercial development. It
decided that investment should be privately financed and market-led
and that regulation would be kept to a minimum, leaving the companies
investing in cable systems the freedom to develop a wide range of services and facilities.

Under this policy, regulation was also kept flexible, so that companies could react to changes in market demand and technology. In
practice, however, the perceived impact of the political culture was that
the policy of a market-led development course had enormous effects on
the actual development of a cable system. The main problem was that
the financial community viewed the development of cable with caution.
As a result, until the late 1980s only little progress was made because of
lack of financing of cable ventures and the unsatisfactory response of the
market.

During this period cable was considered an unsuccessful venture in Britain, despite the supportive role of the government and the favorable political culture. This was the situation in terms of technology and the development of advanced technology, as well. Although Britain saw the long-term future of cable as advancing with interactive services, fiber optic cabling was only encouraged, but it was left for the market to take the initiative in this area.

The approach adopted in Britain recognized that it was the entertainment element that would appeal to the average subscriber in the early stages, and cable providers were free to design whatever system they preferred, although when competing for a license, the operator that offered the more advanced system was at an advantage. Under these circumstances, it was clear that establishing cable as part of an integrated national broadband communications network would be difficult to achieve, and there was no development of advance technology.

France

An almost completely opposite approach was adopted in France, where the government tried to keep its finger on the pulse of cabling. The involvement of the government has to be seen as an integral part of the public role in French communications. According to the traditional political culture, the government had an active role in the implementation of national plans. It had a dominant position both as a client and as a provider of funds with French industry. This applied to the cabling of France too. Political parties of all persuasions endorsed the Cable Plan, as it offered good opportunities for national industries and was in line with the public general support for decentralization policies.

Originally the French plan was based on the relatively ambitious and expensive choice of fiber optic technology, aimed at establishing the most advanced infrastructure and ensuring that France would become the third technological nation, alongside the United States and Japan. But in practice the actual cabling plans made little or no progress. Although after the first announcement many local authorities were quick to volunteer their support for the coming revolution in the field of local communications, there had been unenthusiastic reactions to the Cable Plan.

The initial excitement of many cities had changed to attempts to quit the national plan. Other cities came to the conclusion that their control of the project was more formal than real and that they were merely being asked to support a national plan. By the mid-1980s it became obvious that the main aim was the creation of a national Integrated Services Digital Network (ISDN). Local municipalities also discovered that cable was a complicated area and that they lacked technical competence and had limited capabilities to undertake such a huge project with long-term cultural and technological goals.

Another aspect of the change in attitude that identified most cities was that they had doubts about the social adoption of fiber optic technology. Many cities claimed that the less expensive coaxial infrastructure had more advantages. Under the circumstances and with no progress in cabling, national public authorities also claimed that the Cable Plan would inevitably lead to failure and economic disaster because of the huge cost.[4] They faced the problem that while the aim of using a large amount of fiber optic cables increased cabling costs, local authorities were interested in getting this service from the PTT at reasonable rates.

As a result, national and local authorities had to face the complexities of the Cable Plan, and it was realized that despite the enormous involvement of the government the plan was unsuccessful. In practice, the French cable drive took place at a much slower pace than was originally envisaged. Although more and more cities desired to develop a local communications system, little real progress was made in the development of new networks. Policy changes were inevitable. The new policy had a more realistic and less enthusiastic approach, although the involvement of the government remained substantial. But although financial aid was given to the PTT to start cabling the country, the number of households connected was far short of the original plan.

Germany

In Germany, as in France, the government financially supported cable developments. But different from the French Cable Plan, the initial German plans were not as widely supported by public authorities at the local level. This situation posed a major problem for the federal government as a result of the political culture in Germany.

The main difficulty was that approaches toward cable legislation varied among the states. The postwar constitution gave the states, rather than the Federal government, jurisdiction over all cultural matters. Because broadcasting qualified as a cultural and not a commercial matter, authority over cable and satellite was left in the hands of the states. The control exercised by state governments over broadcasting created legal and technological complexities, and the split political structure affected the development of cable. The Center-Right national government was in favor of commercialization, but also increased investment funds for the Bundespost for the cable plan. New media have also confronted German policymakers with problems arising from the rapid

erosion of boundaries between broadcasting policy and industrial-tech-
nology policy.

The constitutional division of responsibilities between telecommunications and broadcasting, which had been imposed on Germany,
was an obstacle to the development of an agreed-upon national media
policy. Policy differences between the states were substantial, and related to contrasting cultural and commercial definitions of the role of
broadcasting. Conservative states considered the public broadcasting
networks as wealthy and strong enough not to be harmed by competition for revenues and encouraged the development of cable systems and
satellite channels. In contrast, Socialist states conformed to public broadcasting policy and restricted the development of commercial broadcasting and new media channels with the aim of promoting cultural aspects.

This conflict between the commercial policy of Conservative
states and the public policy of Socialist states can be demonstrated by
the fact that in 1985 all Conservative states passed laws allowing local
and regional private broadcasting channels. The largest state—Socialist-
controlled Nordrhein Westfalen, one of the most populated regions in
Europe with a population of 17 million—gave permission for regional
and satellite commercial broadcasting only in 1988, although it had
approved one of the pilot projects. In practice, however, despite policy
differences between the states, commercialization has prevailed over
cultural values.

In order to resolve the problems that had been created by differences in the political culture of the states, the Federal government was
forced to press ahead with the pilot projects and the cable plan. Despite
criticism that the plan was expensive and that there was insufficient consumer demand for the new services, with the cabling of the country by
the DBP and the availability of private channels, the political culture also
changed. By the late 1980s commercial competition started to challenge
the public broadcasting system across Germany. This was the attitude in
terms of technology too, and coaxial cable was chosen as the leading
technology. Although many argued that there was a need to build
advanced fiber optic cable systems, the Bundespost refused to develop
interactive services without proof that a demand actually existed. Policy
changes were completed by the start of the 1990s, with the addition of
new media and commercial broadcasting to the states of the East.[5]

3.2 COMMERCIALIZATION AND GLOBALIZATION

The most distinct development course that identified European broadcasting in the 1980s was the changing structure of new media policies,

from concentration on cultural values to commercialization and globalization—a process that led to policy changes dominated by deregulation, privatization, and convergence. This transition followed the changes that had already prevailed in America, evidently creating the globalization of media policy.

The interplay of international market forces, government departments, champion companies, interest groups, and deregulated domestic markets, led to deregulation of media policies. The development of the American cable system provided an incentive for other nations to adopt public policies encouraging cable and satellite developments. The availability of American capital and expertise stimulated a growing of investments in new media, leading to privatization policies.

This process implies that the objectives of American policy have also prevailed elsewhere, as the definition of culture had been changed. The globalization of new media policies forced a central direction that has become evident. All three of the largest media countries in Europe have regarded finance from the private sector as essential to developing new media and telecommunications services and have adopted policy convergence—the second stage in the adoption of global media policy.

Changing the Definition of Culture

The extent of commercialization of media policies can be related to the shift in the definition of culture evident in Europe. The prominence of this process can be analyzed according to policy changes at the local level and the linkage between cultural issues and technological advancement. In the early stage of media policy, the main role of national plans had been the cultural role of broadcasting, and this aspect had also provided the most significant change in favor of commercialization in later stages.

Commercialization policy involves cultural, political, and economic aspects unique to each country. The differences in the social and political perception and in the political culture of countries that have identified the early period of media policy have diminished to the extent that global policy has become more influential than local impact.

Although the process differed among countries, the conclusion is similar: the changing definition of culture in favor of commercialization policy has been the result of deregulation and privatization policies and the entry of new media and telecommunications interest groups. Social and cultural distinctions and political characteristics were no longer a powerful force as in the early period—leading to the convergence of media policies.

The differing approaches between countries obviously had an enormous influence on the speed of the cabling and the extent of commercialization. The variations in policy are attributable to the different social and political approaches of governments and the extent of commercial and global impact on local policy.

In Britain, the essential principles of development followed the American example of a market-led policy, with the emphasis firmly on a private and commercial industry. It was determined that a range of technologies may be installed, subject only to their meeting specific minimum performance standards. In contrast, in France and Germany cable developments were publicly supported. The French Cable Plan encouraged public ownership of cable systems. The assumption of policymakers was that the fiber optic system would eventually dominate and be used in conjunction with telephone systems to provide information services. In Germany, politics had a major role to play, because the postwar constitution required agreement between the states. The central government had to mediate among the social, cultural, and political differences of the regional states by adopting a policy that granted the DBP the funds to cable the country.

Ten main conclusions can be analyzed from these attempts:

1. A similar outcome can be drawn from all three European experiences, despite the differences in cable policies. Neither the U.K. policy of giving priority to the market nor the state sponsored initiatives of Germany and France have successfully established comprehensive cable networks or attracted the hoped-for subscribers to the networks that have been established. Of the three countries, Germany made the most determined effort to establish cable systems. Both Britain and France also sought the speedy establishment of cable, but failed to achieve their objectives. The cable plans in Britain and France have not succeeded because the main players—in Britain domestic private industry and in France local authorities—did not consider it appropriate to invest heavily in cable systems.

2. Differences in the political culture have been evident as part of the domination of cultural values. In Britain difficulties in take-off arose because the government did not provide financial support for cable, whereas in France and Germany the main problems resulted from the involvement of the government. These problems included the structures of the authorities responsible for cable and the social and financial role played by the government in the development of cable.

3. Only with the elimination of key differences between countries did new media begin to evolve. This followed the impact of deregulation and policy convergence, a process that ended up in the commercialization and globalization of media policy. This development course has been evident in all three countries.

4. Combination of technological developments and market change had been the driving force behind the change of perspective, which led to the development of new media technologies and the globalization of media and telecommunications policies.

5. This process demonstrates the tremendous change in policy. Whereas initially new media developments were characterized by a high degree of regulation in the interest of public service criteria, they have become diversified, with private service providers dominating the marketplace.

6. This trend reflects the process that has identified media policy in Europe: the transfer of influence from cultural objectives, dominated by social and political forces, to economic determinism, dominated by market interests.

7. A major characteristic in the development of new media is that changes in European broadcasting systems can be attributed to the initial unsuccessful results of the national cable plans and to the consequent response of market forces to policy changes.

8. The final structure of global media policy was reached according to the model discussed in Chapter 1, includes deregulation and privatization policies, convergence of policies and technologies, and finally, multichannel competition.

9. This structure has prevailed in all countries leading to public pressure for commercialization of new media markets and demands from multinational companies for new media policies to allow wide-ranging competition of all media and telecommunications services.

10. All countries decided to emphasize the commercial aspects of new media rather than the social and cultural goals of cable policy. These developments combined economic, political, and programming aspects. They took place more or less at the same time, between the mid and late 1980s, and then spread across Europe as part of a continental and global process.

Deregulation, Privatization, and Convergence Policies

In examining the global impact on these policy changes, it is evident that European policy has been influenced by the phenomenal growth of the American cable system. In order to capture social and economic benefits, Europe moved toward the commercialization of cable, with greater involvement for private investors and letting the market guide policy. Following the commercialization of broadcasting systems, changes in national broadcasting structures led to deregulation and liberalization. This process, which resulted from new political and economic ideologies and technological change, was followed by the convergence of technologies. This means that different technologies such as broadcasting, cable, and satellite and other telecommunications systems could no longer be seen as separate technologies, but as different parts of a complex policy-making process.

The changes proved that the transition from cultural values to commercialization and globalization had become prominent. In all countries media policy had changed, as global impact and technological development required policy changes and the avoidance of established broadcasting regulation. At the heart of the debate that surrounded the change in perspective was the fact that the public service principle that identified European media policy for many years came under threat from the dominant impact of global changes. This development resulted in growing adoption of technological advancement and new policy objectives.

The impact of deregulation made the difference. The role of deregulation can be seen as a significant result of the influence of external decision-making centers with a potential for global reach. Despite the social and political significance of media and telecommunications policies, governments decided to secure future national wealth by attracting investment, and this led to a restructuring of media and telecommunications policies. Under these circumstances, cultural values could no longer determine policy objectives.

American policy had an enormous impact on deregulation policies in Europe. The parallel regulatory shifts within the large European media countries were embodied respectively in: the 1986 Liberty of Communications Law in France; the new media laws of some German states and the 1987 State Treaty on the reorganization of broadcasting in Germany; and the 1990 Broadcasting Bill in Britain.

Policy changes were followed by changes in the structures of the regulatory authorities. Perhaps the major significance was the transfer of regulatory powers to a body set by new legislation in Britain and France. In both countries, the new policy structure established an Americanized regulatory regime, based loosely on the model of the FCC. In Britain, the new body operates with a "light touch," and in France it generally acts as watchdog.

With the emergence of these changes, the convergence of new media policies became evident. In Britain, according to the Broadcasting Bill, a new Independent Television Commission (ITC) responsible for licensing and supervising all commercial television services (including cable) replaced the Independent Broadcasting Authority (IBA) and the Cable Authority. In France, the issue of regulatory body became the most important for broadcasting and new media policy. The new ideological direction was initially expressed in the modeling of the CNCL (the TV Authority) on the American FCC. When the Socialists returned to power, the government disbanded the CNCL and established the CSA (Council Superior for Audiovisual industries) as the body that regulates French broadcasting. It had responsibility for allocating television and radio frequencies, drawing up and enforcing regulations and charters, and penalizing offenders by revoking licenses.

In examining the global effects of new media policies in Europe, it is evident that the transformation of powers to market forces, which meant substantial policy changes, had been gradual. On the one hand, the whole process was an example for an attempt to provide the cable industry with the stability and certainty essential to its growth and development. On the other, social and cultural aspects remained influential. Even though privatization occurred in all three of the large media countries in Europe, the extent of this process differed. In Britain it was basic from the outset, in France it emerged when developments failed to keep pace with the original plans and resulted in revised expectations, and in Germany it had been the result of agreements between the states.

These policy changes emphasized the role of free competition and provided the market with the means to determine the course and nature of development according to technological advancement and market demand. Deregulation and privatization policies led to a rapid growth in the number and variety of cable channels, and this process resulted in a growth in the number of subscribers.

The impact of new policies and the globalization of new media technologies and programming led to policy changes around the world. The technology and economics of broadcasting produced a wider choice of channels and increased competition, followed by the rise of cable and satellite distribution. The addition of these technologies meant changes in the role and status of broadcasting and in a multiplication of channels. Competition has made a tremendous impact on further policy changes, as it accelerated the globalization of media policies, promoted multiple channels and transmissions, and reduced social, cultural, and political distinctions.

New policies have combined forces of a technological, ideological, global, political, economic, and domestic political nature, leading to the globalization of new media policies. This allowed for the development of satellite transmissions and telecommunications advancement, which offer cross-national services. The overall result of the transition in new media policies is that cross-cultural differences have diminished with the impact of technological advancement, which crosses the boundaries of culture and politics.

It is consequently argued that the most important aspects of new media policies in Europe have involved economics and programming—the commercialization of new media services and the provisions for a wide variety of transmissions. Policy changes have demonstrated that the rapid growth of American cable, following deregulatory moves, has made its impact on European new media policy thinking. Provisions for private programmers have further increased the number of satellite channels that transmit to cable systems and DBS services. This changed European cable and satellite programming services considerably and led to the domination of deregulation and privatization policies.

The commercialization and globalization of new media services, which is the next step of deregulation and privatization, has been reached through policy convergence. As can be seen from the course of change in cable and new media policy that transpired in the three leading European media countries, initial differences diminished with the adoption of deregulation policies. The transition from cultural values to commercialization had common results in all three countries and made an impact on the commercialization of media policy for all of Europe.

The changes that have occurred in Europe and around the world have been the result of the adoption of new attitudes dominated by policy convergence. The commercialization of new media policy has been part of a global trend, which led to a growing recognition of the need for a new market policy for broadcasting services. This process has endorsed policy changes dominated by commercial competition within a global market in which all information services are in competition.

As a result, national differences in the development of new media have diminished, following the swift development of cable and satellite in America and the European regulatory responses to these changes.

To emphasize this outcome, examination of the transition in Europe explores the contribution of each nation to the technological and economic processes of deregulation, privatization, and convergence.

Britain

In Britain, the combination of these factors created remarkable advancement in new media development and services. The extent of policy changes is best demonstrated by the difference in approach in the second and third stages of media policy.

One of the most important and noteworthy rules of the 1984 Broadcasting Act determined that foreign and media companies could have an equity share in a cable system, but not a controlling interest. Thus, despite the heady optimism, British cable developed with painful slowness, afflicted by a self-reinforcing combination of regulatory uncertainty, lack of investment, low take-up and inadequate programming and promotion. As licensees found it increasingly difficult to finance their embryonic operations, it became clear that the commitment to advanced technology was proving too costly to financial investors who were not sufficiently convinced of cable's future growth potential and profitability to provide the necessary venture capital to make it a success.

This situation changed in 1989, when the removal of the restrictions on non-U.K. shareholding in cable companies opened a much-needed conduit for cash from American and Canadian investors. In 1990, the Broadcasting Bill eliminated all non-EC control restrictions, removing barriers to further North American involvement in British cable. Cable has been further encouraged by the removal of the requirement to interface with both British Telecom and Mercury in providing telephony services at the local level. The decision to allow foreign ownership of cable systems was decisive and provided the main boost for investment by North American companies. Since the start of the 1990s, it has become increasingly clear that the impetus for U.K. cable expansion lay with American telephone companies, because their reasons for investing in cable were boosted by the unique opportunity to offer telephony. The promise of cable telephony, fueled by the liberalization of the telecommunications market, was the result of a well-organized lobbying campaign won by the cable industry in Britain.

The impact of convergence is evident in this process. The government, which was encouraged by the levels of investment pledged by Regional Bell operating companies, gave the cable industry a key role in building up competition with British Telecom. In return for guarantees on construction rates, franchise holders were awarded a local monopoly on the supply of cable services and were able to offer telephony services within franchise areas. In this way policy convergence became a reality, with new media technologies providing telecommunications services.

The conclusion for Britain is that without deregulation and policy convergence it is unlikely that foreign capital would have been made available. It is also unlikely that without the permission for globalization of investments cable would have had much of a future, because American companies in particular have kept faith with cable. In addition to having permission to offer telecommunications services (this was still prohibited in the United States at that time), they have concluded that following the new regulatory framework British cable can follow the same pattern as the United States.[6]

France

Among the various experiences addressed in this research, it is arguable that the most dramatic change took place in France. Since the mid-1980s French policy has shifted almost entirely, with an emphasis on commercialization and privatization in all media and telecommunications sectors. This new approach meant additional commercial channels, more television channels and private investment in cable and satellite, and further competition of all media and telecommunications services— intensifying the role of policy convergence.

Developments in the areas of broadcasting, new media, and telecommunications resulted from political changes. Following the victory of the Right in the elections, the way was opened for more private enterprise in the cabling of the country. The government appointed in 1986 largely deregulated the cable industry, forcing operating companies to review their strategies. They negotiated politically to obtain pragmatic provisions in the new legal dispositions—mainly dealing with the operating conditions of networks. The objectives laid down by the Cable Plan were almost unrecognizable by the time that the new government was passing the Law of Liberty of Communications. The law was aimed at policy convergence, recognizing that broadcasting policy should be based on a diversity of media.

This policy represented an acceptance of the unsuccessful attempt to rely on a particular medium—cable TV. The change of policy in favor of commercialization also led to the privatization of TF1, the main national public service channel, and to the creation of a number of other broadcasting channels. This meant the collapse of the centralized public broadcasting system in favor of a commercial and market-driven approach, and resulted in the establishment of a range of DBS and cable channels. As can be learned from the French experience, despite the return of the Socialist government in 1988, the cabling of France entered the 1990s with a more realistic view, with private rather than public investment, and with commercial rather than social and cultural domination. The conclusion is that the combination of new media technologies and a range of broadcasting and telecommunications services has become a dominant force in French media policy, prevailing over cultural issues and demonstrating the importance of policy convergence.

Germany

A new attitude for the development of new media policy and services was also adopted in Germany. Despite the social and political complications outlined earlier, policymakers at both national and state level gradually had to face the fact that broadcasting was being subsumed into a wider revolution that involves competition of all media and telecommunications services. Policy convergence has prevailed over cultural values and become a prominent process in German broadcasting media.

As in Britain and France, policy changes in Germany also resulted from the political structure. The end of the public broadcasting monopoly was followed by the introduction of a private and commercialized media sector, based on cable and financed by subscription and advertising. This provided the incentive for the development of cable systems, with local and private companies becoming involved in the cabling process. With the progress in the cabling drive, it was concluded that private programmers should be encouraged, and cabling became more economically planned, less bureaucratic, and offered larger channel capacity.

As a result of this commercialization process, private operators were incorporated into the cable drive in order to expand the number of connections as rapidly as possible. A leading aim in developing cable was to increase the diversity of television transmissions to the public, and it was concluded that because the broadcasting channels could reach most households, cable could create only limited interest among potential subscribers if used merely for retransmission of broadcast signals. In order to encourage competition, the national government believed in the capacity of cable and satellite to bypass established channels and to receive programming from other countries. An increased supply of transmissions was essential if cable was to become popular, and following the agreement between the states, both public and private broadcasters have increased their program output.

These developments demonstrate the extent of policy changes in Germany in relation to commercialization. Although public broadcasters continued to dominate, mainly by using their financial and programming advantages, the popularity of private channels has been growing. This trend, which strongly influenced the development of German media, accelerated because broadcasting policy and the national cabling plan have become increasingly interlinked.[7]

3.3 MULTICHANNEL COMPETITION

The common aspect of new media policies today is competition between multichannel program providers and suppliers of advanced services. The American competitive structure has been adopted in Europe and around the world, and with the advent of new technology, multichannel competition is leading global changes. Competition between cable and satellite is the most prominent, because these technologies have traditionally provided multichannel services, although other sectors—telecom and terrestrial operators—are also in a process of entering the new competitive structure.

Commercialization had different versions in each country, although the convergence of policy has accelerated changes leading to commercialization of all media policies and opened the way for new technologies. This has been a global process, in which the nature of new media changed from a service that merely provided better reception of off-air transmissions into a sophisticated operation capable of providing multiple transmission and telecommunications services.

This particular process became evident because national governments and international organizations have become interested in promoting more competition and greater choice in new media and telecommunications services. The transition in media policy also related to other sections of the broadcasting media. It resulted in major changes in the nature of public broadcasting services and the addition of commercial broadcasting outlets operating alongside public channels. The whole process can be considered as the convergence of media policy, according to which all broadcasting, new media and telecommunications services are guided by the same policy objectives.

The new structure of global media policy, which dominates the development of all media systems, is distinguished by widespread competition of all media and telecommunications services. This includes competition of public television organizations with private and commercial operators, competition between new media technologies of cable and satellite, and competition of terrestrial, new media, and telecommunications services.

The adoption of multichannel competition has been gradual in different parts of the world, with technological development and market changes providing the driving force. The ability of new technologies of cable and satellite to offer wider geographical coverage, based on improvements in transmission and reception equipment, means that programming can reach beyond national boundaries, thus creating large global media markets and providing opportunities for policy changes dominated by market-oriented principles.

The resulting increased globalization of media markets and the accretion of commercial competition have made it relatively easy to transmit a variety of channels, changing the political and commercial role of media policy. The permission for satellite transmissions on cable systems brought together technological development and new media policies. Following the start of satellite transmissions, American cable industry experienced a dramatic expansion. The availability of new channels with satellite programming, which subscribers could pay extra for, created a revolution in the media market. Satellite communications changed the cable industry by providing it with the means to develop into a fully commercial competitor to broadcast television. The capacity to substantially increase the number of channels provided the basis for the promotion and development of the media market.

The global impact is related to the adoption of commercial and competitive policy in Europe, too. Although European media policy had been politically significant to governments, the impact of new media technology developments challenged the traditional national media structures and required policy changes from public service goals to a mixed model of old and new media.

The most prominent aspect has been the adoption of open-skies policy, which followed the American open-skies policy and created a global process of free market revolution. This was adopted in the 1989 Television Without Frontiers Directive and the 1993 Cable and Satellite Copyright Directive. Under this uniform policy, the free flow of trans-missions among countries is guaranteed, using all media technologies—broadcast television, cable and satellite, and other advanced services. The agreement to policy convergence has in fact created a policy process common to all advanced countries, which leads to a global revolution of media policy.[8]

Policy changes have diminished the impact of domestic legislation. Following the adoption of new media policies and services in the United States and Europe, technological development and market change have also spread into other parts of the world with a growing number of countries adopting new media services and experiencing a vast increase in the number of channels and services available.

Multichannel competition has become a global issue, but the state of convergence and the competitiveness differs among countries, according to four key elements: local regulation, the number of competi-tors, the influence of new technologies entering the market, and the dominating power of former PTTs and national broadcasting and telecommunications monopolies.

The United States

The United States is a "cabled nation." Around 69 percent of its population is connected to cable systems, which dominate the multichannel video subscription market. The American cable boom of the 1980s proved that the industry has undergone a series of changes that have transformed it from a community reception service into a comprehensive primary communications medium and a powerful rival to broadcast television. The deregulation of American media allowed for their immense growth and made its impact on global media patterns by expanding the range of delivery services available.

Satellite services started in 1994, and reached 22.3 percent of the multicultural market in ten years. Digital satellite services compete with cable by offering hundreds of television channels and advanced services, including cable-type programming, Pay-Per-View (PPV) movies, subscription sports, and local network affiliates from the nation's biggest markets. There are two satellite operators: DirecTV has a share of 71 percent of the satellite market, and Echostar captures 29 percent.[9]

Satellite services are expected to increase further. An annual report by Horowitz Associates for "State of Cable 2000" predicts that 25 to 35 percent of cable subscribers will switch to DBS services due to the increasing popularity of digital interactive services. The study reveals the strong interest of consumers in new technologies such as digital cable services, cable modems and Internet access through the TV. Fifty-six percent interest was demonstrated to better picture and sound quality and new basic channels, and 50 percent interest was expressed in the ability to stop, forward, rewind, and pause TV programming.[10]

Competition among multichannel service providers is intensifying, and cable systems are getting ready for the digital age, mainly through mergers and the addition of new services. AT&T's Broadband Services purchase of TCI and MediaOne makes it the top provider of subscription television services in the United States, passing 27.9 million homes with service delivered to 16.1 million homes.[11]

In early 2003, Comcast merged with AT&T, to form a cable giant serving 21.4 million homes—25 percent of America's pay TV market as well as 17 of the 20 largest metropolitan markets in the country. In 2002 EchoStar, the second largest satellite operator, attempted to purchase its main rival, DirecTV, to form a satellite powerhouse of 18 million homes—the second largest multichannel provider and the largest digital operator in the United States.[12] Concerns about the merger had been that "millions of consumers in rural America have no multichannel video programmming and for Internet service. The rural consumers who presently have a choice between two very competitive satellite providers, could be subjected to monopolistic practices if the merger is approved."[13]

EchoStar and DirecTV claimed in response that the merger would eliminate duplication of channels and have the capacity to provide local channels in all 210 American TV markets as well as advanced broadband and interactive services, "thereby providing a real alternative to cable and helping to address the competitve disadvantages currently confronted by the DBS industry."[14] In October 2002, the FCC and the Justice Department's antitrust division announced their opposition to the merger of DirecTV and EchoStar, and at the end of 2002, the companies scrapped the deal.

Table 3.1. The Spread of U.S. Multichannel Video Subscribers

Total television households:	100 million
Cable systems:	68.9 million
Direct Broadcast Satellite (DBS):	18 million
Satellite Master Antenna TV (SMATV):	1.78 million
TV Receive Only (TVRO):	1.9 million
Wireless Cable Systems:	0.9 million

Figures show the number of subscribers in early 2003

Table 3.2. American Digital Video Market

Total digital subscribers:	31.7 million
Satellite:	18 million
Share:	57%
Cable systems:	13.7 million
Share:	43%

Figures show the number of subscribers in early 2003

Table 3.3. U.S. Top 25 Multichannel Service Providers

1. Comcast	21,714,505
2. AOL Time Warner	13,080,000
3. DirecTV	11,160,000
4. EchoStar/Dish Network	8,010,000
5. Charter	6,698,000
6. Cox	6,238,408
7. Adelphia	5,780,000
8. Cablevision	2,796,000
9. NRTC	1,729,592
10. MediaCom	1,588,000
11. Pegasus	1,375,000

(continues)

Table 3.3. U.S. Top 25 Multichannel Service Providers (cont.)

12. Insight	1,289,000
13. Cable One	731,000
14. C-Band Satellite	636,000
15. RCN	567,000
16. Classic Cable	352,600
17. WideOPenwest	310,000
18. Service Electric	293,000
19. Tele-Media	255,000
20. Armstrong	210,800
21. Subquehanna	205,700
22. Midcontinent	200,200
23. Galexy Telecom	175,800
24. Pencor Services	174,000
25. Northland	109,727

Figures show the number of subscribers in early 2003
*NRTC and Pegasus sell DirecTV in rural markets
Source: *The Bridge*, February 2003, Vol. 2, No. 2, www.SkyReport.com

Table 3.4. U.S. Digital Cable Subscribers

1. Comcast Digital	7,165,000
2. AOL Time Warner	3,700,000
3. Charter Digital	2,530,000
4. Adelphia Digital	1,690,000
5. Cox Digital	1,512,956
6. Mediacom Digital	348,000
7. Insight Digital	317,000
8. Cablevision Digital	79,670
9. Classic Cable Digital	32,000
Total	17,373,760

Figures show the number of subscribers in early 2003
Source: *The Bridge*, February 2003, Vol. 2, No. 2, www.SkyReport.com

Britain

The combination of deregulation, technological advancement, and global investment, have placed Britain as a leader in multichannel competition. Following major political decisions of the European Commission and local regulators, Britain has almost completely deregulated the media and telecommunications industries in the broadcasting acts of

1990 and 1996. The United Kingdom is one of the first countries in the world where both cable and telephone service to households could be delivered, and it is leading advancement in the transformation to digital technology. A majority of the investment by American multimedia companies in Europe has been in British cable, which is a growing industry that has gained access to telecommunications services.[15]

In recent years a series of mergers have established a growing cable industry ready to face competition. Three MSOs—Videotron, Bell Cable Media, and Nynex—merged in 1996 into Cable and Wireless Communications. The 8.2 million acquisition by NTL of the consumer and direct business division of Cable & Wireless Communications in 2000 created the largest cable operator with a customer base of some 3 million subscribers and 200,000 businesses and a combined network reach of 12 million franchise homes.[16] Together with the third MSO, Telewest, the systems are making huge efforts to exploit the full range of cable's capabilities, adding digital television services, telephony, and high-speed Internet. NTL and Telewest co-operate on a pay-per-view movie joint venture. Telewest has 1.1 million subscribers, including 179,000 on digital.[17]

The British cable industry is set to attract subscribers with new services and advanced technology on offer. In addition to television programming, systems offer a range of telephony and high-speed Internet access services. The permission by the ITC for Britain's MSOs to merge was meant to create a cable giant that would offer a powerful alternative to the growing digital satellite market. Penetration rates reach about a quarter of the homes passed. NTL has a rate of 28.2 percent, Telewest 22.7.[18] But the future of British cable is still fuzzy, because it faces competition from other services offering packages of television programs and telephone services—direct broadcast satellite and digital terrestrial television.

In the satellite market, has BSkyB offered since October 1998 a 200-channel direct-to-home digital service (Sky Digital) and leads the multichannel market with dominance in pay TV sports and movies. Sky shut off its analog satellite service in September 2001, 12 years after delivering the service. With the full transition into digital service, Sky reached 5.3 million subscribers.

The 1996 Broadcasting Act deals with Terrestrial Television Broadcasting. It created a licensing system of six television multiplexes. A multiplex is a frequency band on which several program channels and additional data can be provided. Existing terrestrial broadcasters were guaranteed capacity on the three multiplexes with the greatest national coverage. One full multiplex was given to the BBC, one in a joint control of Channels 3 and 4, and the third to be operated by Channel 5 and the Welsh Forth Channel, S4C.

The Independent Television Commission can award the three remaining multiplex licenses to commercial operators, according to certain criteria, which includes: which applicant will do most to promote the development of digital terrestrial television in the UK; the extent of the proposed broadcast area; the ability to establish and maintain the proposed services; the capacity of the services proposed to appeal to a variety of tastes and interests; proposals by the applicant to promote or assist in the acquisition of equipment to receive digital services; and the terms to ensure fair and effective competition.

Digital program and additional service licenses can also be awarded by the ITC. Broadcasters wishing to launch a program service on a digital multiplex need a digital program license, available to any applicant subject to media ownership rules, and broadcasters wishing to provide information services need an additional service license, available on demand and under similar arrangements to digital program service licenses.[19]

The United Kingdom has four commercial digital platforms of terrestrial, cable, satellite, and DSL and it leads Europe's transition to digital TV. One third of U.K. households had digital service by early 2003, compared to a European average of 16.3 percent.[20] A new competitor in the multichannel market, Digital Terrestrial Television operator, ITV Digital (formerly ONDigital), which was launched in November 1998 and has 1.3 million subscribers, was closed down in 2002, unable to fulfill its contract with the Football League. Meanwhile, the ITC received six applications in respect to the three advertised licenses to operate multiplexes B, C, and D. According to the ITC, the government expects all television transmissions to be digital between 2006 and 2010.[21] In late 2002, the BBC launched Freeview, the second attempt at delivering digital terrestrial television. The service is targeting customers who don't want to pay for premium digital content, but desire an increase from the standard five terrestrial channels. Up to 75 percent of the nation will be able to receive the 28 television and 12 digital radio channels for a one-off payment of $150 for the purchase of a set-top box.

Table 3.5. U.K. Media Market Statistics

Television households:	24 million
Cable subscribers:	3.2 million
Satellite subscribers:	5.3 million
Digital terrestrial subscribers:	1 million

Figures show the number of subscribers in the end of 2002

Table 3.6. U.K. Satellite Figures (BskyB)

Total subscribers:	6.562 million
Penetration rate of U.K. homes:	27.5%

Figures show the number of subscribers at the end of 2002.

Table 3.7. U.K. Cable Figures

Homes passed:	12 million
Total subscribers:	3.8 million
Penetration rate of U.K. homes:	16%
Homes passed by digital cable infrastructure	10 million
Digital cable subscribers	1.9 million
Digital cable penetration rate of homes passed	16%
Cable telephony lines installed:	4.4 million

Figures show the number of subscribers at the end of 2002.

France

For centuries the centralized French state guaranteed stability and unity in the country. Broadcasting developed under the same goals, and new technology was perceived as a tool to develop French culture rather than to encourage globalization. Despite the changes that took place in Europe and elsewhere in the world, the state continued to safeguard its privileges to control the development of new media technologies, especially with respect to those functions that made it easier for France to face the challenge of globalization.

For that reason, the changes that took place in France are particularly significant. The main changes have been in the regulatory structure and in the development of new competitive media and telecommunications sectors. The government has changed its policy outlook to allow the market to dominate by encouraging competition and diminishing its role in future developments. In recent years the tasks carried out by the government have changed dramatically, as today many of its former tasks have been taken over by the European Community. France has even suggested that the European Union should play a role in motivating and financing a pan-European interactive television network.[22]

The main policy structure of the government is the move away from the reliance on cable for providing multichannel and advanced services and pushing ahead with new technologies. Legislation throughout the 1990s was aimed at encouraging competition. This included: regulation on television- and radio-encrypted services and a decree on encrypted services through satellite (in 1995), adoption of the European Directive on TV Signals Transmissions (in 1995), the Law on Telecommunication (1996), modification of the Law on Freedom of Communication (in 1997), and authorizations for telephony licenses (since 1997). A new Authority for Radio and Television (ART) and a Public Agency of Frequencies (ANF) were formed, also with the mission of encouraging competition and new services.

Although diverse competition has developed since the European telecommunications market was liberalized in 1998, the multichannel and telecommunications sectors are still dominated by France Telecom. The French PTT, which ended the monopoly status and is progressing with privatization, plays a major role in the development of new media by entering new markets. It is seeking regulatory approval for ASDL services in up to 500 towns, in an attempt to stay ahead of cable high-speed Internet services.

France Telecom is still dominating the cable market. Some networks are owned and operated by the PTT, and in others it is the owner but the commercial business is privately operated. Following the requirement by the European Community that PTTs sell their cable networks, France Telecom is selling off its Plan Cable networks.

Table 3.8. French Media Market Statistics

Population:	58.5 million
Total households:	22.9 million
Total TV households:	21.6 million
Homes subscribed to cable:	3 million
Homes subscribed to satellite:	4 million
Phone lines Installed:	37 million

Figures show the number of subscribers in early 2003.

Table 3.9. French Cable Figures

Number of cable sites:	461
Homes passed by cable:	7,134,469
Projected homes passed when all sites are completed:	9,175,641
Total subscribers:	2,588,618
Basic TV subscribers:	2,580,430
Digital cable subscribers:	219,297
Cable Internet subscribers:	13,464
Cable telephony subscribers:	1,856

Figures show the number of subscribers in 1999.

Table 3.10. French Satellite Figures

Total Subscribers: 4 million
Canal Plus: 2.9 million
Canal Satellite—2.1 million
Television Per Satellite (TPS)—1.1 million

Figures show the number of subscribers in early 2003.

Consequently, gradual competition is developing in the cable market, which is dominated by MSOs: NC Numericable (controlled by Canal Plus), Lyonnaise Communications, UPC (through Videopole and Media Reseaux), and France Telecom. Other major players in the multichannel market are direct broadcast satellite operators Canal Plus, TPS, and Canal Satellite.[23]

Germany

Germany is the world's third largest economic power, after the United States and Japan. Its economy is strong in traditional sectors such as car making and mechanical engineering. Germany is also the largest new media market in Europe with a total of 30 million cable and satellite homes, over 40 percent of all European cable and satellite homes. But although new technology has enabled the country to achieve economic goals, the social elements of market economy have received special emphasis in media policy and technological development.

Germany has a great regulatory complexity in the governance of communications services. Under the Federal Constitution a distinction is made between the responsibilities of the states and the central government. The states regulate broadcasting and media services and the federal government regulates telecommunications and information services. Political parties have always played a significant role in the political culture and competition in media and telecommunications services had been delayed for a long time.

In recent years, along with the adoption of globalization rules, traditional political dividing lines between left and right are fading. The triumph of market principles has made an impact on media policy too, and key legislation was passed in the New German State Treaty on Broadcasting, which came into force in January 1997, and several telecommunications laws. The Federal Cartel Office is also an influential regulatory institution.

Additional competition is the result of regulation by the European Community. Following the liberalization of the telecommunications market in 1998, Deutsche Telekom, the national telecommunications monopoly, is in the process of privatization and entering new markets, including information technology. Deutsche Telekom leads changes in Germany. It plays a major role in the development of new media, including in areas that it had previously dominated as a national monopoly.

Changes in the cable market are the result of competition and European regulation. Following the requirement by the European Community that PTTs sell their cable networks, the German PTT is ending its traditional monopoly status in the cable market. Currently Germany has one main cable network with Deutsche Telekom controlling the technology and many providers operating the systems, and the German PTT has split the network into nine regional companies. As part of the new competitive structure, Deutsche Telekom also encourages competition and diversity policies in its cable services. It is opening up public cable networks for private ownership and encouraging exclusive cable packages, by focusing on new programming services and advanced developments like Pay-Per-View and Near-Video-On-Demand.[24]

Germany is Europe's leading broadband nation, with 2.2 million DSL subscribers, although at the same time it is one of the European laggards in advanced television services, with only 8.2 percent of German households connected to digital services by the end of 2001. A major political battle between regulators and commercial operators—new cable investors and terrestrial broadcasters—has been delaying the rollout of digital services. Deutsche Telekom operates about 95 percent of the country's DSL lines and until recently was the leading force in Germany's cable industry. While Deutsche Telekom admitted it could not upgrade its cable networks, it aimed to sell nine regional networks.[25]

Table 3.11. German Media Markets Statistics

Population:	81.2 million
Total Households:	37.45 million
Total TV households:	32.5 million
Homes passed by cable:	34.5 million
Homes subscribed to cable:	24 million
Homes subscribed to satellite services:	16 million
Phone lines Installed:	45 million

Figures show the number of subscribers in at the end of 2002.

Table 3.12. German Cable Market Figures

	Subscribers	Homes Passed
Total	21.85 million	31.54 million
Callahan Associated International:	6.5 million	9.4 million
Deutsche Telekom Bavaria:	2.2 million	3.6 million
Deutsche Telekom Bremen & Lower Saxony:	1.8 million	2.9 million
Deutsche Telekom Hamburg, Scheswig-Holstein & Wecklnburg:	1.6 million	2.7 million
Deutsche Telekom Berlin & Brandenburg:	1.7 million	2.4 million
Deutsche Bank:	1.5 million	2.24 million
Deutsche Telekom Rhineland—Palatnate & Saarland:	1.3 million	1.9 million
Klesch Investments Co.	1.3 million	1,8 million
PrimaCom:	930,000	1.35 million
Bosch:	1.2 million	not available
UPC:	876,000	1.1 million
Deutsche Telekom Saxony:	70,000	990,000

Source: Satellite Communications International (CSCI), September 2000, page 22.

SUMMARY

One of the most significant changes in the development of media and telecommunications services has been the globalization of media policy. Policy changes have become evident with the growing impact of technological advancement and globalization, led by the availability of new technologies and the establishment of global markets. The main course of transition had been from cultural values to commercialization, and this process has involved new media technologies, deregulation, privatization and convergence.

Changes have been considerable and distinct, with Europe following the American experience of free market approach. Initially European media policies developed with the encouragement of national governments, which saw the establishment of new media infrastructure as a national priority. Deregulation led to a restructuring of media and telecommunications policies, and convergence replaced local policies that had prohibited the development of new technologies. Following policy changes in America and Europe, competitive structure has been adopted around the world. In the new structure of media policy, technological advancement and the enforcement of global trends dominate all media and telecommunications developments, demonstrating that global policy has become common around the world.

Globalization is one of the most principal elements of media policy for the 21st century. With the advent of new technology, multichannel competition is leading global changes, reflecting on the transition of new media into digital technology, guided by commercial and global rather than cultural and local considerations.

Policy changes are gradual in different countries, although the globalization of media policy has accelerated commercialization of all media policies and opened the way for new technologies and further competition. In future terms, global competition between multichannel program providers and between suppliers of advanced services should force governments and television stations around the world to switch to digital technology and to offer a variety of television programs and interactive services.

4

The Technologies
of the 21st Century

The next revolution in television broadcasting is digital technology, which differs tremendously from the analog television broadcast system used for decades. The incentive for broadcasters to advance the transformation from the old transmission system to the new technological revolution is the ability to converge between television and telecommunications services through the use of different digital technologies—terrestrial television, cable and satellite systems, telephone and wireless communications.

These technologies provide new services, which distinguish the new structure of media policy. In addition to traditional services of passive television broadcasting and point-to-point telephone calls, new services include cellular phone, video telephony, teleconferencing, cable telephony, teletext and videotext, multimedia, personal computers, the Internet, and other interactive applications.

Several digital technologies have developed in recent decades. Telephone networks began incorporating digital techniques in the late

1970s, the audio CD introduced digital sound to consumer electronics in the early 1980s, and CD-ROMs and the Web developed sound and video in personal computers in the 1990s. In the 21st century digitalization came into television, combining broadband television-computer and wireless services.

In technical terms, the digital television age is an era in which information increasingly gets stored, retrieved, and transmitted in an electronic form that computers can handle. The commercial applications mean that all providers are free to offer all available services and compete over the same networks. The broadcasting, telecommunications, and computing industries are rapidly converging toward a single multimedia market in which all technologies supply all services. Under the new structure, television operators supply high-speed data and telephony services; telecommunications services provide video and data; and the Internet is delivering voice, video, data, and telephony services.

One of the most exciting developments in the communications industry is the convergence of communications, information, and entertainment. The convergence of television and telecommunications services through digital technology is radically changing the ways society communicates, providing new kind of video and data services and starting new commercial opportunities. The introduction of digital services makes it easier to link television content to interactive and various services on demand. Digitalization is expected to transform the broadcasting industry from the passive medium of the past century into an active information and entertainment medium and a retail sales instrument of business.

With new media technologies, society is now embarking on digital expansion. Technological innovations such as the Internet, multicasting, and interactive applications change the television and telecommunications landscape around the world. The conversion from analog to digital transmission of audiovisual signals allows the delivery of high-quality television and advanced interactive services—high definition pictures and CD-quality sound, and several standard definition television signals over the same portion of electromagnetic spectrum used for analog channels.

The technologies offering combined services include Digital Terrestrial Television (DTT), broadband cable, digital satellite, Digital Subscriber Line (DSL), and wireless communications provided by telecom operators. Additional competition comes from Internet Service Providers (ISP) and Advanced Interactive Multimedia (AIM) content providers offering interactive television applications.

With such intense competition, however, the question remains if there will be enough room for all service providers to attract as many data customers as required for survival in a competitive market. Despite the uncertainty, one major conclusion is certain: competition will be increased, and to survive networks will have to perform at peak efficiency. Competitors will have to provide better services at a lower price, respond directly to customer requests, and correct potential weak spots before failure. Competition will become the name of the game and customer satisfaction will become a key element in the new competitive environment.

This chapter provides a comprehensive analysis of the structure that should dominate the 21st century, with a detailed explanation of the evolving nature of global issues. The main goal is to analyze the current and future technological and social trends; data and statistics on the main forces and trends involved in global media policy support this analysis.

4.1 DIGITAL TERRESTRIAL TELEVISION

The transition to digital television presents the most comprehensive and complicated change in the history of television. With the conversion from the old analog transmission system to digital technology, television is entering the most significant transformation since its inception. The 1980s were a decade of development for cable, with the triumph of multichannel television. The 1990s were a decade of multichannel competition, with the addition of direct broadcast satellite services, and the new millennium is characterized by the launch of digital terrestrial television (DTT) technology and heady growth of interactive services.

Different from all other technologies, which compete for the provision of video and data services to the home, digital terrestrial television is backed up by governments' decrees, and national media policies are aimed at making DTT a leading technology for interactive television in the 21st century.

The Transition to Digital Technology

The convergence of television and computers through digital technology is radically changing the way that we will communicate with each other. The conventional television standards of analog transmissions and the related monochrome-compatible color encoding systems (NTSC, PAL, and Secam) represent the broadcasting technology of the 20th century. The concept of advanced television transmissions, with digital and high-definition qualities, is providing the basis for the interactive television of the 21st century.

Digital television allows broadcasters to provide new kinds of video and data services. It can provide high-quality picture and sound of high-definition television (HDTV) or broadcasters can split their signal to offer multiple channels of standard-definition television (SDTV).

The high definition technology allows to transmission of to six times the information of analog service, including five discrete CD-quality audio tracks. The transmission can offer data and on-line services, subscription television, and full interactive television applications. These capabilities can intensify efforts to turn the Internet into a broadcast medium and television into an interactive service.[1]

The standard digital technology is comparable to the analog transmission but allows an almost unlimited number of channels. Television applications include: multichannel television, a larger distribution capacity and the opportunity to access more television channels with better video and audio quality, electronic program guide (EPG), pay and pay-per-view services, audio-on-demand, near-video-on-demand and video-on-demand, and enhanced television programs with text, graphic, or audio on the top of the screen. The interactive applications include Internet and e-mail, discussion-groups, websurfing, electronic commerce (e-commerce), and other on-line services.[2]

Digital technology has different meanings, depending on the technical and social aspects of the new revolution. A prominent aspect of global media policy is the debate on the technical standard for digital television, between the DVB specifications developed in Europe and the American ATSC system.

The development of advanced television concepts in America was entrusted to the Advanced Television Systems Committee (ATSC), a private-sector organization of corporations, associations, and educational institutions. It was responsible for exploring the need for and developing the documentation of the Advanced Television (ATV) standards, according to which the ATSC standard was developed. This standard was adopted and is being implemented by the FCC. Other countries like Canada, South Korea, Taiwan, and Argentina have also adopted it as the standard for digital terrestrial broadcasting.

Europe has selected the Digital Video Broadcasting (DVB) standard for digital services—DVB-T for terrestrial, DVB-S for satellite, DVB-C for cable, and DVB-MMDS for microwave. DVB systems can deliver a range of picture qualities, multichannel sounds, and multimedia data in a way that can meet the needs of any service provider or particular market.

DVB has been adopted as the digital standard across Europe and in Australia, India and Singapore. Pan-European consensus for a terrestrial interactive TV standard was critical for the further penetration of DVB into new markets and services. DVB started with broadcasting. It was specified to provide a common standard for digital delivery across all transmission media. It gradually moved to the specification of return channels in the telecom domain, and finally to the specifications for interactive and data broadcasting in the software domain. Because interactivity is the defining difference between digital and analog television, each of the new markets will require the deployment of a return channel to complement its DVB broadcasting system.[3]

American and European broadcasters are at opposite ends of the scale in trying to predict what consumers will want from digital television viewing. The main question is whether the majority of the public will take the opportunity to benefit from the advantages of digital television, and which system will be most popular. Past experience demonstrates that only a small percentage of viewers have subscribed to analog pay services of cable and satellite.[4] The question is, then, is there a real need for additional multichannel services in the SDTV system, or would it be better to take the opportunity to make a new viewing experience available in the HDTV system.

The policy thinking behind the adoption of SDTV is to enhance the production and distribution infrastructure by multiplying the number of channels available to the public. Contrary to this policy, the FCC decided that because multichannel television already exists in the United States, digital television should be used to enhance the quality of the services and introduce high-definition television and advanced interactive applications.

The debate relates to future applications of digital television. DVB and ATSC differ in the way audio is compressed, the way modulation format is issued, the way program guide information is incorporated, and the way error correction is used. DVB is most concerned with digital broadcasting of multiple standard-definition pictures, and will bring Standard Definition Television (SDTV) to European homes. ATSC is primarily concerned with transmission of HDTV pictures, while acknowledging transmission of multiple standard-definition pictures in one channel. It should develop into High Definition Television (HDTV) in the United States.

The ATSC system is an all-digital terrestrial broadcast system that includes provisions for a wide range of formats at various frame rates. Resolutions under 720 are considered Standard Definition and those at or above 720 are considered as High Definition. The members of the ATSC did not agree on a single picture format concept and the ATSC standard supports a range of formats. These include HDTV level with 720 and 1,080 active lines and SDTV with 480 active lines (compared to the 525 active lines of analog Pal system and 625 active lines of the analog NTSC system). The FCC's rules allow broadcasters great flexibility to use digital technology to offer whatever services they want to, as long as at least one free digital television signal of SDTV quality is available at the same time.[5]

Powerful Coalition of Supporters

The transition to digital terrestrial broadcasting is beneficial to and backed up by several key sectors, and thus has gained general consensus:

1. *Governments and Official Organizations.* The role of regulatory authorities has been the most crucial in the transformation from the analog transmission system, led by key agencies: the Federal Communications Commission (FCC), the European Community (EC), and the Independent Television Commission (ITC).[6]

Globalization and technological advancement have become the two most striking aspects of the new structure of media policy. Digital television, which brings the global information superhighway to the home, combines broadcasting and interactivity and opens up new opportunities for national governments. The combination of new technology and the enforcement of global trends mean that new media services dominate all media and telecommunications policies in the leading media countries as they move to digitalization. It also demonstrates that the main principles of global policy have become common around the world.

The global government-mandated transition to digital television is the biggest national-technological changeover ever backed by government decree. It will eventually affect everyone around the world. In the future today's television stations will go off the air, to be replaced by all-digital stations, and when the global process is completed only digital stations will operate.

2. *Multichannel Service Providers.* The digital revolution presents many advantages to program providers and the production industry. Multichannel services have created significant changes, mainly in Europe, with its long tradition of state-owned national broadcasting monopolies. Traditional regulatory regimes have had to adapt to the erosion of boundaries between television markets and between cultural and economic sovereignty. Satellite and cable operators and pay-TV providers have seen the transition to digital television as the opportunity to restructure the television marketplace and establish a new leading position in the competition with terrestrial services.

Many program providers have stressed that digital television does not necessarily mean high-definition, because the advantages of a greater number of channels are enormous. The overall result of policy changes is that new media are of a commercial type, with programming as the main attraction to customers. Experiences around the world have demonstrated that success of different technologies depends on programming and service content, rather than on the physical infrastructure by which programming is being delivered or the cultural perspectives dominating new media policies.

Following the conversion into digital infrastructure, more broadcast space is available, with new services and more competition among broadcasters. The greater number of programming and potential services creates narrowcasting—the process of searching for increasingly specific audiences. New audience groups can be differentiated based on factors such as age, gender, or interest. Broadcasters and advertisers can beam their transmission to a more specific group of customers without having to pay for sending their signals to millions of viewers who are unlikely to watch the particular program or buy the advertised product.[7]

3. Economic Interests and Commercial Forces. New technologies increase the complexity of broadcasting and telecommunications issues and complicate the task of regulation, giving way for global commercial forces to dominate. The concepts that make up the new structure are liberalization, deregulation, reregulation, privatization, convergence, open-skies, free market, and market-led approach. Under this structure, commercial forces have gained priority in delivering new services.

Global policies have resulted from the interplay of public policies and market forces led by giant international firms. Global and technological trends—the cost of switching into digital and pay-per-view television and of marketing integrated bundles of television, telephone, and Internet services—are forcing relatively small players to join forces. The role of global policy means the surge of American and European conglomerates, as a common media market is evolving.

The combination of global economic forces and the power of new technology spur global links and encourages the development of global services also because commercial channels and advertisers can reach wider mass audiences. In this way, commercial advocates have become more powerful than regulators. They are investing in digital projects and have influenced the adoption of a commercial approach in the transition to digital terrestrial television.

4. Public Organizations and Audience Groups. Public organizations have recognized the opportunity to provide additional capacity for more program choice and interactive services. The social aspects of the transition are related to the quality of the transmissions, which enable viewers to have more control over the television viewing experience and to have access to entertainment and information services. The proliferation of cable and DBS made many voices available to television viewers, and the assumption has been that with digital services the variety of options will become even greater.

The changeover has some major potential benefits for consumers: a wider variety of channels, sharper and clearer television images, high-definition transmissions, and interactive services. Advances in digital compression technology allow reception of a greater number of channels and advanced services using only a fraction of the valuable spectrum resources that are used in analog technology. Demand by consumers for integrated services that are provided through broadband infrastructures is also expanding with the opportunities offered by digital technology.

5. *Equipment Manufacturers.* The transition to digital technology opens up attractive technological and financial opportunities for equipment manufacturers. Although the cost of the new services is still questionable, because competition for the supply of new services is only starting, there are significant differences in converting to SDTV or HDTV systems. Manufacturers emphasize the cheaper services and simple use of SDTV: all that is needed to get standard digital services is a set-top box decoder on top of the analog television set or a new set with a decoder device. This gives access to multichannel television services, including free channels at relatively low cost.

In contrast, high definition transmission is designed for display on a 16x9 ratio screen (as opposed to the analog 4x3 ratio). Special digital receivers and digital-capable television sets are required to display the full resolution of digital broadcasts. Television manufacturers, who have to supply HDTV receivers and television sets, and television studios, which have to transfer films to videotape with high-definition recorders, support advocates of the new system. In America alone, about 260 million television sets nationwide will have to be replaced or updated with a converter box by 2006.

Digital Timetable

The conventional model for transfer to digital terrestrial television is to determine an extended intervening period of service in which both analog and digital services are available, with an announced switch-off date for the analog service and conversion into digital. Most countries, however, have not set a firm date, because of the uncertainties and possible differences between the predicted diffusion and actual adoption of DTT. Because the technology has not been fully implemented anywhere, there is no firm data on consumer reactions, on equipment costs, or on the practical difficulties in implementing the new technology at large.

The United States is leading the transition to digital television. By 2006, all terrestrial broadcasts will become fully digital and the current NTSC form will be turned off for a new digital ATSC system. DBS and cable operators are not required for this timetable, although they already offer digital services and some high-definition channels.[8]

On December 24, 1996, Congress approved the Telecommunications Act, which sets a timetable for the completion of a new system of broadcast television. In April 1997 FCC gave broadcasters $70 billion worth of spectrum to broadcast digital alongside analog until 2006. Each television station is eligible to apply to operate a new digital station serving a geographic area with any mix of digital TV standards including HDTV. FCC also mandates that during the transition period stations will air both analog and digital signals, and in 2006 all broadcasts must be fully digital. This change means that in the second half of this decade, today's American terrestrial television stations will go off the air, to be replaced by all-digital stations, and every household will need a digital receiver to continue watching television.

The transition is gradual, according to a strict schedule, which includes the following timetable:

1. First digital stations went on the air in November 1998.
2. Stations affiliated with the top four networks (ABC, CBS, NBC, and FOX) in the 10 largest markets began digital service by May 1, 1999 (30% of the viewers).
3. Stations affiliated with these networks in markets 11-30 began digital service by November 1, 1999 (50% of the viewers).
4. All commercial stations had to begin digital transmission by May 1, 2002.
5. All noncommercial educational stations must begin by May 1, 2003.

The law requires that at least one digital channel must be free and of the same quality as the analog channel but not the same program, according to the following timetable:

1. By April 1, 2003, 50 percent of analog programming must be simulcast on one of the digital channels.
2. By April 1, 2004, broadcasters will be required to simulcast at least 75 percent of their video programming on both the analog and digital systems.
3. After April 1, 2005, broadcasters will be required to transmit all their video programming on both analog and digital services.

4. By the end of the transition period, in 2006, licensees will cease analog broadcasts and return their spectrum to the government. The analog transmission will be shut down, although this will depend on how many people still rely on analog television.

During the transition period viewers with conventional sets can still watch television as usual, but only viewers with digital television receivers will be able to receive the high-definition version. By 2006, all 1,600 terrestrial television stations in the United States will be able to use only a single digital channel and consumers will then have no choice but to use digital television sets. Broadcasters will have to relinquish extra broadcast spectrum and broadcast only digitally. Old analog channels will then go off the air and be given back to the government for possible auctioning.[9]

The government-mandated changeover to digital broadcasting is unprecedented in the extent of national technological transition backed by government decree. This change will eventually affect almost every household in the United States and perhaps the world as a whole, enabling viewers to receive sharper and clearer television images than with analog services and use interactive services through television rather than only on computers. As a result, HDTV may be mostly influential in the computer industry, as the Internet and other interactive services will be offered on television.[10]

The market is poised for long-term growth with the addition of Internet-Protocol (IP) application (services which include high-speed Internet access, voice telephony, and streaming video). In addition to broadcast services interactivity has become a crucial issue for TV operators and an opportunity to add new services, increase the loyalty of subscribers, and obtain new ones. Digitization and broadband are changing the very foundations of the traditional business model of broadcasting, by increasing the average revenue per subscriber and changing the way people watch television and use advanced services. Although broadband technologies are having difficulties with commercial realization, broadband infrastructure is being developed as a multiple service of broadcast, satellite, and cable.

The transition to digital television is taking place in all sectors of the broadcast market, although it is a multifaceted, complicated, and evolutionary process involving multiple industries. As a December 2001, approximately 223 terrestrial stations were transmitting a digital signal in 79 markets. Operators have invested billions of dollars to upgrade their facilities, and program networks have launched new digital channels. Several program networks are pushing ahead with the deployment of high-definition HDTV programming, although the transition to digital remains slow. The broadcast industry as a whole has made no major commitments to use the digital channels primarily to provide HDTV, with many broadcasters preferring to provide SDTV services and use the rest of their spectrum for commercial applications.

The cable industry is also implementing digital services. Cable networks have launched more than 60 new digital channels, some of them providing high-definition digital services. According to FCC Chairman Michael Powell, cable's commitment to delivering HDTV programming will present new business opportunities for MSOs: "HDTV presents an enormous opportunity for cable, as well as anyone who hopes to be accessing consumers in their homes wit the products of the future."[11]

While all of satellite's 18 million customers have digital service, according to the National Cable and Telecommunications Association, 13.7 million American subscribers had digital cable by the end of 2001. Comcast had more than 1 million broadband telephony customers, and more than 1.9 million high-speed data subscribers—10 percent of the homes passed and 15 percent of its basic cable subscribers. It also had 3.3 million digital subscribers. Cox Communications has achieved 1 million high-speed data subscribers and 500,000 broadband telephone customers.

The European timetable differs from that of the United States, primarily because different policies have been employed around the continent. Digital Video Broadcasting has already started in Europe, and terrestrial, satellite, and cable viewers in different countries are able to have a multiplicity of channels.

Digital terrestrial licenses are being issued all over Europe. The leading country is the United Kingdom, and its policy is based on multiplex licenses that have been authorized to cover 70 to 90 percent of the country. Other major markets are Sweden and Spain, although other countries have already announced their intentions to start DTT services. Policies differ according to the competitiveness of the market (cable and satellite penetration) and operating rules for digital multiplexes.[12]

Competition for supplying future services is also developing in Europe, although it has been slow. The European satellite broadband venture is aiming at becoming Europe's leading provider of two-way satellite broadband services. Their competitors, cable operators, offer new services of high-speed Internet access, voice telephony and streaming video, aiming to generate new sources of revenue for firms that in the past had only sent analog video services. However, less than 1 percent of the population in Europe has access to broadband connection, compared to 3.24 percent in the United States. According to report by Astra, Europe's leading DBS service (with 33.7 million customers, 41.6 percent of them getting digital services), digital television is now accessible to 25 million homes—more than 70 percent via satellite.[13]

4.2 BROADBAND CABLE

The cable industry has changed dramatically in the last five decades, transforming from a locally oriented service into a sophisticated and advanced technological network providing universal service and creating new markets with interactive applications and global appeal.

Cable systems started as a community service that offered subscribers more channels than were available off-air. With the provision of satellites, cable technology became a means for delivering new types of programming through specialty channels, which also included video broadcasts of local origination and community services. Channel capacity has grown similarly, from only a few to hundreds today. Additional services include pay channels and special-interest programming aimed at smaller audiences.

Cable has become an important industry around the world. With penetration in most countries, including all top media markets, it has the technological capabilities to explore interactive services and compete with terrestrial broadcasters, satellite operators, and telecom services. Cable is dominant in the multichannel market in the United States, with penetration in over two-thirds of American homes. Cable is also a growing industry in Europe, although the European cable market differs from the American market in the size of the cable network. Total European cable households number only about a half of the American market.

Another difference is that the implementation of European multichannel services differs from country to country. It constitutes three main models of development. In the first model (best represented by the United Kingdom) satellite has a dominating position in the local broadcast market. The United Kingdom was the first country in Europe to launch a satellite service with almost no cable penetration and just four terrestrial channels. It was also the first country to offer digital satellite services (through Sky Digital). In the second model (such as in the Benelux and Scandinavia) cable penetration is high and satellite is an alternative or complementary service mainly in remote areas. In the third model, which exists in leading countries such as France and Germany, cable and satellite are equal and competitive services.[15]

The New Structure of Cable

The new structure of cable systems differs from the old one in two major areas: the competitive environment under which cable systems operate, and the technological capabilities and services provided.

Table 4.1. The Penetration of Cable in the Top 10 Media Markets

Rank	Country	Cable Penetration
1	United States	69%
2	Japan	28%
3	United Kingdom	34%
4	Germany	56%
5	France	12%
6	Brazil	5%
7	Italy	0%
8	Australia	14%
9	Canada	77%
10	South Korea	8%

Source: Advertising Age International, June 2000

Competitive Environment. The competitive environment is changing dramatically for the cable industry. Contrary to past experience, when cable used to be a monopoly or had a dominating status in many markets, today competition is dictating operations in the multichannel and advanced services markets. Following the opening of new markets and the development of competing technologies capable of providing advanced services, cable operators must diversify their services and offer customers greater choice of programming to become full-service providers of integrated television and telecom services.

Competition among multichannel service providers is growing. Cable systems face competition mainly from digital satellite operators providing interactive and high-speed services. According to the FCC's sixth annual report on Multichannel Video Program Distributors (MVPDs) competition, although cable remains the dominant multichannel video provider in the United States, two out of three new multichannel video subscribers are going to the satellite industry. New media services of cable and satellite have an unprecedented reach across the United States and promising potential growth in Europe. European cable also faces harsh competition from satellite operators such as Astra, Eutelsat, BSkyB, and Canal Plus, which focus on digital television and broadband access while gaining growing shares of the television and telecommunications markets.

Traditional competition between cable and satellite services had been over price and programming offerings, and is now also over advanced services. The new competitive structure of digital satellite services and broadband cable is more interactive and more tailored to individual consumer interest. Integrating cable and satellite into the Internet started the momentum for broadband services, providing combined broadcast, Internet, voice and data services, including telephony, multi-casting, e-commerce, distance learning, banking, and video games.

Advanced cable systems have an essential communications infrastructure that puts them in good position for the future. The new cable system will eventually deliver much more than the old structure of one-way video programming, including interactive programs, high-speed Internet, and telephony. It is the new competitive environment that cable operates within that forces technological deployment of the industry into an integrated network capable of transmitting not only entertainment, but also advanced information and interactive services at high speed.

Technological Capabilities.   The technological structure of cable systems is also changing dramatically, because advanced cable systems can deliver more channels and high-quality voice, video and data. Interactive services are now the key to the digital future. With the spread of digital terrestrial services and the competition with satellite, cable systems must switch to digital and advanced interactive services in order to survive in the competition.

Digital technology enables cable subscribers to have a greater diversity of programming options aimed at targeted audience groups, including greater choice, and advanced programming services of pay-per-view and high definition television. The expended services include high-speed Internet access and data applications, and advanced trans-mission options like near-video-on-demand (NVOD) and video-on-demand (VOD).

Video-on-demand is like a digital video store, which allows sub-scribers to select from a wide range of programs and events for viewing at their own convenience. Near-video-on-demand allows customers to view programs with start times every 15 or 30 minutes. Additional inter-active provisions include services such as electronic program guide, video games, home shopping, interactive commercials, teleconferencing and transaction processing, personal travel planning, and other multi-media on-line applications.

Broadband and interactivity are becoming the leading terms in the development of new media services, and high-speed interactive cable services are inching around the world. The rapid pace of techno-logical change has been fueled by the opportunity to add new services of high-speed access to the Internet and telephony. The technological change means the convergence of image, voice and data and the combi-nation of entertainment, information and commercial services through a single system.

The new digital infrastructure will connect homes, businesses and government and social agencies through a broadband telecommunications network. Rather than programming, which identified cable services under the old structure, the emphasis today is on the ability to deliver high-speed data, voice and video services and phone calls over advanced communications networks.

The Next Generation of Cable

The next generation of cable means an integrated data, voice, and video (DVV) strategy. Rather than cable, the new term is broadband—delivery of high-speed data services, video, and potentially phone calls over advanced communications pipelines. Delivering integrated services has become the main goal of all communications companies, led by cable systems, which aim to operate on the same playing field as the giant phone companies.

The forecast is that broadband cable systems will compete with telephone companies while delivering a basket of advanced services and practically becoming communications companies. Such combined systems would offer an integrated service of television programming, data, the Internet, and telephony. For that reason, the battle is between the cable and local telephone industries to determine which sector will provide Internet links to homes and businesses.

The face of cable is changing in the new competitive structure. Cable has entered an era of competition for the system that will be used to deliver digital media content and interactive services. Operators around the world upgrade into broadband networks to become DVV operators—rather than concentrating on their traditional business of multichannel service.

For cable, the future of telecommunications is evolving with fiber optic cables that replace coaxial cables, transmissions systems that are computerized, and digital services that provide much more information and interactive options. Broadband technology allows cable significantly faster transmission speed than traditional telephone lines (50 to 100 times faster than telephone-based modem technologies), but not from DSL systems. By 2005, more than 67 million American homes are foreseen to be connected to high-speed services through cable. The number of digital service customers could increase from 9.8 million homes at the end of 2000 to 38.6 million by 2006. The cable industry is also providing local residential telephone service in most American markets.[16]

Worldwide digital cable TV deployment is leading manufacturers to ramp up compatible set top boxes. The number of digital units to be distributed in 2003 was expected to reach 60 million, compared to around 20 million in 1999, 28 million in 2000, 36 million in 2001 and 46 million in 2002.[17]

However, the stakes are still high, and in the new competitive environment cable faces many difficulties. The main problem is that only about a quarter of America's homes are linked to the Internet. Secondly, telephone companies are generally bigger and have more customers and money than cable companies. Although cable modems are often faster than high-speed modems developed by phone companies, local phone companies have increased their Internet access services and secured many of the households that could have become customers of advanced cable services.

There are additional major differences between telephone and cable companies as they enter into broadband services. Cable has developed in most markets as a local service, while telephone companies have developed in most countries on a national or regional basis. Telephone companies have traditionally served the entire population in their franchise area, whereas cable provided limited services. Telephone companies have traditionally provided a monopoly service, whereas cable companies faced competition from terrestrial and satellite services.

There are also technical differences between high-speed services of cable and telephone companies. Cable modems are faster than the modems developed for telephone, but whereas cable modem users share transmission capacity with their neighbors, high-speed telephone lines users can get their own private data pipe. The concern for cable operators is the high investment required to upgrade systems that have traditionally been built to serve residential customers and to compete in a new territory against dominant existing carriers (telephone companies).

Developing the right technology to deliver a digital service is the main problem that cable operators face in upgrading systems for the new digital age. The American cable industry has the broadband capacity to transmit high definition services, and several cable systems already have experimented successfully with the delivery of high definition. The cable industry is also launching initiatives with the computer industry to combine high-capacity transmissions, which will allow cable to offer advanced services and transform systems into telecommunications companies capable of providing telephone and high-speed date services.

The role of the American cable industry in the transition into digital is particularly critical, because more than two-thirds of the nation's television viewers subscribe to cable and the industry is providing a significant part of the technological infrastructure that will dominate future developments in data broadcasting. This means that unless cable subscribers are able to watch digital broadcasts, the government-mandated transition could not be guaranteed.[19]

Although forecasts are still undecisive, one thing is clear: size is extremely important in this competitive structure.[20] For cable, the solution is mergers with telephone companies, to balance the television and data services and to become multiservice providers rather than local television operators.[21]

As the American cable industry faces an increasingly competitive telecommunications market, it is moving into consolidation. The competition to bring a combined telephony, television, and Internet service to the home is forcing mergers of telecom and television companies, which have resulted in major deals in recent years. Consolidation seems to be the answer for the growth of Internet traffic and broadband services.[22]

4.3 DIGITAL SATELLITE

The satellite industry has also undergone dramatic changes in the last several decades, transforming from a technology that only delivered programming services to cable systems into a multichannel service offering direct broadcast television. Today digital satellite services offer advanced interactive services, such as specialized content services suitable to the tastes of individual customers, and a variety of information services, including high-speed Internet access.

The first satellite television systems were TVRO (TeleVision Receive Only). These systems require large mobile dishes and make it possible to view programs on the many satellites that are positioned in the Clarke Belt (there are over 20 C-Band and KU-Band satellites that can be received in the continental United States). They started in the late 1970s and early 1980s and are still widespread today, despite the proliferation of digital cable and satellite services.

Satellite transmissions used for television and telephone services reached an economic breakthrough in the 1970s, when it became dramatically less expensive to use satellites to deliver information. During that time, however, satellite had not been a competitor to cable because large dishes were required to receive transmissions. During the 1980s analog services began in Europe. Medium and high-powered satellites allowed subscribers to pick up scrambled signals on a small dish. The wide variety of programming included three types: over-the-air transmissions, free services, and subscription channels aimed at cable subscribers.

The 1990s were a decade of development and heady growth for satellites. With the start of digital broadcasting, dozens of satellites were built and launched around the world. Asian countries became the biggest customers for many satellite companies; American DBS services were launched; Europe saw tremendous advancement of new satellite services; and digital services were initiated around the world. Satellite has made quick and steady entrance into the multichannel market, turning away from a complementary role to cable into a competitive service offering the most advanced services.

Today digital television and advanced multichannel offerings are available via satellites. The industry gained a competitive position to supply advanced services including Internet access and data broadcasting services. In the competition with cable systems, satellite providers have been focusing on increased programming packages and advanced services to attract a growing number of new customers.

Direct Broadcast Satellite (DBS) has become a viable alternative to cable TV, mainly because of its digital capabilities. These allow an average of ten channels to be broadcast from a single satellite transponder, up to 300 channels from a single orbital location in the sky, and a total of hundreds of channels from satellites close together in space where a single dish can pick up signals from all.

The popularity of satellite services can be explained in that the available number of channels is constantly growing. Digital satellite services offer 500 channels with a single dish, including pay-per-view and video-on-demand programming, interactive television services, and high-speed data. Like digital cable, satellite services offer almost no HDTV capabilities, as they use a digitally transmitted analog signal that is displayed back into a conventional TV set. Both multichannel services digitize the analog signal for transmission and the receivers in viewer's homes convert the digital signal back into a standard analog signal for display.[23]

Digital television in the United States began with Direct Broadcast Satellite in 1994. Five service providers had been in the market: DirecTV, USSB, Primestar, EchoStar, and the DISH network. With the advent of competition and with the start of digital broadcasting by terrestrial and cable services, only DirecTV and EchoStar survived into the 21st century.

Satellite TV became the fastest selling consumer electronics product ever to enter the American market—faster then color television, CD player, or VCR. According to the Consumer Electronics Association, the American DBS industry has created the fastest growing major consumer electronics product in history—with a rate of a new subscriber every 12 seconds.

The advent of direct satellite services has changed the television industry in Europe too. Until the late 1980s, the ability to offer multiple programming services was generally limited, and broadcasters had only two options to deliver content: terrestrial transmissions or cable networks. These technologies were limited in spectrum capabilities and as a result of the number of available channels and the ability to collect advertising and subscription revenues. Since the end of the 1980s, high-powered satellite services have made it possible to reach large numbers of viewers with small dishes and to deliver multiple channels of attractive programming to new audience groups. Further technological advances and regulatory changes in favor of free market competition have established an environment in which different platforms operate with a variety of technological analog and digital formats, including cable, satellite, and terrestrial services.

There is a big need for satellites in Europe, for direct-to-home and Internet services. About 100 satellites with regional or international coverage were serving Western Europe in 1999, providing 1,100 transponders with 111 of them, or 11.2 percent, categorized as access capacity. Predictions are that more capacity will be needed for Europe and a big shortage will develop toward the end of the decade, unless more spectrum is located and more satellites procured.

Satellite services are prominent in the European broadcast industry, and the major European Pay TV companies operate via satellite. Two major players dominate satellite infrastructure: the Société Europeene des Satelites (SES), which operates the Astra service, and Eutelsat, the European Satellite Organizations, which operates the Hot Bird services. These pan-European satellites cover most of Europe and

Table 4.2. Western Europe Market Share of Satellite Operators

1. SES Astra	29.5%	$548	million
2. Eutelsat	23.0%	$427	million
3. Intelsat	12.1%	$225	million
4. France Telecom	8.6%	$160	million
5. Deutsche Telecom	7.0%	$130	million
6. Telenor	5.8%	$108	million
7. Hispasat S.A.	4.1%	$75.6	million
8. Nordiska Satelit AB	2.6%	$49	million
9. Panamsat Corp.	1.7%	$32	million
10. Colombia Communications	1.4%	$26.5	million
11. Arabsat	1.2%	$23	million
12. New Skies Satellites N.V.	1.1%	$20	million
13. Turk Teleckommunikasyon	0.7%	$14	million
14. Lorak Skynet	0.6%	$10.4	million
15. GE Americom	0.5%	$10	million

Total 1998 market: $1,858.5 million

*1998 figures.

Source: Euroconsult, in: Via Satellite, September 2000, page 20.

parts of the Middle East and North Africa. They offer the potential for a wide variety of pay services with digital technology and enjoy an unregulated environment and large capacity.

Besides the established services, new operators are entering the market, representing a new global outlook for satellite services.

There are three major satellite television service providers, based in the three largest media countries in Europe. The French Canal Plus is the biggest pay TV operator in Europe, providing services in 10 countries. The second largest European satellite operator, British Sky Broadcasting (BSkyB), provides a 200-channel digital service for the British market. The German Premier (analog pay-TV service) and the digital Digitales Fernsehen service are dominant in the German satellite market.[24]

Satellite services are spreading globally, with penetration in the world's major media markets.

Table 4.3. Worldwide DTH Platforms

Rank/Service	Country/Region	Subscribers	
1. DirecTV	United States	11,000,000	(December 2002)
2. Echostar/Dish Network	United States	7,500,000	(December 2002)
3. BskyB	U.K./Ireland	6,562,000	(December 2002)
		11,000,000	DTH/cable
4. Sky FerfecTV	Japan	3,352,000	(January 2003)
5. CanalSatellite	France	2,100,000	(January 2003)
6. DirecTV Latin America	Latin America Region	1,669,000	(June 2002)
7. Telepiu	Italy	1,376,000	(January 2002)
8. Premier	Germany	1, 368,000	(January 2002)
9. Canal Satellite Digital	Spain	1,230,000	(January 2002)
10. Bell ExpressVU	Canada	1,117,000	(June 2002)
11. TPS	France	1,090,000	((January 2002)
12. Via Digital	Spain	806,000	(January 2002)
13. Star Choice	Canada	755,000	(January 2002)
14. DStv	South Africa	733,400	(January 2002)
15. Stream	Italy	700,000	(January 2002)
16. Sky Net Sat	Brazil	700,000	(January 2002
17. Sky/Innova	Mexico	690,000	(July 2002)
18. C-Band Satellite	United States	636,000	(December 2002)
19. Wizja TV	Poland	600,000	(January 2002)
20. Viasat	Scandinavia	550,000	(January 2002)
21. Canal Digital	Scandinavia	530,000	(January 2002)
22. Sky Television	New Zealand	503,229	(July 2002)
23. Austar	Australia	417,196	(July 2002)

Data from: www.SkyReport.com and analysts.

The New Generation of Broadband Satellites

Until recently satellite technology had been used as a point-to-multi-point technology, ideally suited for television distribution. The satellite industry now moves into the delivery of broadband technology, which includes high-speed interconnection to the Intranet and digital interactive services.

The new generation of satellite communications means convergence with interactive services. As a wireless technology that is particularly adept at the delivery of voice and data, satellites are well positioned to play a leading role in the new evolving broadband market. Competition is expected to accelerate also because terrestrial services, cable modems using fiber optic technology, and digital subscriber lines (DSL) by telecom companies are already able in some markets (or will be able in other markets) to provide the same services to both residential customers and businesses.

Interactive Services.   The growing premium role of broadband satellites is largely based on the increasing demand for advanced services. Satellites are already established in the residential market, offering direct-to-home (DTH) television services, and the next generation of broadband satellites is expected to offer digital and high-definition television (HDTV), high-speed data transmissions, and other advanced services to both the consumer and residential markets. The competitive position of satellites in the telecommunications marketplace is based on the advantages of broadband services, which—unlike land-lines ser-

Table 4.4. Satellite Penetration in the Top 10 Media Markets

Rank	Country	Satellite Penetration
1	United States	18%
2	Japan	30%
3	United Kingdom	17%
4	Germany	32%
5	France	9%
6	Brazil	1%
7	Italy	5%
8	Australia	Not Available
9	Canada	4%
10	South Korea	15%

Source: *Advertising Age International*, June 2000

vices—can offer wide coverage with potential global reach and an instant infrastructure that can be deployed quickly and economically because it is small and installed at an end user's premises.

One of the most exciting developments in the communications industry is the combination of broadband satellite services with global coverage and the Internet. The Internet has changed the global market for communications and the addition of interactive services to traditional video broadcasting opens up a new array of data services. The availability of broadband satellite services will enhance the infrastructure for delivering Internet services and multimedia applications—the combination of text, graphics, audio, video, and animation into a single, interactive computer-based environment. These include services such as datacasting (delivery of data services through broadcast technologies) and webcasting (content developed for television delivered over the Internet).

Satellites and the Internet have changed the way new media markets operate. These are two global services capable of providing interactive applications. New global satellite services would enhance even further the infrastructure for delivering Internet services and create new global markets, changing the concept of localism in broadcasting. In this way social and economic differences diminish as information is transformed through global networks and broadband structure.[25]

In Europe, although new media markets are developing swiftly, growth in the availability of easily affordable broadband access is tied to the intensity of competition between suppliers of telecommunications services. The potential for high-speed services also exists in Europe, where SES Global, Gilat Satellite Networks, Alcatel Space and its SkyBrodge subsidiary have formed a joint company that will provide two-way satellite broadband communications services to entrepreneurs, consumers and small office/home users throughout Europe. SES Americam, an SES global company, has also filed a petition with the FCC to allow it to offer American television program owners and consumers a new satellite platform. The service will allow content providers to lease capacity in order to offer program and interactive entertainment directly to customers.[26] A key element in advancing competitiveness in the market comes from satellite operators and independent service suppliers operating through open access to broadband infrastructure.

Satellite operators in the United Kingdom, France and Spain are leading the way in terms of interactive satellite video. In the United Kingdom, Sky Digital includes interactive content from two principle sources: Open . . . is an interactive shopping mall, and Sky Interactive offers advanced services such as Electronic Program Guide (EPG) and Pay-Per-View (PPV) channels. According to Sky, 73 percent of Sky Digital customers use EPG and the expansion of PPV channels from four (in the analog service) to 74 (in digital) has improved buy rates tremendously. In France, Canal Satellite offers services such as interactive games, interactive advertising, and C:Direct—a service allowing users to download software via the decoder. In Spain, the two main satellite players offer interactive services. Via digital provides up-to-date localized traffic information and Canal Satellite Digital provides banking services.[27]

Global Satellites. The role of satellite networks in global communications is growing at an unprecedented pace. With the ability to offer direct broadcast satellite services to residential customers, satellite phones to businesses and high-speed Internet access to both residential and commercial markets, the industry is working to make satellite services as accessible and convenient as terrestrial broadcasting and ground telephone services.

A vast number of regulatory decisions have affected global competition in the telecommunications market. Following the first successful geostationary satellite put into orbit in 1963, the Eutelsat and Inteslsat agreements started the development of international satellite services. The decision of the FCC in 1972 to license domestic nongovernmental satellites initiated the open-skies policy and proposed no limits on the number of satellites that could serve the American market. Additional American deregulation was initiated in 1985: the decision to minimize orbital spacing opened up additional orbital slots and the decision to open international markets for competition by authorizing international satellite networks separate from Intelsat initiated global competition.

Further global competition was reached in the Television Without Frontiers directive adopted by the European Community that provided a framework for cross-border television signals and created a market for pan-European satellite services. Other decisions in Europe liberalized the satellite market and determined the rules for satellite personal communications services (S-PCS). The different rules for domestic and international service were abolished in the United States, too, and open-skies policy was made as part of the World Trade Organization (WTO) agreement to liberalize the provision for telecommunications services. The Agreement on Basic Telecommunications Services obligates its signatories to open their markets for satellite-delivered services and ensures that global satellite networks have practical access to global markets, in a way that prevents local regulation from curtailing the development of new technologies and global services. It establishes pro-competitive regulatory systems and nondiscriminatory regimes for licensing and spectrum allocation and ensures that global satellite networks have virtually global market access to deliver Internet services.

The drive to achieve a cost-effective, satellite-based digital broadcasting and telecommunications infrastructure has been employed through the development of small aperture terminal (VSAT) systems. This term typically refers to a class of earth stations with a small diameter in the range between 0.95 meters and 2.4 meters, used by corporations and institutions for remote access. The system offers affordable and reliable services to both consumers and corporate uses. They are used mostly as private networks to distribute enterprise-specific documents, sales and credit data for a variety of specialty applications—to a great extent decreasing the digital divide. New broadband VSAT services provide advanced bandwidth-on-demand systems allowing corporate network and Internet service providers to offer cost-effective and rapidly deployable high-speed communications solutions.[28]

Next-generation broadband satellite is moving from VSAT to SIT—satellite interactive terminals. The systems have both received and transmit capability, and have seen great demand with the growth of Internet access. New satellite services will be able offer digital and interactive television that will successfully complement terrestrial broadcasters and telecom providers. The most important advantage of satellites—universal service—is providing a major benefit over competitive services. Signals from space delivered through satellites do not care whether they land on urban or rural antennas, on rich or poor population, or on a leading culture or developing country, and they enable satellites to provide universal and global service to multiple countries.

Satellite technology is becoming a leading broadcast and telecommunications service provider. The worldwide market for satellite products and services topped $66 billion in 1999 and is experiencing 15 percent annual growth. The satellite services sector is the largest and fastest growing segment of the industry, worth $262 billion. Services delivered to the end-user, such as satellite TV, have been the prime source of the revenue growth. Of the total, end-user services accounted for $20.1 billion, satellite manufacturing accounted for $12 billion, and ground equipment accounted for $15.2 billion.[29]

The globalization of satellite technology is leading to changes in the business plans and in the operations of global communications satellite system providers, as they move from the supply of combined voice, video, data, and Internet services. This means the development of global satellite services. SES Global, the biggest global satellite company in the world, with 29 operational satellites and access to 42 satellites (including partnership and ownership stakes), was formed following the FCC's approval for SES Astra to acquire GE Americom. The global fleet of the union covers Europe, the Americas, and Asia, offering a complete spectrum of broadcast, video, broadband, multimedia, Internet, and telecommunications services with a footprint that covers most of the world (more than 90%), offering transoceanic capacity and global connectivity.

Another key development in the global satellite market has been the privatisation of both Intelsat and Eutelsat. Following Panamsat, which operates 22 satellites, Intelsat operates 20 satellites and Eutelsat 18. The competition of these four major global players is due to grow with the launch of new satellites and global services. Intelsat has announced that it is now offering global services, combining the company's global satellite fleet with terrestrial capabilities, delivering voice, data, Internet, and video content to customers.

4.4 TELECOM SERVICES

The new structure of media policy is changing the way telephone companies operate. Traditionally telephone has been a monopoly service, which controlled telecommunications, advanced services, and maintained universal basic telephone services. Today national telecom companies are moving from monopoly to competition, experiencing privatization, and supplying a handful of new media and telecommunications services.

Telephone companies are being privatized worldwide as part of the telecommunications revolution. The change in policy began in the United States, continued in Europe, and then spread into other parts of the world. American long-distance markets became competitive in the 1970s, and in the 1980s the world's largest telephone operator, Bell, was broken down. The 1996 Telecommunications Act permitted open-access to supply telecommunications services on local telephone networks, opening the market for competition. In Europe local telephone infrastructures were liberalized in 1998 as part of a wide-European policy directed by the European Community. In other parts of the world privatization is also progressing, although the rate differs among countries according to local policies.

Privatization is changing the nature of telecommunications markets, which are now in the process of being owned and controlled by the giant phone companies that once had a monopoly over national tele-

Table 4.5. Privatization Rate of Telecom Companies Around the World

United States: 100%
Latin America: 70%
Europe: 55%
Asia: 46%
The Arab states: 33%
Africa: 28%

Source: International Telecommunication Union (ITU), June 2000.

phone services. The sell-off of national telephone companies is raising tens of billions of dollars, some of which are being used to finance third-generation mobile licenses. The result is that telephone services become competitive and former monopolies are free to enter new markets—in some of which they traditionally had a monopoly status. These companies are privately owned by giant global forces or by the public, depending on the privatization system.

Despite the massive degree of privatization witnessed since the late 1990s, European telecom markets differ from the American for two main reasons: Firstly, competition is growing more rapidly in the United States. Broadband access is new field in America, which has not been dominated by a leading technology or service provider. As a result the market is highly competitive and diversified, service providers and legislators alike are fighting for open-access for broadband networks, and new entrants are entering the broadband market with no prior advantage to any single technology or service provider. In contrast, the European telecom industry is still dominated by former state monopolies, which have traditionally gained prior access to the provision of advanced services.

Table 4.6. Percentage of Telecom Companies Owned by Governments in Europe

United Kingdom	0%
Ireland	0%
Denmark	0%
Italy	0%
Spain	0%
Hungary	0%
Croatia	0%
Portugal	10.5%
The Netherlands	45%
Slovakia	49%
Belgium	50.2%
Greece	51%
Czech Republic	1%
Slovenia	54%
Germany	59%
Finland	60%
France	63.2%
Switzerland	65.5%
Poland	70%
Austria	75%
Sweden	75%
Iceland	100%
Luxembourg	100%
Norway	100%

Source: International Telecommunication Union (ITU), July 2000.

The results are still limited competitiveness and potential services, relatively high cost of Internet access, and low adoption of online and interactive services.

Secondly, the American market has always been privatized. In contrast, European governments are moving toward privatizing their incumbent telephone carriers, but public holdings remain a mixed structure, as countries differ in their privatization rate. In some countries privatization has been completed and other countries are in an active process of privatization.

The New Competitiveness Position of Telecom Companies

In the new structure of media policy, competition between telecom companies and other technologies is intensifying. Although traditional advantages still provide a good starting point, monopoly status or technological advantage no longer protects them. In addition to telephone calls, a market still largely dominated by telecom companies, the growing worldwide demand for advanced services—Internet access, interactive multimedia, and videoconferencing—has created increased competition for additional broadband solutions.

Telecom equipment hardware and software sales are constantly going up, and Web exchanges are expecting increased revenue as they facilitate many of the lucrative transactions between providers and vendors. Telecom equipment sales are expected to reach about $200 billion in 2003, compared to about $100 billion in 1997 and $150 billion in 2000, while developing new markets and supplying advanced services.[31]

Despite these figures, however, the competition for the future structure of advanced services is yet to be determined. Telecom services are getting ready to meet the new challenges of a combined broadcast-telecommunications market by developing business strategies that involve broadband wireless. They are entering new fields, concentrating on the delivery of high-speed Internet access, interactive applications, and television programs. Competition with multichannel service providers (cable and satellite) is predicted to grow, as all services intend to provide telephone and television services.

Advanced telephone companies use Digital Subscriber Line (DSL)—a digital technology that uses special telephone lines to deliver a basket of media and telecommunications services. In technical terms, it is possible to squeeze television pictures down the existing copper pair telephone lines by using DSL technology. This makes use of a pair of modems at each end of the copper pair to create a digital line that has greater use of the potential bandwidth available than traditional transmission methods.

The more advanced operators use Asynchronous Digital Subscriber Line (ADSL) technology, which allows telephone companies to deliver simultaneously high-speed Internet access, hundreds of digital television channels, and traditional voice services over existing twisted-pair copper telephone wires. The same as cable, telephone companies aim to become VVD providers, offering voice, video, and data services. The system will enable customers to download movies and video games and receive digital television programs, video-on-demand, and pay-per-view options directly from their local telephone company.

In the United States, following the passage of the Telecommunications Act, there are no statutory or legal barriers preventing telephone companies from entering into cable or offering cable services. European telecom companies, mainly former state monopolies, are likely to become increasingly important competitors to cable and satellite operators for the provision of television programs following the liberalization of telecommunications services and their strong position in the market.

Britain is leading the competition between cable and telephone service providers. The national telephone service, British Telecom, is permitted to offer video programming services (such as video-on-demand) and to compete directly with cable licenses over delivery of television broadcasts by the use of its fixed telecommunications network. BT will certainly play a major role in delivering digital television services because its network reaches the entire nation.

Interactive services are the key for competition in the digital age, and competition of different technologies and services dominates the future of British media. The new regulatory environment, under which all technologies operate, including British Telecom, represents the growing competition in the high-speed Internet market and other multimedia and broadband services to homes and offices. The former state monopoly has reduced its total share of the telecommunications market on the one hand, but also entered new areas on the other, such as a deal with Microsoft to develop wireless technology.

Competition for Internet services in Britain is between broadband cable and the ASDL service of British Telecom. BT openworld, BT's global Internet service, has successfully positioned itself as a leader in broadband in the United Kingdom, providing a range of ADSL broadband access products through fixed and satellite services for around 100,000 businesses and residential customers. NTL and Telewest have produced a joint marketing strategy encouraging the take-up of broadband services throughout Britain. Broadband cable is available in 9 million homes—covering 37 percent of Britain and Ireland, and is expected to be available in all cabled homes in the United Kingdom, 11.6 million. The combined force on NTL and Telewest has insured that cable opera-

tors provide 70 percent of broadband connections to residential customers in the United Kingdom. One of the key advantages of cable is the
possibility to offer the triple play of fixed telephone, Internet access, and
digital television services. NTL, which has 1.25 million digital customers
and 50,000 high-speed customers, has even become a fourth play operator, after forming an alliance with mobile telephone operator Orange
UK, to offer mobile phone services to NTL's customers.

To compete with the cable industry, British Sky Broadcasting
has announced a marketing agreement to subsidize subscription to Sky
Digital for BT residential customers. BskyB has also been granted a
"non-exclusive local delivery license in all parts of the UK," to provide
multichannel TV and related telecommunications services, including
over the networks of duly licensed systems operators, using DSL equipment via local telecommunications networks, such as BT.[32]

One certain result of the free market approach is global competition. The competitive environment is changing the way telephone services operate because although new unprecedented opportunities to
expand globally exist, the stakes are high. Competition for telephone
comes from media companies becoming telecommunications providers
and offering customers multiservice applications. On the other hand,
telephone companies offer on a trial basis or intent-to-offer combined
broadcast-telecommunications service.

In this competitive environment, telephone companies have
three major advantages over rival technologies:

1. The main advantage of telephone is universal service, because
   the technology connects almost every home around the globe.
   The current global telephone network is the biggest home-
   delivery broadband distribution system, and as telephone
   companies enter the television business, the technology is
   expected to become an alternative to current multichannel
   providers (terrestrial, cable, and satellite).
2. Telephone is in many countries more popular and more profitable than television. However, this applies to countries with
   low penetration of multichannel services (telecom services are
   obviously popular and widely adopted in all countries).
3. Telecom markets are being liberalized around the world and
   media companies have the opportunity to seize new markets.
   Cautions in these countries are the terms of liberalization and
   the level of free market principles applied to new markets.

In contrast to these advantages, the stakes are high. Telecom companies are in a transition period into the next age of information services
to the home and have the opportunity to enter new businesses and create

new revenue streams. Both services of multichannel and telecom are within the same technological arena and multiservice companies can distribute telecommunications and television services in the same packages. Concentrating on new services in areas where companies have existing networks may, however, result in offering subscribers new services and abandoning their stable profitable business for new and risky businesses.

A new market is high-speed Internet access. Internet services can be viable only through the convergence of other technologies—digital terrestrial television, satellite services, cable TV, telecom services, and wireless communications. Competition among all service providers for the supply of high-speed Internet access to the home is growing at an unprecedented pace. Broadcasters and telephone companies are working out how to fit into the new realities created by the Internet explosion that should result from the high-speed revolution, and wireless operators are also entering the market.

DSL has strong position in the American and European high-speed access market.[33] The competition is with cable.[34] According to the FCC, high-speed Internet connections to homes and businesses using cable modems, DSL, or other broadband technologies increased to 16.2 million by mid-2002. Cable services had 9.2 million lines, and DSL reached 5.1 million homes.[35] Total number of subscribers to DSL broadband services in the United States is expected grow to 15 million in 2003 and almost 20 million in 2004.[36] Predictions are that DSL will dominate the high-speed Internet access market in Europe, with a 53 percent share. Cable modems are expected to take 27 percent of the market, and other services, including wireless communications and satellites, will acquire the remaining 20 percent.[37]

In addition to providing fast access services, telecom companies have a good starting point as the boundaries between media, telecommunications and Internet services blur and increased data and traffic are in need. The potential areas include e-commerce, wireless services, combined wireless and commerce services (mobile-commerce), web portal, billing services and other online, wireless, and advanced applications.[38]

4.5 WIRELESS COMMUNICATIONS

Wireless communications is predicted to become one of growing areas in the telecommunications industry in the 21st century. The massive global deregulation of local and long distant telephone services and cable, video, and broadcast services, with new spectrum becoming available for wireless, is making the new technology one the fastest growing industries around the world.

Wireless communications is a technology that encompasses two leading technologies: fixed and mobile wireless services. Fixed wireless includes the technologies of Multichannel Multipoint Distribution Services (MMDS) and Local Multipoint Distribution Services (LMDS). Mobile wireless includes devices like cellular phones, two-way pagers and Palm hand-held computers and advanced services like wireless Internet and mobile-commerce.

Wireless growth is predicted in long run, not in the short run. A new wave of wireless sophisticated Internet applications is being promoted by governments and giant companies, mainly telephone operators, and distinct technical shortcomings are being resolved, to create combined wireless-broadband-Internet service that will become a dominant player in the evolving global telecommunications market.[39]

Fixed Wireless

Fixed wireless systems have the potential to supply competitive multichannel and telephone services. The technology of Multichannel Multipoint Distribution Systems (MMDS) can provide service at a relatively low spectrum to homes within a 30-mile radius. The technology of Local Multipoint Distribution Services (LMDS) has a range of two to three miles. These technologies can send data, video, and voices services through the air, as an alternative to fiber optic lines or copper telephone wires. Services are available through an antenna placed on the roof of homes to receive the transmissions.

The fixed wireless technology was used in the past to provide wireless cable services. It was also known as wireless cable and included multichannel services with fewer channels than a standard cable system in areas where cable services did not exist or as a replacement to cable in closed neighborhoods. In some markets cable services are still the primary use of wireless systems, although penetration is low. New applications include everything from cellular phone calls to broadband wireless services of Internet, data, and voice services at high speeds. The technology can be a cheaper alternative to providing communications services to rural areas or other markets that lack high-speed networks.

The focus of broadband fixed wireless companies is moving to interactive services and high-speed Internet access. The strategy for acquiring MMDS spectrum is to allow long distance carriers to bypass local incumbent networks and connect directly with the customer. Spectrum became very attractive to long-distance telephone companies as a way to bridge the gap between long-distance networks and customers' homes or businesses, so that they are willing to pay huge sums to acquire wireless licenses.[40]

The long-distance telephone companies WorldCom and Sprint dominate the fixed-wireless market in the United States. Together they spent around $2.5 billion in acquiring MMDS licenses that will service 54 million homes with one-third coverage of the American market apiece. Another key player is Netlink Communications, which covers 95 percent of the top 30 markets and owns 40 additional LMDS licenses. Additional LMDS operators are Winstar Communications (16 licenses) and US West (licenses in eight markets).[41]

Forecasts are that fixed wireless is going to be a big business in the next few years. It is estimated that in 2005 MMDS will be the leading fixed-broadband wireless technology, covering 70 percent of the American wireless market (a growth from 57 percent market share in 2000), whereas LMDS will reach 21 percent (a draw back from 32% in 2000).[42] However, the growing fixed wireless market requires regulatory scrutiny, as a "leapfrog" infrastructure deploying a jump over the normal stages of development of wired services. WorldCom's proposed $129 billion merger with Sprint was called off in July 2000 by American regulatory authorities because of fears that it would create a huge company that would dominate the wireless market.[43]

Mobile Wireless

The mobile wireless industry is dominated by the heady growth of cellular phones around the world. Additional mobile devices included two-way pagers and Palm hand-held computers, although these are not as popular. Penetration of mobile services is boosted by the new generation of advanced services such as wireless Internet and mobile commerce (m-commerce).

Cellular technology is in a transition period from the second to the third generation. The first generation was the analog technology that the original cellular industry used in the 1980s and 1990s. The second generation is digital technology widely used today, serving the majority of cellular customers around the world. The third generation is the technology of the future. It will allow creation of a global wireless industry with much higher data speeds and will offer advanced applications such as high-speed Internet access, video conferencing, and m-commerce.

The Second Generation (2G). The current digital wireless technology has three different technological standards used in different parts of the world. Most of Europe uses the digital technology of GSM, which stands for Global System for Mobile communications. In Asia, a mixture of standards is in use. CDMA, which stands for Code Division Multiple Access, is dominant in Japan and South Korea. GSM is used sporadically elsewhere, including the Arab World. In the United States standards have been the most fragmented. AT&T uses a format called TDMA, which stands for Time Division Multiple Access. But because TDMA does not support data transmission, AT&T was forced to overlay an older format to provide Internet access through its cellular phones. Other American carriers such as Sprint and Verizon use CDMA, and still others like VoiceStream and Pacific Bell use GSM.

Most creators of wireless Internet have agreed to use a format called WAP (Wireless Access Protocol), which works with any of the transmission formats. The WAP is a program that takes Internet information and displays it in a special format for the small screens available on mobile telephones and hand-held computers such as Palm III.

But currently the different standards make the development of a common mass market for wireless communications an almost impossible mission. This means that unless special measures are taken to enable a wireless phone to use several formats, a device designed to work with one wireless technology cannot be used on a network that employs another technology. Another problem is that speed limits of the second generation of wireless technology mean that users can only send and receive a few lines of Internet text or send a short e-mail through their cellular phones.[44]

The Third Generation (3G). Over the next decade the global wireless industry expects to move into the third generation (3G), with formats that will allow much higher data speeds and be compatible with one another. The next-generation mobile cellular phone is going to lead mobile telecommunications. The new UMTS standard has a transmission speed nearly 40 times the existing GSM standard, allowing mobile phones to be used for high-speed Internet access and video conferencing. UMTS is also expected to open the door for m-commerce, where mobile phones are used like credit cards to make payments from vending machines.

Global telecom companies see the next-generation mobile phones as a must-have in the predicted explosive growth in mobile telecommunications. The sale of spectrum for high-speed wireless Internet transmission is rapidly spreading around the world, mainly in Europe, which has made a strong commitment in spectrum allocation to 3G.[45]

In Europe there are two formats for license award: a beauty contest or auctions based on competitive financial bids. A beauty contest requires an entrance fee or a nominal fee for each license and a yearly charge. Countries such as France, Ireland, Portugal, Spain, Norway and Sweden lead this process, in which the government awards a selected number of licenses. Generally most of the licenses are awarded to incumbent operators with one reserved for a new entrant to the market.

Auctions are taking place all over Europe. Britain, Germany, The Netherlands, Austria, Belgium, and Switzerland have collected heavy fees for UMTS licenses in a process based on competitive financial bidding rounds that end when all available licenses become available to single contenders. The Czech Republic, Denmark, Italy, and Poland use a combined system of prequalification requirements based on beauty contest principles with a bidding process for all or some of the licenses on offer.[46]

The bidding system for 3G frequencies has been a lucrative source of revenue for European governments. The two biggest auctions were the multiple-round processes in Britain and Germany. The British auction raised $34 billion, and the German auction raised $46 billion. The bidding process in Germany was the most lucrative, because Germany has Europe's largest economy and is its most populated country. Germany is also the world's third largest telecommunications market, with 81 million households and low penetration of cellular phones.[47]

The United States is the world's largest telecommunications market, with 100 million households and 53 percent penetration of cellular phones,[48] although it has fallen behind Asian and European countries that have managed their airwaves more efficiently and have already conducted licensing auctions. According to former President Bill Clinton, if the United States does not move quickly to allocate 3G spectrum, there is a danger that it could lose market share in the industries of the 21st century.[49]

Spectrum has become a valuable asset in the American economy, as most of the spectrum is already in use. President Clinton took on the task of freeing up spectrum by issuing a memorandum that instructs federal agencies to work with the FCC and the private sector to identify the radio spectrum needed for 3G wireless communications.[50]

The American system is due to change dramatically. Under the current system, the Federal government licenses each user and regulates the frequencies and signal power that can be used. The Federal government is developing a plan to open up the airwaves for wireless communications by treating frequencies as commodities to be bought and sold in the open market. The FCC is promoting the trading system to sell airwaves and to create a whole new market, in which telecommunications companies of all kinds could bid.[51]

The wireless market is expected to reach new highs by 2006, when the transfer to digital technology is completed. Broadcasters will have to relinquish extra broadcast spectrum received on loan from the FCC, and old analog channels will then go off the air and the government will use them for wireless communications.[52] In the meantime, auctions are being delayed, mainly because broadcasters have the right to stay on their current channels until digital television catches on widely.[53]

Japan is the world's second largest telecommunications market, with 126 million people and 50 million cellular phones. There are between 20 and 27 million Internet users in Japan, approximately one of every five people in the nation. Of that number, nearly half are connected to the Internet wirelessly. Wireless communications is going to dominate the high-speed access market as Japan is moving quickly to a second generation of wireless Internet technology with higher data speeds and a variety of commercial services compatible to the second-and-a-half-generation.[54] Official plans are to introduce 3G technology, too. An advisory panel appointed by the Posts and Telecommunications Ministry has recommended deregulation to allow more competition and to introduce wireless license bidding. The government is expected to present relevant bills based on the panel's proposals.[55]

Wireless Internet. Expectations for rights to operate wireless technology have been elevated by the huge potential of mobile services to provide high-speed Internet transmission. The boost for wireless has been two-way delivery approval, which could unite several technologies: the Internet, personal computers, and cellular phones. Mobile access to the Web could be the next Internet revolution, which will take over the strong position of the personal computer.

Wireless Internet is expected to spread more quickly than the wired technology for four simple reasons.

1. Every cellular phone sold today already has standard Web-browser software built in, and adapting existing Web sites for use by these wireless browsers is a relatively small additional expense.
2. Tens of millions of people around the world are already used to surfing the Internet, so the transition to wireless access should seem like a natural next step for them.
3. Third generation (3G) transmission can carry vastly more information at high speeds and allow a full Internet page to reach a screen in a split second.
4. The volume for Internet traffic is doubling every 100 days, and that traffic has been rapidly migrating into on-line and wireless services.[56]

Wireless Internet provides Web access on devices such as pagers, cellular phones, and Palm hand-held devices. It is being promoted as the most promising technological development since the Internet itself started taking off in the 1990s. Global growth estimates for mobile Internet are promising. In 2003 an estimated 300 million of 900 million cellular phones around the world will be Internet-ready.[57]

The technological and financial implications are equally challenging. The potential for wireless communications is unprecedented and will continue to grow with the transition to digital terrestrial television. As television broadcasters gradually convert to more efficient digital transmissions, they will need narrower slices of spectrum to transmit the same signal, and an enormous chunk of airwaves could be offered for sale to wireless carriers.

The spectrum is particularly useful, because it allows transmission around buildings and other obstacles, much like a television signal. The Third Generation wireless systems promise mobile voice and wideband data communications with global reach. The technology is designed to provide high-speed mobile access equivalent to the speed of a cable or DSL modem. With the market demand that exists around the world, the transition is hard driven by the need for Internet access.[58]

Currently only fewer than 2 percent of Internet users subscribe to the Internet via wireless technology and there is little consumer demand for wireless Internet services, although forecasts are incredibly optimistic with the expected launch of 3G technology.[59]

As Internet access evolves from wired to wireless, predictions are that both mobile subscription and Internet penetration will dominate the three largest telecommunications markets. In Japan, mobile subscription penetration will reach over 80 percent with almost 40 percent Internet penetration. In Western Europe, mobile subscription penetration is expected to reach over 70 percent with about 40 percent Internet penetration. In the United States, mobile subscription penetration could reach 65 percent and Internet penetration is predicted to be over 55 percent.[60]

Despite these figures, however, both services are not predicted to become truly global. In the rest of the world, predictions are that mobile subscription penetration would reach only about 12 percent and Internet penetration would be about 8 percent. It is estimated that the mobile phone will experience the same stages of development of wired telephony, and only at the start of the next decade will mobile phones also penetrate less affluent countries. By then, 3.5 billion people worldwide could have access to mobile phones.[61]

4.6 INTERNET SERVICE PROVIDERS

In the forefront of information technology in the third millennium is the Internet, which is transforming computing, communications, the broadcasting and telecommunications markets in a way as profound as the telephone and television accomplished last century. The current Internet is still largely based on terrestrial telecommunications infrastructure serving primarily local societies, but through global links and combined with new technologies with unlimited coverage across the globe, the Internet has the potential to fundamentally change the shape of its commercial, political, and cultural agendas.

The Internet is growing to be a mass medium in many of the largest markets around the world. Combination of the Internet and other platforms can create successful convergence of new media services that will dominate the new broadcasting and telecommunications markets. In some respects the computer and the television are rival technologies, because the time spent on the Internet is being substituted for television viewing time. However the significance of Internet penetration to the broadcast industry is the delivery of interactive services and the ability to use television as the reception platform for the delivery of digital interactive services—combining voice, video, and data.

The use of Internet services is growing rapidly. History shows that the number of users doubles approximately every two years, and Internet traffic doubles every six months.[62]

Table 4.7. Worldwide Internet Users (in millions)

Country	Year-End 2000	Share (percentage)
1. United States	135.7	36.2
2. Japan	26.9	7.18
3. Germany	19.1	5.10
4. United Kingdom	17.9	4.77
5. China	15.8	4.20
6. Canada	15.2	4.05
7. South Korea	14.8	3.95
8. Italy	11.8	3.08
9. Brazil	10.6	2.84
10. France	9.0	2.39
11. Australia	8.1	2.16
12. Russia	6.6	1.77
13. Taiwan	6.5	1.73
14. Netherlands	5.4	1.45
15. Spain	5.2	1.39
Worldwide Total:	374.9	100

Source: Global Telephony, June 2000

Table 4.8. Internet Penetration in the Top 10 Media Markets

Rank	Country	Internet Penetration
1	United States	33%
2	Japan	16%
3	United Kingdom	20%
4	Germany	8%
5	France	4%
6	Brazil	2%
7	Italy	6%
8	Australia	33%
9	Canada	37%
10	South Korea	12%

Source: *Advertising Age International*, June 2000.

Open-Access Policy

The technological revolution of the information society has brought into existence a political conflict around open-access for Internet Service Providers (ISPs), allowing them to compete with the services provided by infrastructure operators over the same networks. Open-access policy carries important advantages. It allows a wide range of services and a handful of service providers, many of them serving niche audiences, to compete in new markets while providing interactive and information services. It also encourages global service providers, who will be free to provide services on different infrastructures, as opposed to giant operators providing both the infrastructure and content and using their powers to dominate different local markets.

Open-access is an issue debated around the world,[63] although the most heated campaign occurred in America. According to the Telecommunications Act, local telephone companies supplying high-speed Internet services using Digital Subscriber Line (DSL) technology are required to allow other Internet Service Providers to provide dial-up access to the Internet over their phone lines. The debate relates to cable, which is considered as an alternative technology to telephone. Advanced cable systems provide digital cable TV and high-speed Internet access, and many organizations argue that they should also be allowed access to digital cable, although the cable TV industry claims that forcing them to open their networks will decrease their profits and slow investments in new digital networks.[64] There are about 7,000 Internet Service Providers operating in the United States and the number of global operators is growing too.[65]

In early 1999, the OpenNET coalition backed by AOL campaigned for open cable networks for multiple Internet service providers. The merger of AOL and Time Warner in early 2000 set off concerns about the future of broadband and how best to ensure that no single company abuses its control of the Internet's infrastructure and global television market.[66] The convergence of the world's largest Internet service provider (AOL) with the world's largest news, entertainment, and cable television operator (Time Warner), launched increasingly urgent discussions about the way to ensure that no single company abuses its control of the Internet's infrastructure. The reasons for concerns about open access revolve around the issue of how to open privately owned broadband access to all comers and the danger for free speech when a single or dominant entity controls both a transmission medium and the information that flows from it.[67]

The political campaign to allow other service providers open access to compete over the same networks of the combined AOL and Time Warner was partly resolved in February 2000. AOL and Time Warner signed a memorandum of understanding to let customers choose from several Internet service providers, including AOL, on Time Warner's broadband cable systems.

The AOL-Time Warner Open-Access Memorandum includes four key elements. The first is aimed to offer customers choice among Internet Service Providers, so that customers don't have to buy service from AOL-Time Warner affiliates to get broadband access. The second is to support diversity of Internet Service Providers, in a way that AOL-Time Warner does not limit the number of Internet Service Providers with which it has relationships and offers those providers the choice to partner with its systems on a national, regional, or local basis. The third is to provide Internet Service Providers with a direct relationship to the customer, so those providers and cable operators be allowed to sell broadband services directly to the customers. Providers can bill and collect from the customers directly. The fourth aims to permit video streaming, so that AOL-Time Warner does not block Internet Service Providers from providing streaming video to their customers.

Since the signing of the nonbinding memorandum, rival companies have lobbied for government officials to make that promise a condition of approving the merger, claiming that AOL-Time Warner might lock competitors out of its cable networks and dominate the emerging high-speed Internet service and interactive television markets. After federal regulators pressed the company to explain how its merger would be no barrier to open-access, Time Warner announced an agreement giving independent service providers access to its cable television subscribers.[68]

Despite the agreement, open access is still to be resolved, the networking element of a cable modem system is a telecom service that is not tied to cable services.[69] Former FCC Chairman William Kennard, an advocate for letting the market dictate the open access issue, applauded the agreement: "For sometime now, I have encouraged the fast-moving broadband marketplace to find business solutions to customer demand as an alternative to intervention by government. The agreement is a significant step in the right direction. It is that Time Warner and other cable companies continue to listen to their customers and foster a robust ISP market. I will keep a close watch to determine if we can continue to forbear from regulation in this area."[70] He explained his position in that "I think everybody agrees that the broadband platform should be an open platform. This is a question of how we get there."[71]

The FCC must, however, take action in the debate over which federal regulators should govern high-speed Internet access over cable, and has formally opened an inquiry on the issue. The inquiry into opening cable lines for Internet Service Providers encompasses all forms of cable services, including satellite.[72] It is conducted in an attempt to create a national political and legal framework and examine how to promote the use of high-speed services while also preserving an open market.[73]

The AOL-Time Warner merger was approved by the European Union on October 11, 2000; by the American antitrust agency (FTC) on December 14, 2000; and finally, by the Federal Communication Commission (FCC) on January 11, 2001—a year and one day after it was originally announced—subject to key conditions. The FTC accepted a settlement that requires Time Warner to open its cable lines to Internet rivals that compete with AOL. The condition effectively turned the privately owned system of AOL-Time Warner into a kind of public channel for the delivery of information over the Internet. The decision of the FTC followed an antitrust review by European regulators, which led to approval of the merger by the European Commission. The FCC approval required AOL-Time Warner to open its instant-messaging system to rivals.[74]

Advanced Interactive Multimedia (AIM) Content Providers

The growing penetration of Internet access in the largest media markets is advancing competition for the supply of advanced interactive services by giant firms. New interactive offerings of Advanced Interactive Multimedia (AIM) content providers aim to mold online services to television, using the impact of the Internet on broadcasting and the desire to deliver television programming combined with the interactivity of the Internet. Internet Service Providers intend to form a television portal in the same way they provide an Internet portal, making interactive television a reality.

This is the future of broadcasting, and many companies are trying to secure a leading position in the evolving new structure. Under the
new model of broadcasting, cable, satellite, and telecom operators, and
advanced interactive multimedia (AIM) content providers are joining
forces to offer customers hundreds of subscription channels with interactive capabilities. Interactive content is the key to formulating new
audience groups with specific interests, as specific content can be delivered to and sent back by separate members of these groups. From the
customer point of view, the new competitive structure will create the
information society, in which all of the leading platforms will provide
essentially the same services: Web browsing, interactive programming,
online gaming, e-mail, and basic communication.[75]

The most ambitious plan to change the structure of media services was launched by the $183 billion merger of America-OnLine and
Time-Warner. The merger raises hopes that cheap high-speed Internet
and broadband access will be available everywhere through television.
The company is looking ahead to the next generation of technology,
when all the content of Time Warner libraries will be made available to
people over the Internet.

Among the different services that will become available is
AOLTV—a broadband service that offers two-way, high-speed Internet
access to a captive audience of 30 million AOL and 21 million Time
Warner Cable subscribers (in more than 40 systems). With this service,
AOLTV has the capability to combine an extraordinary customer reach,
with over 40 percent of the American online access market, a massive
portion of cable subscribers, and the majority of satellite customers.[76]

British AIM content providers lead the European market. Yes
Television launched a broadband Internet-television portal, which delivers video-on-demand over both ADSL and cable. In March 2000 it was
awarded a nonexclusive local delivery license in the United Kingdom to
provide television broadcast services over broadband cable or telecom
networks. It has launched several commercial projects providing
enhanced television and VOD services including a pilot project with
British Telecom offering VOD, Internet access, and e-mail services.
Video Networks provide another service. The service offers interactive
television services on ADSL networks. It launched its first full commercial service in London at the end of 1999, including video-on-demand.

Cable television operators are also launching interactive trials.
NTL is providing the services of several AIM content providers
(Liberate, Two Way TV, and OpenTV) on its networks, and is launching
its own interactive services. NTL has started an innovative television-
Internet service for customers who prefer to use television rather than a
PC to access the Internet and new digital services. The second cable

operator in Britain, Telewest also has formed an interactive joint venture to offer services to television channels, advertisers, retailers, and government departments waiting to capitalize on the growing market for interactive television services.

Global operators like OpenTV, Liberate Technologies, Wink, and Two Way Television provide services through existing platforms. Common to these services is that content is delivered directly from the service provider (telephone, satellite, cable, or terrestrial) to customers' television, adding active applications to television viewing. Interactivity is part of the broadcast and thus allows the end-user (the TV viewer) to interact directly with the television set without a computer or Internet access. The cost is also attractive. Operators generally don't charge customers for the services, and profit is made from direct purchases made by customers.

OpenTV delivers interactive content and online functions such as web browsing, chat, e-mail, shopping, and commerce. It is considered a leading provider of interactive television software. The service reached twenty-three million subscribers at the end of 2001, addressing different markets in over 50 countries. OpenTV is also developing the practical applications for the software. These include uses such as video replay, interactive advertising, and information services on different shows, such as movies, entertainment, music, and sports. The system operates through an electronic program guide (EPG) that appears on the screen as a picture within a picture and enables individual viewers to select information.

The main operations of OpenTV are in Europe and the United States, although it also reaches platforms in Latin America, the Middle East, and South Africa. The service in Europe is provided in: France (France Telecom Cable, TPS and Lyonaise Cable), Germany (Free Universe Network), Spain (Via Digital), Sweden (Senda and Telia InfoMedia Television), Denmark (TeleDanmark Kabel TV), Italy (Stream), and Turkey (Teleon). In the United States the project provides complete end-to-end Internet solutions via cable, satellite, and terrestrial broadcasting. The most advanced plan is on the EchoStar DISH Network, providing a hard-drive storage and playback capability to accompany the service. In South America the service is provided through Galaxy South America, provider of DirecTV in the region. In the United Kingdom, the interactive service of BskyB is run by Open—the first interactive digital television e-commerce system in the country launched at the end of 1999. It runs through (and is owned by) the BskyB digital satellite pay network, using OpenTV software and application tools.

Wink is an information-on-demand (IOD) service provided on television without Internet connection. The service allows subscribers to interact with their content providers in all available markets—terrestrial, cable, and satellite. The system provides a small icon that lights up whenever the broadcast signal has additional information embodied in it for shows and ads and viewers can select at no additional cost information as they prefer. To get information, the viewer has to hit a button on the remote control and the requested information appears on the screen. The Wink system is operational through DirecTV and several cable systems around the United States.

Another interactive service is provided by Liberate Technologies. Liberate enables cable programmers and operators to provide enhanced programming and applications based on open-standards with access to interactive content and services.

Two Way Television specializes in adding interactivity and "play-as-you-watch" games to existing programming across any platform, making digital terrestrial, cable, and satellite platforms viable targets for distribution to countries throughout the world. The service started providing interactive games in the United Kingdom, and formed joint ventures to deliver its services to North America and Australia. The deal with Interactive Network (called TWIN Entertainment) will deliver live interactive games in the United States and Canada, and with Australian partner ITVA in Australia and New Zealand.[77]

SUMMARY

Digital technology is leading the development of media policy for the 21st century. Under the new structure, all providers are free to offer all available services and compete over the same networks, involving wide-ranging competition between technologies that offer combined television and telecommunications applications. The broadcasting, telecommunications, and computing industries are rapidly converging into a multimedia market in which all technologies supply all services. These include Digital Terrestrial Television (DTT), broadband cable, digital satellite, Digital Subscriber Line (DSL), and wireless communications. Additional competition comes from Internet Service Providers (ISP) and Advanced Interactive Multimedia (AIM) content providers offering interactive television applications.

The digital revolution will transform the broadcasting industry from the passive medium of the past century into an active information and entertainment medium and business retail selling instrument in the 21st century. Several key global players support the transition to digital technology: regulatory authorities such as the FCC, ITC, and European Union; multichannel service providers; global economic interests and commercial forces; public organizations and audience groups; and equipment manufacturers.

DTT has not succeeded thus far, mainly in Europe, for two key reasons:

1. The technology started late, as opposed to cable and satellite, which had opportunities to capture the multichannel market. For that reason, DTT is associated as "old media," although it presents many new media advantages.
2. Terrestrial networks tend to concentrate around densely populated areas and for that reason are considered as local, whereas cable and satellite are identified as global technologies or as ones that provide global service and programming.

In the United States the situation may be different because of the government's heavy commitment to bring DTT to the market. The United States is leading the transition to digital television, and by 2006, all American broadcasting services are due to become fully digital. The current NTSC form will be turned off for a new digital ATSC system providing full high-definition interactive television. Digital licenses are being issued in Europe, too, using the Digital Video Broadcasting (DVB) system for terrestrial, satellite, and cable services. DVB is the standard for digital video broadcasts in Europe, and according to European regulation all video broadcast streams should be DVB-compliant.

Digitalization is spreading in other parts of the world, with new services provided by different technologies and new global services. However, transition to digital technology is provoking new social and global issues, with the merger of America-OnLine and Time Warner demonstrating the impact of global networks. The combined service provided by the world's largest Internet Service Provider (AOL), with 30 million subscribers, and the world's largest provider of news and media services and one of the largest cable operators (Time Warner), has been subject to stiff debate on the future of television.

The debate concerns the technology that will dominate the digital age. The digital revolution is certainly going to change the way people live around the world, although the technologies of the 21st century and the actual adoption of advanced services are unclear. The question remains whether interactive services will dominate the future structure of media policy and which new services will be provided by the broadcasting and telecommunications industries.

5

The Social Adoption
of Information Technology

The social implications of information technology have always been the focus of intense debate on the feasible adoption of advanced services. Similar to the general development course of media policy, the development of new media technologies has also gone through distinct stages and policy changes in regard to their capability to provide additional services to the traditional supply of programming services.

Throughout the development of media policy, these conceptions included requirements for local and community transmissions, and actual trials were implemented through narrow-cast television and interactive cable services. In examining the prospects for media policy for the 21st century, it is evident that the ideas that support advanced services have not changed despite the relative unsuccessful results of the community and interactive trials of the 20th century. Rather, the plans are flourishing again in the digital age on the assumption that new digital technologies can actually establish the information society.

The information society implies a culture in which information and entertainment are used and delivered intensively through a wide range of technologies and services of media, telecommunications, and information technology. Globalization, commercialization, pluralism, and technological advancement dominate this culture, with access to information and communication being the most essential public utility in the new information society.

In the new digital age, the conception of information technology is undergoing a new social formation, following the relationship between information infrastructure and participation in public discourse. The combination of new information technology and democracy leads to the building of social capital and the advancement of social networks of democratic participation. Despite the differentiation between telecommunications and mass communication issues, globalization issues have created options for a new structure of democracy and public participation involving advanced technology.

The implications of information technology on social transformations are related to the adoption of advanced technologies and to the utilization of their cultural role in implementing democratic and public participation. The possibility of new media and telecommunications applications to serve local communities through interactive television has stimulated social changes. This social and technological combination, which identifies the new information society, aims to involve participants in the viewing process. Interactive applications relate to the ability of advanced systems to learn individual viewers' tastes, provide them with their preferred services and offer more choices per channel and more services per system.[1]

The argument made here is that the idea of an information society served by telecommunications services has changed with the growing impact of technological and policy changes, and is likely to be revolutionized with the spread of digital technology. In that respect, the common elements at work in the relationship between digital technology and the information society demonstrate the changing structure of new media and telecommunications policies.

This chapter examines the social adoption of information technology, which leads to the implementation of the information society. While concentrating on the implications of advanced services, which have identified attempts to create the information society, the research provides an overview of the course of implementation of advanced technology in society. It also illustrates how digital television and the multiplication of channels and services change the social development of media policy and markets. The main focus is on the counterrelations between digital technology and the information society, which have changed dramatically following the course of change of media policy and the globalization of technology and culture.

The examination is undertaken according to the three-stage course of media policy examined in Chapter 1. It demonstrates that the transformation in the social adoption of information technology and the changing structure of the industry within local markets have occurred in three main stages of development. This course started with perceptions of localism in broadcasting in the early period of media policy. It changed in the second stage into a comprehensive perception of social change while concentrating on the role of interactive applications of new media and telecommunications services, and is now moving into the digital age while operating within a global market.

The three-stage development of the information society demonstrates that whereas past experience included initiatives to insert advanced services that had been implemented mainly by national governments, in the current stage new technology and market forces dominate future applications of advanced services in the form of digital democracy.

1. First Stage: Localism in Broadcasting

In the first stage of media policy, which is equivalent to the first stage of the social adoption of information technology, applications of advanced services were aimed at establishing community services. In this structure, attempts to dominate social and cultural developments identified the use of information technology trials. This phase is identified by perceptions of localism in broadcasting, which was exploited after citizens' movements and practices started to challenge the relationship between new media services and democracy. In practice however, despite the attempts to exploit the social and cultural potential of new media technologies, the democratic potential of new media projects with community and interactive appeal was rarely explored.

2. Second Stage: Interactive Trials

In the second stage of media policy, experiments to implement interactive applications in community and public access television took place in the United States and the leading media countries of Europe. These experiments concentrated on establishing a new cultural order that could be utilized with the adoption of new information technologies. The notion of interactive television that could create social change developed with the growing technological ability of new media to utilize interactive services. In this form, the new services attracted governments and commercial entrepreneurs, who claimed that the social adoption of information technology would become common around the world. In practice, however, although the adoption of new means applied to the development of advanced technology, the experiments with cable transmissions proved unsuccessful as far as public response and cost effectiveness of these services.

3. Third Stage: A New Digital Society

The concept of information society is changing dramatically in the digital age. New technology has established a new social structure, broadening the base of community communications and involving interactive technologies with global potential. This course of change suggests that the move to adopt the objective of global media policy has challenged the concept of localism in broadcasting. The triumph of digital technology is creating a different version of the social adoption of information technology—through a new digital society.

The social and technological implications of the digital age are particularly relevant to the development of media policy for the 21st century. The role of information technologies can be seen in the changing social nature of localism. The new structure of media policy is dominated by digital services that operate within a global market.

A new digital society is created by this revolution. Digital technology is going to transform broadcasting and telecommunications through its ability to significantly increase the number and variety of the services on offer. These applications include programming, information and advanced services, increased resolution of television signals, and vastly improved picture quality—with interactive capability that simultaneously provides different services to each customer.

The new age of digital technology is identified with dramatic changes in the relationship between technology and social development. Governments and global regulatory institutions that aim to create a new social and technological order encourage the convergence of digital services. The new digital society means that a new structure of information technology is expanding globally with far-reaching implications for the digital divide between leading nations and less technologically advanced countries.

5.1 LOCALISM IN BROADCASTING

This section examines experiences in localism in broadcasting, which took on importance in the first stage of media policy. Throughout this period, local perceptions characterized media policy, led by obligation to maintain public interest principles in local applications of the information society. This policy advocated the implementation of the various functions of narrowcast television, which resulted in requirements for local and community services.

The perception of localism in broadcasting was developed as a result of the relationship between media policy and society. One of the outstanding characteristics of the evolving concept of information society is the degree of access that local people can acquire with the help of technology. In that sense, the definition of community is usually discussed within the limits of society, and community media are meant to represent community interest. Within this structure, attempts to impose the perception of localism in broadcasting took place while using advanced applications of new media.

According to this policy, the social adoption of advanced technology can make the implementation of localism in broadcasting accessible in the framework of community television and interactive services. The impact of new technologies has arisen because they have the potential to allow both interior dialogue and outward self-expression of social and political movements.

Local transmissions had been explored through community and public access channels as most cable systems, even those with a limited capacity, had spare channels that could be used for community and public access programming. In both America and Europe, communities were offered opportunities to make their own programming and to reach a local audience via television.

The potential of cable systems began to catch the attention of the public, and community leaders saw it as a means of providing programs to neighborhoods, particular segments of the community, and special interest groups. In most cases, local channels relied extensively on the voluntary efforts of members of the local community. These ranged from coverage of local sports, music, and events, to documentary and discussion features of direct relevance to the community, and provided an opportunity for many groups to have true narrowcast television transmissions, even on a small scale.

Differences between American and European perceptions of local and community television were in the extent of social and cultural aspirations. These differences have been evident mainly in terms of the programming aspect of community television. In America, public access channels were common between the late 1960s and the late 1970s. These channels provided an outlet, free of charge, for program production by people within the community.[2] In Europe, the requirements were for local origination transmissions, and this identified cable systems in the 1970s and 1980s. These channels contained transmissions actually produced by the local cable system, while both the channels and programming policies remained under the control of the cable system.

Differences were also evident in the role played by governments in endorsing social and cultural perceptions through the imposition of public access and community programming. In all countries alternative services had been endorsed by national governments, although at a different phase and approach.

The American objectives behind local transmissions date back to early policy on localism in broadcasting. In the 1960s, the FCC was worried that CATV's continued diffusion would discourage terrestrial television by reducing stations' audience and the amount their operators could charge advertisers. The FCC saw its function as guarding the revenues of local broadcasters from direct competition of cable systems offering programming and advertisements from stations in nearby cities, and restricted cable to carrying signals of local origin. The policy was intended to promote cable as a supplementary service and to protect broadcast interests. It was supported by the Supreme Court, which ruled in favor of the FCC, holding that they had the right to preserve local broadcast services.

In terms of regulation, public access channels were common during late 1960s and early 1970s, but were not a requirement. In 1972 the FCC made public access channels a statutory obligation, but in 1979, following the general deregulation of cable, it dropped its access rules, leaving local municipalities free to negotiate with franchise applicants as they wished. Lobby groups and minorities without other access to broadcast media saw major attractions in community and public access channels. But the government claimed that cable's increasing technical capacity to serve a multiplicity of interests justified its policy of not making a specific requirement for local channels in the 1984 Cable Act.

The lack of enthusiasm evident in the operation of local and community channels was also reinforced by the advent of satellite transmissions, which revolutionized the cable industry. The open-skies policy, announced in 1972, permitted the import of distant transmissions and gave permission to private companies to launch commercial satellites. With the growth in the number of channels, the attraction of public access channels diminished, and deregulation and commercialization conceptions have since characterized American cable policy. Accordingly, the policy of not requiring public access channels did not change.[3]

In Europe, broadcasting largely conformed to a dominant model of public service broadcasting with common values and principles of regulation, and the perception of community television was initially perceived as an integral and essential element of this policy thinking. In practice, however, these conceptions were not realized to their full extent because of the restrictive nature of the broadcasting policy, which had made an impact on the development of alternative services through CATV systems.

Within the general model of public service broadcasting, a monopoly status was given to national broadcasting services. This policy concentrated on local social and cultural aspects and reflected significant differences of historical experience and regulatory culture between European countries. The public service aspects had been designed to protect the national broadcasting services and local broadcasters. They addressed the concern that commercial transmissions could limit the ability of public television to serve their intended audience. In the approach for local and community transmissions, in addition to prohibition on private channels, European media policies limited the reception of additional channels by requiring cable systems to carry a specified number of local television signals. For that reason, although cable offered local organizations the chance to reach wider audiences, cable operators have generally not explored the full potential of local transmissions.

European experience demonstrates that because media policy was under strict public supervision and the initiative was left in the hands of governments, few community experiments survived the first stage of media policy. The main difficulty was that communities and localities rarely felt that they could afford to fund local transmissions, and operators had to provide technical equipment and funds. Because subscriber interest in local origination and community transmissions was not sufficient to justify increased expenditure on these services, local transmissions have not expanded much. The elimination of these rules has also differed among countries, although the obligation for community programming was lifted with the commercialization of the media sector during the second stage of media policy.[4]

5.2 INTERACTIVE TRIALS

Initial results of the social adoption of information technology had been similar in all countries, proving the unsuccessful attempts to impose the perception of localism in broadcasting. But in spite of the failure to redefine the public interest in local applications of the information society, the experience with local and community television has highlighted the important role of information and interactive services in society. This role was due to be explored in the form of trials to create social change through the implementation of interactive services.

This section concentrates on the renewed attempts to exploit the social implications of information technology. These were implemented in the 1980s based on the various applications and capabilities of interactive cable systems. But the interest shown by policymakers to facilitate participatory democracy at the local level had gone beyond the growing significance of media and telecommunications services, relating to further attempts to formulate a long-term process of social change through the various applications of information technology.

The potential of new technologies and localism, which had not prevailed in the early stage of broadcasting, was explored again in the second stage, although with different perceptions. The ability of television and telecommunications services to offer educational and narrowcast transmissions with social and community appeal has always caught the attention of policymakers and social groups. Whereas the primary function of alternative media, namely cable and satellite, has been the provision of programming services, other concepts, such as community and interactive services, have been explored through both broadcast and cable transmissions.

Experiments with interactive cable took place between the late 1970s and the early 1980s, aimed at creating new technological means that would lead to social changes. They proved that the historical development of the broadcast media is related to their shifting structure toward social and cultural change. However, following the adoption of open-skies policy in America in the early 1970s and in Europe in the late 1980s, media policies have become influenced by new technology, stimulating new thinking about the social and cultural capabilities of information technology.

The main lesson that can be learned from the early experiments with local and community television is that although new technologies have increased competition within the broadcast media, they did not develop programming produced for local markets. This conclusion is particularly evident when examining the development of the broadcasting and telecommunications industries in relation to interactive services, because they did not change the commercial-type national television transmissions that had already dominated the American television market and were later adopted across Europe.

Experiments with interactive cable applications have been most prominent in Europe, although they took place also in the United States.

France

France initiated the first major trial of interactive cable. The motivation behind the development of interactive technology was political and social, with further global outlook. The experiment, launched in the city of Biarritz in 1979, started an attempt to establish an interactive nationwide cable infrastructure, with sophisticated applications of telecommunications. The project aimed to establish a fiber optic system that would provide two-way capability in the form of images, high-fidelity sound, voice, and data, to users of the public network. The goal was to give France a competitive economic advantage via early research and development and move its industry into the development of a broadband video-communications network.

The policy sought to take advantage of a growing demand for audiovisual services and telecommunication in order to accelerate the installation and interconnection of local video-communications networks. The strategy of the pilot project had been to build an Integrated Services Digital Network (ISDN), providing its 1,500 subscribers with television channels and various advanced services, such as videophone, an electronic directory, and an exchange of videocassette content by telephone.

Following Biarritz, many systems asked to join the project as part of the national Cable Plan. This plan desired to establish interactive cable systems throughout France and change French culture by allowing people within communities to communicate. This was an early version of an information system that offers potential for interactive democracy within a whole range of nontelevision services. Although local authorities were given a main role in the establishment of local video-communication systems, local authorities and the public did not respond according to the national government's plan, and it soon became clear that the cable experiments were stagnating and fading away.

Germany

Local and interactive projects endorsed by public authorities were also launched in Germany where the primary reason was not to build an advanced industry, as in France, but to establish local means of communications and enhance the variety of television channels on offer. Experiments started after the Federal government decided on an ambitious plan to install new technologies and to test the feasibility of a wide range of new services. Pilot projects started in 1984 in four major German cities. Although each experiment tested different aspects, their main goals were to assess user acceptance of services and technologies and to provide answers to the technical difficulties that would arise.

The interactive potential of cable was tested in seven sites. The fiber optic experiments tested the technical integration of data and telecommunications for the second period of the German cable plan, which was to start when interactive services had enough demand to replace the distribution function of the coaxial cable systems.

German experience with interactive cable demonstrates that fiber optic and two-way systems were not built, despite the Bundespost's belief that such systems would eventually come into their own when costs came down. Evidently, with the start of the cable plan in the mid-1980s, it was claimed that interactive systems were to be developed when fiber optic cables were to be laid over coaxial systems, mainly promoted by business communications. But the unsuccessful experiences with interactive cable led to a growing recognition of the inevitability of wider regulatory changes promoting liberalization policies and letting the market, rather than public authorities, determine the pace of new technology development.[5]

Britain

The prospects of advanced technology and social change were evident in Britain too, although British policy differed from that of France and Germany in the implementation of these objectives. The long-term goal was to promote all possible applications of information technology for the national economic advantage, but on the basis of private capital and market demand. This policy was based on the American example of free enterprise and the notion that the social implementation of information technology was based on commercial motivation.

On the part of the government, the social and cultural objectives that led the development of the cable infrastructure had been initiated as part of a national plan to advance information technology. The Conservative government based developments in information technology as the main goal of new media policy, although in practice implementation of advances in technology was bound to the role played by the financial community.

The role of the government was limited to providing the regulatory means to develop advanced technology, and it was left for commercial operators to invest in cable systems and services. The government formed the Information Technology Advisory Panel (ITAP), which examined the industrial potential of cable systems and the broadcast and regulatory implications and announced 1982 as the Information Technology Year. The government also formed the Hunt Committee, whose aim was to explore the practical implications and industrial benefits of cable technology.

This policy gave prominence to the private sector and free enterprise while permitting cable systems to carry a wide range of entertainment and other services. Although the government was reluctant to privilege any particular system, it formulated a liberalized policy with the aim of promoting the legal environment that would allow the market to direct developments in the field of information technology. But the goal of letting the market dictate advancement and at the same time be consistent with the public interest proved unsuccessful. Commercial undertaking was not sufficient, because the development of information technology systems proved to be too costly and lacked satisfactorily certain future growth potential.

The United States

American experience with advanced technology differed considerably from European development. Whereas in Europe public authorities promoted interactive cable to meet public interest objectives,[6] in America experiments with new technologies were private initiatives.

The main goal of American experiments was to examine the application of interactive services and their commercial potential. Early cable projects took place in the 1970s, and were conducted on a limited basis. They demonstrated that interactive cable could be used to provide a range of services to a community, although their commercial capability was not tested.[7]

The most advanced, city-oriented, two-way interactive cable experiment was the system in Columbus, Ohio, called Qube. It provided audience members a terminal that allowed subscribers to select the programming and to send signals back to the programmers when the latter presented prompts to that feedback. This system was interactive in a fuller sense but most of its subscribers did not participate in the two-way offerings. The primary goal in designing the system was to allow television viewers the chance to tailor the system to their own personal likes and dislikes, although it was finally downgraded into a much simpler cable and pay-per-view system because of low consumer interest and high expenses.

Qube was privately operated by Warner-Amex. Although it came into an existence in other American cities, the interactive project folded in 1984.[8] After the merger of Time-Warner, additional interactive trials took place in the first half of the 1990s, although these were also shut down due to lack of financial certainty.

5.3 A NEW DIGITAL SOCIETY

As can be seen from the analysis of the development of advanced technology the trials with interactive cable did not prevail. It became clear that the overall potential to serve the interests of local communities is limited as far public response and commercial outlook. The experience gained with the various applications of the social adoption of advanced technology was however beneficial, as it showed that the attempts initiated by both public authorities and commercial entrepreneurs proved unsuccessful in terms of public response and commercial potential of the proposed services.

The conclusion that can be drawn from this development is that the concept of an information society served by interactive cable did not prevail, although the ideas behind these plans did not fade away. It became clear that cable technology could not realize the social potential of an information society, and despite the growing impact of new technologies, the concept of advanced services and localism could not prevail because interactive cable was not attractive and cost effective enough to both the public and commercial forces. The experiments also proved that the perception of localism in cable transmissions could not be achieved through interactive services.

Despite the insufficient results with interactive cable, it became evident that the concept of telecommunications and localism should be explored in the future, stimulated by additional advances of digital technology. This trend identified the start of the third stage of media policy, with the increased impact of advanced technology in society, and would become dominant in future applications of information technology.

This section investigates new forms of localism in broadcasting and the employment of future advanced applications. It is argued that advances in technology, mainly digital television services, have brought policy changes with global impact, creating a new concept of localism within a global market. This concept means that information technology is being advanced by commercial initiators at the global level, mainly through digital applications, even though the actual adoption of these developments and their consequent social changes differ in each country according to local policy.

The New Structure of Information Technology

With new technology, the implementation of new forms of broadcasting has captured greater interest and attention. The social implications of the experiences with community and interactive services employed in earlier stages, coupled with the characteristics of new information services, created an efficient platform to establish the infrastructure for both domestic and global telecommunications markets. The commercial spread of information technology is related to global media trends, because new developments are likely to dominate in the technologically advanced countries. In this form, they pose a major challenge for public policies in less advanced countries, as a global force of change that tends to ignore local restrictions.

Common to all countries is that the new structure of information technology is being implemented as a service that encourages the adoption of localism within a global market. The current state of media policy provides the assumption that if digital television penetrates a majority of the homes, society should be transformed. Because this process influences all counties, the new definitions of public interest and participatory democracy would change social policies and provide the means to implement the concept of digital democracy on a global scale.

The resulting global development of telecommunications services involves the complex transformation of technology, markets, and politics. The experience with new applications of alternative and new media services and the triumph of market forces and deregulation policies have increased the globalization of media policies and had a tremendous impact on the adoption of telecommunications services. The role of public authorities has also changed, as new technologies are no longer characterized by a high degree of regulation in the interest of public service and social criteria. Thus, the role of public authorities in the new global and commercial environment is limited to dictating the rules under which advanced services operate.

The combination of global and local impact is particularly significant to this transition in policy. At the global level, future developments depend to a great extent on global forces promoting deregulation and commercialization. At the local level, social implications involving major aspects of technological, ideological, political, commercial and domestic political nature should be considered.

This process has established the concept of localism within a global market, according to which local versions of information technology are being adopted. The most prominent example is that many countries face a long transition period to convert from analog to digital technology, although the role of leading authorities in determining global media and telecommunications policies is still critical, and it can be assumed that an agreed closure date for all analog services would accelerate the transition. It is for that reason that examination of the social changes that identify the new structure of media policy, which dominates the global impact on local media systems, demonstrates the alternative role of advanced technology.

It is clear in that sense that despite important policy changes and technological advancement, the cable industry remains mainly a distribution system for programming services. Although the scope of the distribution function has changed dramatically, the present role of cable within the mix of the broadcasting media has to be seen in this light as a distribution system for programming services.

Following the unsuccessful experiments with community and interactive services the role of narrow-cast and local transmissions has remained alternative to the main purpose of television—the supply of entertainment and information programs at the national and global levels.

The television industry as we know it today is largely built on the supply of entertainment and information programming in the form of movies, sports, news, special events, and the like, as well as local and public service programming. Both the habits of viewers and consumption of programming have been growing at a steady and continuous phase, and advanced services are still considered as alternative media. The consumption of the traditional uses of television is easy to operate, well known, and common, and in this form has great advantages over new services.

The structure of information technology is changing gradually and a new social order is expected for the broadcast and telecommunications market in the 21st century. Whereas traditionally cable and satellite have been considered as alternative technologies, new global actors and new technologies are making an impact with the advancement in digital technology. In the years ahead we will see the coming of new technology and services, which will make easier use of television and advanced services. Coupled with regulatory changes encouraging and in practice enforcing common use of digital technology, new developments are also likely to make an impact on the alternative role of advanced services and change the social consumption of media services.

The traditional role of media services is undergoing a major transition following the coming of digital services. Although it can be argued that the initiatives that had been exploited with local media during the 20th century can provide important conclusions for future applications of new technology services, technological and policy changes demonstrate that the future potential of telecommunications and localism is related to digital developments.

The applications of digital technology are likely to change the social role and definition of cable, satellite, and telecommunications from alternative to mainstream media. The new competitive structure is also likely to change the nature of social consumption of advanced services, as the reliance on cable technology, which had for many years dominated the social adoption of information technology, has now been transformed with the advent of new technologies. In contrast to digital satellite and digital terrestrial services, which are in progress, the cable industry needs huge investments to digitize systems or to become interactive so that it can compete in the new digital age. Whereas the attractiveness of cable has been its ability to offer a variety of channels, with digital terrestrial and digital satellite offering multiple-channel services, other capabilities of cable, such as local and community services, could also be offered by its competitors.

Another aspect of the digital revolution is that governments encourage digital broadcasting at the local level, in response to the growing impact of global transmissions, which are outside their control. Digital services with local capabilities provide security to national governments and national broadcasting services, because the right to issue licenses remains in the hands of local authorities.

Global impact on the employment of localism in broadcasting is especially noteworthy in the adoption process of digital democracy. The social attractiveness of digital transmissions is that the technology endorses localism, in place of global transmissions, offering a wide range of transmissions and serving a handful of local groups and tastes.

In this way, a new digital society is developing on a global scale, influencing all countries—both advanced and underdeveloped societies. The availability of many channels delivered through digital networks should be beneficial to densely populated countries with limited terrestrial frequencies that would be able to explore local aspects. In that respect, the new digital society is developing into a new mix of a global and local nature. The vast number of channels that would become available—hundreds in each country—would certainly be in need of programming. This will be distributed globally, to digital services around the world, in addition to local programming, thus establishing a new concept of localism within a global market.

What has changed in less than half a century, from the European two-way trials of the 1980s to interactive services of the 21st century?

Firstly, social adoption of advanced services has changed and interactivity is becoming widespread.

Secondly, global institutions rather than single governments are involved in the transition to digital television.

Thirdly, technology has changed, from the limited capacity of the past to broadband access with a hugely powerful force and the potential to bring a massive video and audio library to every network subscriber.

Fourthly, the globalization of policies and technologies and advancement in information technology, which dominate the new era of global media policy, have created the foundations of the information society.

And finally, perhaps most importantly, interactivity is becoming an option for consumers, as a "second force" to television programming. This means that although digital infrastructures replace analog networks, the actual adoption of interactive services could be limited to a complementary service.

In assessing the way the new digital society would evolve, there can be no argument that the stakes in the transition to digital technology are high and there is certainly no clear evidence that consumers are willing to pay for interactive television itself. But the optimistic outlook may be that because past experience shows that customers are willing to pay for multichannel digital services, it can be assumed that if interactivity is additional to that, they would also be willing to buy interactive services. One thing is certain: digital technology is about to establish a new global society, a digital society, which presents many advantages over the traditional analog-based society.

Digital Expansion

The new age of digital technology is identified with dramatic changes in the relationship between technology and social development, changing the nature of society and public participation. For the last five decades, despite the tremendous power of television to influence the way we see the world and how we learn and communicate, the basic technology of television has not changed. The concept of interactive television has been around for decades, although it did not catch the interest of the public. Interactive technology has been available since the 1970s, but it has not been widely adopted and has failed to succeed to reach a mass audience. Today, digital technology, interactive television, and the convergence of digital services have become central issues in the policies of leading governments and global regulatory institutions, and analysts believe that they can finally reach the mass market.

Interactive technology is becoming available in the form of digital services. Although there are obvious problems in rolling out advanced services, as with any new service, it can be predicted that interactive services are the future of television. This assumption can be made based on the direction of the television industry. There is practically no system upgrades, rebuilds, or new builds that are not activating interactive services, as the continuing cost reductions and performance improvements in fiber optic and digital technology are able to keep up with the needs of the media and telecommunications markets.

The social implications of the digital revolution are enormous. Digital technology is changing the way we look, listen, and use television—but mainly the way we consume the products of television, and over time various interactive applications may become common in addition to television broadcasting. The convergence of online services with broadcast television presents many profitable niches once Internet access is not seen as limited and becomes available through cable, satellite, and telecom modems.

New technologies offer major benefits to broadcasters and television audiences while providing a more effective way of transmitting and consuming television services. Digital television brings to an end the direct relationship between one television program and one frequency. The compression of digital signals, which allows multiplication of channels, is the most important application of digital television. Compression technology allows up to 12 channels to be transmitted over the same spectrum of a single analog channel. It increases the number of channels and services available to be carried on any given transmission channel, thus offering far greater choice to viewers.

The other major social impact is the huge amount of content delivered through the large number of channels and transmission services that become handy to customers. Digital television brings a wider choice of channels, expands the range of programming available to the public, improves picture and quality, and allows a wide selection of data services.

The digitalization of transmission channels and the cheaper supply of broadband capacity change the technological development of the mass media dramatically. The multiplication of channels allows digital editing, reduces the cost of production of programming, and improves the quality of sound and picture. Sale of content will probably be a significant source of revenue as the number of channels and production increases. This includes the addition of subscription channels and programs, because the ability of content providers to become broadcasters and to offer programs to smaller audience shares is one of the significant advantages of digital technology.

The technical advantage of digital television is the offering of new interactive services to be delivered to the home in high quality. Digital technology can provide better reception of television services and higher quality picture and sound through high-definition television (HDTV). The technology offers approximately twice the vertical and horizontal resolution of the current broadcasting systems, providing a picture quality approaching 35mm film and a sound quality approaching that of a compact disc. HDTV has an aspect ratio of 16:9 and at least 1,100 lines (in contrast, the existing conventional television pictures use a 4:3 aspect ratio and 525 to 625 lines).

In the new digital age, consumers will be able to use the new television service box to efficiently maintain major activities from home. They will be able to receive e-mail, pay bills, handle bank accounts, and use other applications, such as order groceries, check information about available transportation routes and time-tables, consume information services, and play online games. Consumers will be able to select information services, including an entire edition of a newspaper, and select information such as stock market updates or exchange rates. They will also be able to access other specific information suited to each viewer's preferences and needs—ranging from general news such as current events, sports, culture, and politics to general information such as telephone directories, interactive educational material, and other information that can be translated into digital bits.

Digital technology also changes the consumption of advanced applications and services, because it carries a range of multimedia services in the form of audio, images, data, and text. The supply of enhanced services means that technologies are converging, offering combined services of television, Internet, and multimedia.

The convergence of digital technologies breaks new grounds by providing direct access to consumer homes, allowing much more data to be packed onto a signal than the analog transmission system. The combination of traditional television and new telecommunications services opens up new interactive applications, and broadcasters can offer consumers a selection of preferred programs suited to the liking of each viewer. These include services such as Pay-Per-View (PPV) and Video-On-Demand (VOD), Internet-television options, streaming video, on-screen overlays, and datacasting.

What are the prospects for digital expansion and the establishment of a new digital society?

The immediate social motive for the launch of digital services is larger distribution capacity and more effective handling of broadcast material. Viewers have the opportunity to access more television channels, enjoy a wider variety of programming (including pay services and special events), receive better picture and audio quality, and use interactive services from home. Other social benefits that societies will be able to adopt in the coming future, as the new technology spreads around the world, are the ability to bring the global information superhighway into businesses and homes and the development of a higher-speed global digital medium offering electronic marketing and commerce.

Digital television changes the way traditional broadcasting operates, while exploiting interactive television and the Internet on television. In the age of hundreds of digital channels, competition between multichannel and telecommunications services will have to rely on the quality of advanced services. This means an upgrading of the services provided by television: in addition to more channels and higher definition, digital television will bring a wide variety of interactive services to the home. In such competition, interactive television would offer better opportunities for the public and advertisers, combining video programming and data services.

The transformation into digital technology is expanding global-ly. The imposition of digital television by leading regulatory authorities means that the notion of an information society is in a transition period into digital technology. The social implications of this involvement will force television stations around the world to offer digital high-definition transmissions and a variety of television programs and interactive ser-vices.

The global dimensions of the digital revolution are important also because the debate that has been raised in many countries. This relates to the social impact of advanced technologies, due to the fact that the counterimpact of globalization and localism increases with the grow-ing penetration of telecommunications services and the transition into digital democracy.

The social aspects of these technological and policy changes have become widespread with the development of information technol-ogy. In reviewing the social implications of the digital age, it can be con-cluded that the development of digital technology and the availability of digital services in each home are likely to increase the potential and use of advanced services. With hundreds of channels on offer with interac-tive capability and other nontelevision services, society is due to under-go a transition period, as the transformation into the wider concept of the information society is utilized through digital technology.

Desire to Close the Digital Divide

The tremendous growth in the broadcasting and telecommunications fields has been the result of the new digital society that identifies the 21st century. The advent of the Internet has blurred the lines that separated broadcasting (radio and television) and telecommunications (data and on-line services) and opened up new opportunities for nations and insti-tutions, even individuals, to enter global markets. The fundamental revo-lution the world of broadcasting is undergoing with the new dominance of information technologies and global media policymaking is changing the relationship between developing and industrial countries and creat-ing new opportunities for economic, cultural, and political integration.

Digital technology is likely to transform the global broadcasting market, as subscription to digital television will take off rapidly and interactive services will become a main competitor to analog television. All U.S. satellite subscribers receive digital services and the digital upgrade of cable differs among systems (see Tables 3.2-3.4). There were 13 million interactive TV homes in early 2003, with satellite services leading the way. Echostar Dish Network had 5 million households con-nected to its 14 interative TV channels (the Dish Home Service), and is the top provider of interactive television in the United States, offering "in-demand" access to news, weather, entertainment, sports, and other information.[9]

According to ITC, in the first quarter of 2003, one third of U.K. households had already subscribed to digital television, and more are signing up everyday. Evidently, all television transmissions in the United Kingdom will be digital. According to Oftel, the rate of growth for broadband services in the United Kingdom is higher than in France, Germany, Sweden, and the United States. The United Kingdom is the leader when it comes to the penetration of interactive TV services among those with digital TV. A little more than 65 percent of digital households have access to interactive TV, compared with a little more than 40 percent in the United States. One third of the houses connected to digital cable had previously had neither analog cable nor satellite services, according to a report from U.K. telecoms' watchdog Oftel.[10] BskyB has the most interactive customers. Its service, Sky Active, offers applications such as Sky News Active, Sky Sports Active, Sly Movies Active, e-mail, messaging, games, banking, shopping, and betting.

Sixteen million Europeans are using enhanced TV applications. Interactive TV technology was estimated to be in 31 million European households at the end of 2002. European customers spent a total of $92 million on interactive applications and services in 2002, representing an increase of 121 percent when compared to 2001 numbers. Interactive TV games captured $36 million of the total, enhanced TV $35 million, while TV betting/gambling and TV messaging/e-mail reached $10 million each.[11]

According to a report by Datamonitor,[12] the number of European digital television households will increase by 39 million in 2004 and analog television is likely to be switched off by 2010-2015 in many European countries. The report predicts that new interactive services will become one of the key drivers for the uptake of digital television in Europe, attracting new subscribers and generating new revenue streams for digital broadcasters.

There is uncertainty, however, about which services would be most attractive. According to Oftel, new subscribers are encouraged by the greater choice of channels, but are less enamored of interactive services. According to Datamonitor, the most attractive applications will be interactive services—home-shopping, games, information and data services, and e-mail, whereas services such as interactive advertising and interactive banking will attract revenue.

Predictions are that the Internet will also attract European customers during the first decade of the 21st century, according to a report released by market research firm Forrester Research.[13] The report shows that 18 percent of European households (representing 27 million people) will subscribe to a high-speed Internet access service by 2005. Denmark, Norway and Sweden are expected to lead the way, with about 36 to 40 percent of the households subscribing to high-speed services.

Estimates are that 70 percent of American households will be online in 2004, and that the number of worldwide Internet users will grow 21 percent annually, reaching 1.9 billion people in 2009. Tremendous growth is expected in the transmission capacity and the new services of the Internet. Worldwide bandwidth—the capacity of the Internet's transmission lines to carry high-speed data—will increase 100 times by 2009, mainly because more people will spend more time online.[14]

These figures demonstrate a tremendous potential growth of advanced services. The reasons for the slow take-off evident for many years in leading media markets had been limited availability and high prices. In recent years, however, deregulation and increased competition have sparked expansion of Internet services and customers. In addition to less expensive services, broadband providers have stepped up their marketing efforts and introduced expanded services. Another reason for the growth is the domination of large telecommunications companies, mainly former PTTs, in the European market.

But despite the new development course, in which telecom companies are moving toward becoming Internet and telephony providers and cable companies are moving away from traditional cable services, public reaction is still hesitant and the adoption of digital television and high-speed Internet access is slow.

The predicted penetration figures of advanced services may be confusing, because digital divide is also growing. At the start of the century, only 8 percent of European households could receive high-speed Internet access, and fewer than 1 percent actually had the service.[15] A report released in May 1999 by the ITC found that 90 percent of nondigital subscribers were not interested in subscribing to digital service.[16] In the United States, despite aggressive marketing by consumer electronic companies, only 230,000 digital high-definition television monitors were sold by August 2000.[17]

Whereas most Americans have access to high-speed services, in Europe the spread of advanced services is not as high because the reception of national analog television networks has generally provided a suitable solution for most homes. In other regions, such as Asia, Africa, and Latin America, advanced services serve only small portions of the population. Although broadband satellite services may provide the only solution in rural areas in advanced countries, the question remains whether competitive satellite-based broadband services would serve less-profitable parts of the world.

The danger of digital divide remains significant not only between developed and less-developed countries, but also within advanced countries. In the United States, an estimated number of 30 to 35 million homes are not served by digital cable, DSL, or wireless cable, mainly in rural areas. According to a FCC report, although more Americans than ever have access to advanced, high-speed Internet connections (91% of American households), those in rural, inner-city and tribal areas lag behind. The report found that the availability to at least some access to broadband telecommunications services allowing high-speed transmission of video, data, graphics, and video over the Internet is concentrated in affluent urban and suburban areas. In contrast, areas with high concentrations of minorities and low-income residents have little high-speed access.[18] In Britain too, according to a Oftel report, subscription to digital TV is greatest among higher income groups, and lowest among older customers and lower income groups.[19]

Efforts are also taking place to bridge the digital divide in the use of computers. The American National Information Infrastructure (NII) plans to connect every home, school, college, and business in an electronic communications network. The impact of these developments is that new technologies would become readily available in each home, making the potential transformation into digital democracy a reality.

However, the mission is complicated. A U.S. Commerce Department report of July 1999 documented a wide digital divide in America. Black and Hispanic households are only two-fifths as likely to have Internet access as white households.[20] U.S. government studies have also shown significant differences in Internet access between rich and poor. Households with incomes above $75,000 in urban areas are 20 times more likely to have access to the Internet than the poorest households.

In response, former President Clinton proposed a national plan of connecting every American to the Internet. The plan included tax initiatives of $2 billion over 10 years and expanded grants to encourage the private sector to donate computers, sponsor technology centers in poor neighborhoods, and train those not yet connected to the Internet.[21]

The plan aims to make high-technology advantages as universally available as the telephone. The aim, according to former President Clinton, is "finally to slam shut the digital divide, between the computer 'haves' and 'have nots'. We must connect all of our citizens to the Internet, not just in schools and libraries but in homes, small businesses and community centers. And we must help all Americans gain the skills they need to make the most of the connection."

As part of the struggle to answer the technology gap in struggling communities, the plan directs the federal government to commit itself to work toward universal access to the Internet. The President asked: "What do you believe the economic impact would be if Internet access usage were as dense in America as telephone usage?" and answered: "I think it's clear that we need to keep working until we achieve this goal."[22]

In his last State of the Union address (the first in the 21st century),[23] President Clinton described his digital divide plan as "a national crusade" to create "opportunity for all" in trying to bring more people into the world of the Internet. Desire to close the digital divide is strongly supported by Americans, who want the federal government support for computer literacy programs in high-schools and assistance in education and the extension of computer access and training to lower-income areas.[24]

The contribution of the information society to the new economy is growing at an unprecedented pace, mainly in industries such as media services, telecommunications, wireless communications, and the Internet. The importance of the social adoption of information technology is widely supported. U.S. Federal Reserve Chairman Alan Greenspan claims that the technological boom transforming life in American cities is also touching lives in rural areas. "Like all the previous episodes of technical advance, the revolution in information technology already has improved living conditions in numerous ways, and it will likely bring future benefits to rural communities that we now can only scarcely imagine."[26] Former FCC Chairman William Kennard says that because the Internet technology is vital to economic development, "we have to carefully make sure that no one is left behind."[27]

Global digital divide was one of the top agenda items at the United Nation's Millennium Summit in September 2000. According to the UN, the growing technology gap between developed and developing countries has inspired the UN Secretary General to urge world leaders and private companies to action. According to a study released by the World Bank, the lack of computers in developed countries means that 98 percent of Asians, 98 percent of Latin Americans, and 99.5 percent of Africans are not connected to the Internet. The report indicates that without help, the economies of developing countries are likely to become less diverse and further entrenched in the production of agriculture and raw materials, while developed nations race ahead to become information specialists. The conclusion is that in the long term access to and production of technology by poorer countries may boost their economy.[28]

SUMMARY

The relations between digital technology and the information society have become an important issue in forecasting media policy for the 21st century. New technology is creating a new social structure that can be designated as a new digital society. The new age of digital technology is identified with dramatic changes in the relationship between technology and social development at the global level, increasing the divide between digital nations and less technologically advanced countries.

Following the triumph of globalization and new technology, the new structure of media policy is forcing society to examine the social adoption of information technology. This structure is examined in this chapter in terms equivalent to the three-stage development course of media policy. Initially social and cultural developments identified the use of information technology. This phase was dominated by percep-tions of localism in broadcasting. Later experiments to implement inter-active applications in community and public access television took place in the United States and Europe. These attempts were aimed at creating social change, although despite the growing technological ability of new media to provide interactive services they did not succeed in attracting public attention.

In the third phase, which is considered as the digital age, the concept of information society is changing dramatically, because infor-mation and entertainment are being delivered intensively through a wide range of information technologies. The social adoption of informa-tion technology and the opportunities posed by new technology are cre-ating a new social structure dominated by digital services operating within a global market.

Although future development is not certain, it can be predicted that digital technology will establish a new global society. This is the digital society, which presents many advantages over the traditional analog-based society. In this society information will dominate and interactivity will become an option for consumers, as a "second force" to television programming.

In examining the way the digital society might evolve, it is already evident that the social adoption of advanced services has changed and interactivity is becoming widespread. Global institutions rather than single governments are involved in the transition to digital television. This process includes changes from the limited channel capacity of the past to broadband access with a hugely powerful force and the potential to bring a massive video and audio library to every subscriber. The result of this social transformation is that the globaliza-tion of policies and technologies and advancement in information tech-nology are dominating the new era of global media policy.

6

The Globalization
of Media Markets

The impact of commercialization and globalization on the development of media markets has been phenomenal, creating global media markets dominated by a free market approach and commercial competition of all media and telecommunications services. This course has been further influenced by the development of an open-skies policy and new media technologies, which have created changes in the nature of media markets, from domination of social and cultural perceptions to a common structure of global policy.

The role of new media technologies can be seen as a catalyst in the changing attitudes toward broadcasting policy. Examination of the role of governments brings up the conclusion that new media is a policy area where social, cultural, and political considerations have for many years prevailed over technological determinism. The result is that differences in the social and political perceptions of countries have identified new media policies up until the 1980s. During this period of development, social and cultural perceptions dominated new media policymaking, although changes became evident with the growing impact of technological advancement. Following the adoption of new media policies in Europe, with the aim of deregulation and influenced by the American experience, it can be said that broadcasting is increasingly becoming a global rather than a national domain.

This has been intensified by the transformation of both technology and culture. The consequent technological convergence of new media policies reflects the impact of changes in the global field—the transition from viewing cable as having mainly social and cultural goals to deregulation policies that combine cable, satellite, and telecommunications developments.

The globalization of new media markets has developed as part of the transition in the relationship between technology and cultural values. This process followed the introduction of new media technologies of cable and satellite and changed the dependence of cultural identities on new media policy to the extent that global media culture is now dominating media policies around the world.

Although the impact of new technology and cultural changes on local media markets can be seen in the change of perspective of media policy toward globalization, the distinction should be made here between commercial and public service broadcasting policy. This distinction also relates to initial differences between American and European policies.

In the United States, broadcasting systems were always based on commercial conceptions and companies that intended to make a profit, whereas in Europe a strong commitment among broadcasters to public service broadcasting determined media policy. The public service intent, which dominated European broadcast policy until the 1980s, influenced the nature of cable and new media policies through the domination of social and cultural perceptions. In the new structure of global media markets, which is now dominating broadcasting systems around the world, the adoption of the main commercial objectives of American media policy has provided a common set of principles to which all countries are headed—creating a global course of change in media markets.

The globalization of culture and technology indicates that American media policy has been an example for commercialization elsewhere, creating global media markets dominated by advanced technology and common cultural characteristics. The globalization of media markets means that policies of all countries have converged with the domination of free speech and global competition. In practice, the adoption of the American free speech tradition has provided the basis for global competition with common perceptions of free flow of information.[1]

This chapter examines the change of course on media markets by providing a context within which the cultural impact on the evolution of new media policy can be understood. The transformation has been implemented according to the three stages of the development of media policy examined in this book. It is argued that despite differences in approach among countries, the main course of development has been from a social and cultural project to global media culture. The next stage in the globalization of media markets has begun in the new millennium, following the triumph of information technologies—the establishment of the global information superhighway.

1. A Social and Cultural Project. The first section examines the linkage between culture and technology. It reflects the recognition that technology is a cultural product and examines the ways that social, cultural, and political factors have shaped technology. In the examination of the social and cultural impact on cable policymaking as it relates to the relevant experiences of the large media countries in Europe, the focus is on the main ideals of cable policy that existed in the 1970s and early 1980s. The impact of these perceptions can be seen as an attempt to meet broader social and cultural goals: requirements for community transmissions, imposition of Must Carry channels, and establishment of pilot projects to test the structure of future systems. In this way the leading European countries saw the main role of cable as fulfilling cultural objectives, creating a social and cultural project.

2. Global Media Culture. The second section analyzes the changes in media policy that have allowed for new forms of competition and led to the creation of new media markets dominated by global and commercial convergence of new media technologies and policy. The role of new media policy can be seen to a great extent as a catalyst in the changing attitudes toward a new broadcasting policy, as the impact of new media developments on the overall perception of broadcasting is related to the combination of cultural considerations and technological determinism.

The argument made here is that following the globalization of media markets, the ability of governments to endorse social and cultural requirements has diminished, because such policy aims tend to clash with opportunities for commercial distribution. This course of change in technology and culture confirms that commercialization and globalization developments have made their impact on media polices and markets around the world. Along with globalization, the media sector has become commercial, with programming the main attraction to customers, leading to the creation of global media culture. This structure, which combines the impact of global economy, global culture, and global politics, now dominates the global and commercial flow of information and entertainment and the development course of media markets.

3. Global Information Superhighway.   The third section describes
the new global society that is being created by the global network of
information delivered through new technology and the Internet. The
information society is a distinct product of globalization and technological advancement, which is blurring the differences among societies and
changing everything we do on a scale never before seen. Information is
now delivered globally, through global networks, changing the concept
of global economy, culture, and politics. The spread of communications
networks has brought about the growth of multinational media conglomerates that dominate movies, television, information, and music
worldwide, while forming global links to control the next technological
revolution that will serve the information society.

The global information superhighway is changing the way global economy, global culture, and global politics are perceived. In the 21st
century information technology dominates all media markets so that a
global world dominated by new technology is evolving.

As information can be moved around the world at the speed of
light, the whole concept of the nation-state is being challenged. Global
media services pose new dimensions that society has never seen before.
For decades scholars have been talking about the coming of the global
village; information technology provides the means to make this concept
a reality. The global network of information is now based on various
forms of new technology that allow us to do what humans always wanted to do—combat and defeat time and space. Words, pictures, and video
constantly travel the globe through communications technologies and
the Internet, creating a global society dominated by the global information superhighway.

6.1 A SOCIAL AND CULTURAL PROJECT

Social and cultural aspects dominated the development of cable TV policies until the 1980s and set the stage for new media policies thereafter.
This phase of development is identified foremost with powerful system-
atic and ideological pressures that changed public policies in the field of
cable. The process resulted in the collapse of the social and cultural
nature of cable systems and policies and the triumph of commercial perceptions. These aspects are common to the three largest media countries
of Europe—Britain, France, and Germany—despite local variations that
can be attributed to social, cultural, and political differences. In theoretical terms, it is argued that the social and cultural requirements initiated
by governments, although varied among countries, have largely determined that cable be developed as part of a social and cultural policy.

The main argument made in this section is that all three largest media countries in Europe have followed the same general model of viewing cable as a social and cultural project. Within this structure, programming was directed to community and public access appeal, development was restricted through Must Carry rules, and the establishment of cable systems was tested through pilot projects. It was not until these experiences proved unsuccessful that commercial competition and market policy was adopted in all the countries examined in this research. The early experiences of the social and cultural perceptions of cable were decisive to this transition, however, because they were followed by deregulatory policies for the entire broadcast media.

The experience of the social and commercial aspects of cable policy had a profound impact on changes in media policy and was a prominent element in the shift in balance between public service and commercial broadcasting. In the old structure of broadcasting, which dominated European broadcasting until the 1980s, broadcasting was a public service system under national monopoly; it was noncommercial and had social and cultural goals.

This model also had an impact on attitudes toward cable developments. Initially, television was designed to encourage participatory society, and in the 1980s European broadcasting and new media policies shifted their emphasis from a public service conception of the audience and public needs and services to a consumer-driven broadcasting and telecommunications market. Consequently, changes in cable policy can be seen in light of the overall changes in media policy in Europe.

This section examines the social and cultural impact on cable policymaking as it relates to the relevant experiences of the large media countries in Europe. This focus represents the main models of cable policy that existed in the 1970s and early 1980s and provides a context within which the social and cultural impact on the evolution of broadcast and cable policy in later years can be understood.

Community Transmissions

A central issue in the early development of the technology of cable television is the way in which changes that relate to the programming have resulted from wider ideological and political shifts. In the 1970s, a new cultural orientation for cable was adopted, paying greater attention to the potential of cable systems to provide local and community transmissions.

The objectives that identified media policy intended to explore the cultural aspects of the cable technology. Within the rules that controlled the development of cable systems, a duty to provide community channels was imposed. Although details varied from country to country, the major underlying philosophy was similar: local cable channels were intended to reflect the real desires and needs of local people within the community and provide local means of expression.

As a general model of policymaking, Europe experimented with local and community transmissions in the form of specific projects initiated by national governments. These experiments took place in Britain and France in the 1970s and in France and Germany in the 1980s. The outcome was that the perceptions of the community role of cable systems did not become predominant as policymakers had hoped. Despite local differences, the common result of these experiences was that commercial perceptions prevailed over community and public service conceptions.

In Britain, calls for community and public access television by groups interested in the idea of alternative media matched the strategy of commercial cable operators. They were willing to demonstrate the local potential in providing community services in order to gain political benefits that would allow them to provide more profitable forms of programming, such as pay-TV channels and commercial services.

The Conservative government endorsed these objectives, although it had no active role in community transmissions, and it was left for cable operators and the public to determine the actual nature of local television. In 1972, the Minister of Post and Telecommunications announced the granting of experimental licenses that allowed local programming services on the condition that no public money would be provided.

The projects took place in four locations: transmissions began in Greenwich in August 1972, in Bristol in May 1973, in Sheffield in August 1973, and in Swindon in March 1974. But although companies hoped that these initiatives would be the first step in the direction of wider permission for commercial services, change in the political structure caused change in the political perspective, too. The return of the Labour government in 1974 squashed hopes for community transmissions and narrowcast television. Following the policy of the new government, the cable companies were forced to reduce their services, and most community initiatives closed down at the end of the original three-year licenses.

The main difficulty for the systems in Britain involved programming and finance. The British community services produced new and valuable ideas but no new sources of revenue. They had problems financing the projects, because subscription, sponsorship, and advertising were not permitted. By the mid-1970s it was recognized that in these circumstances the projects could not pay their way, and it became evident that the community initiative had failed.

In France and Germany, community projects were also developed by the national governments, which provided financial means to support local transmissions. This approach was part of a social and cultural policy thinking that supported the establishment of cable systems with the aim of encouraging social participation. In both countries however, despite the financial support, the plans were not realized into their full potential.

In France, experiments with community cable systems, which started in 1973, were suspended in 1975 due to lack of government commitment. The plans were renewed a decade later, when the government encouraged and supported the establishment of local cable systems as part of the Cable Plan. This policy was instituted to achieve the goal of establishing an advanced interactive network across the country with the capability to offer local and community transmissions and explore social and cultural aspects. But this project failed because of lack of support by the public and local governments.

In Germany, community transmissions were tested during the pilot projects in the 1980s. These projects tested the social and cultural aspects offered by cable, and required local and community transmissions. Despite initial support by the national government and the public, the addition of commercial transmissions diminished the impact of community transmissions and made it a service secondary to satellite and commercial transmissions.[2]

Must Carry Rules

In addition to community transmissions, the idea of a social and cultural project had also been identified with the requirement for Must Carry rules, which were imposed on cable systems on behalf of terrestrial broadcasters. These rules were usually the most popular resolution for countries whose broadcast system was founded on public service principles. They required cable operators to retransmit all national channels to protect the priority status of broadcast television and the continual impact of public service broadcasting.

Must Carry rules were common in all three largest media countries in Europe in the first two stages of the development of cable policy, aimed at promoting a comprehensive media structure, but in reality they had also delayed the development of cable for a considerable time because the relatively limited technology of cable did not allow systems to provide additional channels much beyond the Must Carry services.

In Britain, the rules made their impact on the development of cable systems to the extent that the British cable industry made little progress. The early experience with relay exchange led to the immediate prohibition on signal importation before British cable got under way, with the result that even in the early 1980s expansion was impossible.

This had a decisive impact on the development of cable, because the technology of British systems limited them to only 4 to 6 channels, leaving no room for services beyond the Must Carry package.

One of the main reasons for the marginal development in Britain was that due to the limited offering of cable the new market-led policy adopted later lacked an initial customer base. Another reason for the lack of success of British cable was that the 1984 Cable and Broadcasting Bill required that all national television services would be included as part of the Must Carry package of cable systems. It was not until the 1989 Broadcasting Bill, which eliminated these rules and initiated a market-led policy for cable and the entire broadcasting sector, that cable systems and services started to develop.

In France, although the development of cable systems was restricted until the mid-1980s, the Cable Plan initiated in 1984 represented an attempt to reconcile conflicting interests of public service and advanced telecommunications services. According to the Must Carry rules required by the Plan, cable networks had to provide all public broadcasting channels. Other rules determined that local programming had to be part of a system's capacity; foreign channels could occupy up to 30 percent of a system's capacity; films could be shown only three years after their release to public broadcasting networks; and 60 percent of the films shown had to come from the European Community and 50 percent from French-speaking countries.

The Cable Plan did not succeed, however, and by the end of the 1980s cable's development was also marginal. It was not until policy changes were enacted and commercial considerations gained a dominating influence on the broadcasting policy that the requirement for Must Carry channels and programming were eliminated and French cable became commercialized.

Process along the same lines took place in Germany as well. But because of the constitutional complexities and the control of the local states over broadcasting, Germany was one of few countries that even attempted to go beyond the Must Carry rules. According to the agreement instituted after the Second World War, broadcasting comes under the authority of the German states, and all other telecommunications aspects, including broadcasting facilities, are the responsibility of the Bundespost. The Must Carry rules were intended to ensure the continuity of the national and states' broadcasting systems.

The conflict of interests between Socialist and Conservative states over the content of cable programming delayed cable developments. The Conservative administration wanted cable and satellite to compete with public broadcasters in order to resolve two main problems: the shortage of over-the-air frequencies and the control of the states over the transmissions received within their boundaries. But in practice, the Must Carry rules imposed by Socialist states made the development of cable virtually impossible. The situation changed after four pilot projects started in 1984 and an agreement among all states was reached in 1987. The agreement established the commercial nature of German cable by permitting transmissions to be received across the country. This meant the de facto elimination of the Must Carry rules imposed by states and the practical adoption of commercial perceptions.[3]

Pilot Projects

Another important aspect that emphasizes the social and cultural perception of European cable relates to cable pilot projects. This perception required prior experimentation to test major aspects of the proposed infrastructure, and pilot projects took place in all three largest media countries. They aimed to test new technologies and assess the social and cultural impact of cable television on a given environment, before the actual establishment of new infrastructure.

The most elaborate experiment, with sophisticated applications of telecommunications, occurred in France. The Biarritz project, which began at the end of 1979, was the most advanced experiment in Europe, with new applications that ventured into areas such as motion video services and video-telephony. This project aimed at the construction of a fiber optic system as part of the official interest in establishing a multiservice network that would provide two-way capability in the form of images, high-fidelity sound, voice, and data of the public network while giving France a competitive economic advantage via early research and development.

The project was also intended to provide industrial benefits and to create a cultural revolution by enabling France to move its industry into the construction of a national broadband videocommunications network. The policy sought to take advantage of a growing demand for audiovisual services and telecommunications, in order to accelerate the installation and interconnection of local networks. The lessons learned from the experience helped in the development of the Cable Plan that was initiated in 1982. Following the Biarritz project and the launch of the Cable Plan, many cities and systems asked to join the huge national project, and in May 1984 the PTT announced that 133 urban areas, representing four million households, had officially applied to be cabled. The initial response was enthusiastic, but it soon faded away, after it became clear to many cities that the establishment of advanced technology was too expensive and that public response was insufficient. By the end of

1984 it appeared that this policy had not succeeded, and that cable experiments were stagnating while nonpilot projects were starting to develop rapidly.

Germany also put high priority on experimenting with cable, although the primary reason was not to build an advanced industry as in France, but to mediate the different policies of the German states. Experiments with advanced technology started after the Federal government decided on an ambitious program to install new technologies and to test the feasibility of a wide range of new telecommunications services. Cable was a primary concern in this development, and the launch of pilot projects matched the social and cultural role of media policy. The cable experiments took place under an agreement among the German states. They were aimed at testing the various aspects of cable, including the social, cultural, technological, political and commercial nature of future developments, prior to the full implementation of the industry on a nationwide basis.

The pilot projects started in 1984, in four major German cities. Two of the projects—in Dortmund and West Berlin—were situated in Socialist-controlled states and the other two—in Munich and Ludwigshafen—in Conservative-controlled states. The first two projects were directed entirely by public broadcasters because the ruling governments in these states were opposed to private television. The project in Dortmund tested the possibility of extending the existing public broadcasting services, and the project in Berlin tested the implications of interactive services. In the other two projects a large part of the marketing was privately controlled. The Ludwigshafen experiment was coordinated by a public organization. It offered 24 channels and had permission for offer private programming. The project in Munich was coordinated under the authority to the Bavarian Broadcasting Corporation. It offered 16 channels and was advertiser-supported. The goal of this experiment was to open up the market to private programming producers.

In practical terms, the objectives of the pilot projects were to study viewer responses to the new services and to assess the effects of the services on social life, the family and local communities. They also examined the impact on existing broadcasting channels, the press, and cinema. The projects concentrated mainly on signing up single houses as the best target market and encountered a number of technical problems.

The overall impact of the pilot projects was noteworthy in Germany, as the experiences gained were very helpful to the cabling of the country. These initiatives marked the entry of private industry into the delivery of television programming and had long-term implications for the future development of the new media infrastructure. On the basis of the pilot projects the Bundespost formulated an approach that aimed to increase the number of cable subscribers as rapidly as possible through the expansion of existing systems and the use of a well-tested technology, thereby abandoning the intention to establish interactive networks. Several cooperative cable projects started after the first cable experiments, with private firms or communities doing the cabling. The Bundespost tried to standardize these cable systems in order to lay the foundations for an institutionalized national network.

Britain also initiated pilot projects, but adopted a less enthusiastic approach than France and Germany in terms of testing the prospects for new technologies. The significance of pilot projects in Britain is of no less weight, however, because despite its policy of letting the market determine the pace of new developments the government played an active role in experimenting with cable systems.

One of the most important aspects of the industrial strategy for cable was the government's readiness to license a limited number of pilot projects before the creation of the Cable Authority. This was required to provide a real indication of the government's commitment to the future development of cable systems and to take full advantage of the interest and enthusiasm of the market for cable.

In 1984 the government invited applications for 12 pilot licenses to build new systems. Thirty-seven applications were submitted and 11 were awarded franchises. The process was constructed as a test of the degree of private-sector interest in the development of cable, particularly in view of the financial risks involved, and the results justified the government decision to launch a cable plan. Another step prior to legislation concerned the existing narrow-band cable systems that served 1.4 million households. Operators were invited to submit applications to provide up to four new channels over the systems. These two initiatives enabled companies to move ahead with cabling; stimulated the design and production of more advanced equipment and new programming; and provided a better view of the market. This was a combination of new systems and new services aimed at building up the audience level required to justify investment in new cable construction.[4]

6.2 GLOBAL MEDIA CULTURE

As can be seen from the foregoing discussion, commercialization has been an issue for debate around the world, and so has been the threat to local cultures from an increase in foreign programming. Whereas in the early phases of broadcasting social and cultural perceptions dominated media policies, following the change of perceptions from public service to commercial domination, local distinctions were no longer a powerful force, as they once were.

Policy changes have been implemented with the adoption of new media policies, changing the relationship between cultural issues and technology advancement. This development confirms that expansion of new media technologies and policy revision leading to commercialization had their impact on broadcasting policies and media systems around the world. The resulting changing nature of policy means that globalization dominates the present course of development of media systems, and that global media has become a major force for reconstruction of media markets.

The global impact on local societies has been the focus of a wide range of research. It is commonly agreed that globalization offers a vast increase in the numbers of channels available, together with options for a wide range of advanced services, provided on a global scale. But the extent is related to the relative impact of global economy, global culture and global politics.

Three major developments have established the new structure of global media culture: the triumph of market forces and the global need for free flow of information; the diminished role of governments and increased role of international organizations; and the spread of global media systems and advanced technology. The result is that globalization has become the main force in the development of media markets, bringing into play the effects of global economy, global culture and global politics.

The impact of global economy is examined in relation to the integration of new technology and global markets, a process that has largely caused the globalization of television broadcasting. This takes place when the same television signal becomes available simultaneously in a large number of countries.[5] It involves several commercial factors: the intention of broadcasters to reach a larger audience; the flow of capital and investment funds across frontiers; and deregulation and cooperation of broadcasters and regulators.

The cultural impact is examined following the development of common cultural markets and the transformation of technology and culture. This approach takes into consideration the cultural aspect of globalization and defines the global flow of information as the transnational proliferation of mass market advertising and entertainment, which affects most if not all human beings and stretches out to all parts of the world.

A new politics is developing with globalization, as new technology and communications are stretched across the globe creating a recomposition of social relationship. Global politics involves the triumph of leading global regulatory institutions over local regulators and interest groups. Through global networks of information, it encourages global issues to become more important than local issues derived by the growing impact of the global media.

Global Economy

Global economy has evolved as a result of common financial markets and the expansion of global media services. The new structure of global economy has been the result of three major developments:

1. *The Triumph of Market Forces and The Global Need for Free Flow of Information.*   The counterrelations between global media services and global economy and markets have changed the traditional role of governments as a central force in domestic and foreign affairs. This development has created uniform markets for the distribution of economic flows and products, dominated by commercial atmosphere and acceptance of market rule. The result of this change in perspective and commercial operation is that multinational corporations dominate the new global media market. These forces advocate a free market and competitive approach under which differences among nations diminish.

The commercial environment created globally is also supported by local societies, which adopt new policies of liberalization and capitalism. The development of global markets has been widely supported, as local societies enthusiastically adopted American and global commercial environments and the availability of new opportunities in new markets.

The effects of global economy create a new and more equal structure of global trade in which consumers are able to purchase cheaper products through new markets. New opportunities are also available for the distribution of products to global markets. This includes opportunities for local manufacturers to compete with multinational companies through the advent of information technology and global services.

The development of global media networks can be measured in the transfer of influence to international financial institutions, which has encouraged swift technological development. The forces that develop and control technological developments are financial institutions and market forces with global interests guided by financial rather than national interests. Their global operation is made possible with the combination of global media services and other key factors: improvement in production, growth of population, growth in the consumption of energy and information, development of global trade, improvement in transportation, and the consequent growth of tourism. In this way globalization has become the dominating drive in the growth of media markets offering new opportunities for economic change.

The links between global economy and global media services illustrate the change from a social and cultural policy to the globalization of financial markets. The use of global economy allows operation in different exchange rates, around the clock, in different timetables, without geographical barriers, and with no bureaucratic limitations. The impact of local authorities has diminished because each product can be manufactured according to benefits provided by local governments and local policies and then distributed to specific markets. This demonstrates that the impact of global economy has become more influential than local political and financial institutions, and that global trade has no limits in terms of production and distribution of goods and services.

Global media services have had an important role in the establishment and growing impact of global markets. The "domino effect" of stock markets around the world is related to the fact that a growing number of companies have global operations. In this way changes in local markets have implications for global economy flows. Since information is available constantly and around the clock, though on-line services and television channels dedicated to financial news, local markets can operate within a common market which is being driven particularly by global media services and advanced technology.

2. A Diminished Role of Governments and Increased Role of International Organizations.   Global economy and the globalization of media markets have also swamped local media policies. With the addition of commercial outlets, the role of public television organizations has changed broadcasting and media policies. In all advanced countries, the primary source of income of public broadcasting—the license fee—was not sufficient to withstand the growing competition of commercial outlets. Public channels had to rely on advertising to operate in the new competitive environment as the increased number of competitors and the parallel weakening of public broadcasting forced them to adopt a more commercial outlook both in advertising and commercial-type programming.

The inevitable changes in the nature of public broadcasting services can be seen as part of the growing impact of market forces and global economy. This trend has changed the relations between local markets and established the course of the media sector as one of commercialization and globalization. The shift has particularly gone from perceptions dominated by social and cultural aspects to a market-led industry dominated by commercial considerations and technological advancement, thus creating common markets of technologies and programming dominated by global economy flows and market forces.

Changes are also the result of international investments in media products and services. The globalization of new media markets and technologies has been propelled by the fact that American interest in other markets has been reinforced since the early 1990s, as opportunities for expansion in the United States seemed to be exhausted and profits came under pressure. The growth in investments was a response to the perceived imperatives of the increasing globalization of markets and the intensification of global competition, as the promise of multiple broadcasting channels revivified the prospect of public policy with a potential for global reach.

The triumph of capitalism and the fall of communist regimes also contributed to globalization and to the growing role of global media in developing markets. Commercialization has become a common policy structure in all countries, including those that previously relied on public broadcasting as a leading system; governments could not oppose the growing demand for commercialization and the increased role of global economy.

3. The Spread of Global Media Systems and Advanced Technology. The combination of global markets and global media services stem from the availability of advanced communication technologies such as satellites, computers, the Internet, videoconferences, telephone, fax, and e-mail. These services are not restricted by time and place and influence global economy flows dominated mainly by American programming and firms.

In addition to the distribution of programming and the spread of investments, American domination is evident in advanced technology, which is based on the Internet economy. The Internet is dominated by American influence in terms of language, contents, culture, and economic operations. The way new products are distributed to new frontiers is also based on American marketing and advertising conceptions. In this way global values have, to some extent, become more influential than local imperatives, and they are changing the nature and uses of technological advancement and economic developments. One of the fastest-growing services is business-to-business (B2) online trade between businesses. The market is expected to grow from $406 million in 2000 to $2.7 billion in 2004.[6] Another estimate is that business-to-business will reach $7.4 billion in 2004.[7] According to a study released by Anderson Consulting,[8] American businesses generate the lion share of worldwide electronic commerce revenue. American operations generate 67 percent of global business-to-business and 76 percent of business-to-customer revenue, compared with Europe's 14 percent share.

Around the world e-commerce revenues reached $132 billion in 2000, and are expected to grow to nearly $2000 billion annually during the first decade of the 21st century.[9]

Another growing industry converging in telephone, wireless communications, and the Internet, is mobile e-commerce. The new service of m-commerce combines the growing wireless market and Internet adoption to deliver access to the Web anywhere around the world, and thus to create a whole new industry that did not exist in previous decades.

The figures show the great potential of mobile e-commerce, the number of mobile devices in use will exceed the 1 billion mark by 2003 and a large proportion of these devices is capable of m-commerce. The service is important to a wide range of industries and end users, and provides the convenience and flexibility of mobility. Predictions are that by 2005 mobile e-commerce users will reach 33 percent in Western Europe, 26 percent in Asia-Pacific, 22 percent in North America, 6 percent in Central and South America, 6 percent in Central Asia, 4 percent in the Middle East and Africa, and 3 percent in Central and Eastern Europe.[10]

The entire mobile data market is also expected to grow, at an annual rate of 21.5 percent, from less than $10 billion in 2000 to over $20 billion in 2004 and up to almost $40 billion in 2007.[11]

The globalization of television and the growth of global economy provide the means for the rise of a new service of television commerce. Due to the popularity of television services, t-commerce is expected to top e-commerce. According to estimates, television services around the world should generate $20 billion by 2004: $11 billion from advertising, $7 from commerce, and $2 billion from subscriptions. It is also estimated that there will be 150 million interactive television households in the United States and Europe in 2004, compared to 10 million in 1998.[12]

These figures demonstrate the tremendous change in the economics of television broadcasting in less than a decade. Whereas at the end of the 20th century revenues were only from broadcasting services (advertising and subscription), by the start of the 21st century revenues almost doubled with the addition of new services. With the move of Internet information into technologies other than the computer, such as television and cellular phones, financial applications will create a new industrial revolution of the global economy.[13]

Global Culture

The concept of global culture refers to the formation of cultural values common to different societies. These values are distributed through global media networks and local television channels that transmit programming with global impact and reach. The vast increase in the number of channels available, together with options for a wide range of advanced technological and information services provided on a global scale, have changed the relations between technological advancement and cultural aspects in broadcasting. The impact of global media culture has followed the growth of new technologies to the extent that common media markets dominate the current state of development of new media and telecommunications services.

The new structure of global culture has been the result of three major developments:

1. The Triumph of Market Forces and the Global Need for Free Flow of Information. The main avenues of the distribution of global culture through global media services are television programs and cultural products. The overall impact of these powerful forces has created tremendous changes in local cultures. Television programs spread new commercial values and stimulate the purchase of commercial products. They encourage the adoption of liberalization and deregulation policies and capitalism as the leading form of democratic life, with the result that cultural products are being adopted by societies that consider the values that these products symbolize as serving their interests.

The new global environment of free speech and the proliferation of programming and culture across the globe has created cultural characteristics common to many societies. This process has established a global society in which global issues are considered more important than national values and social unity. In this atmosphere, the distribution of cultural products and television programming by multinational corporations is aimed at influencing local societies.

The cultural impact of global media is evident in that the same programming and some of the same programming services are available simultaneously in many countries. They bypass the authority of local governments by providing transmissions and reception of channels not in their country of origin, and they are operated by international broadcasting organizations. The content of global media services offers a dominant structure that includes competitive and commercial transmissions, live transmissions around the clock and programs with characteristics which are common to a large number of countries (such as: news, sports, music, entertainment, fashion, science and movies).

In this process, global media products (programming and cultural trends) can be supplied to a growing number of countries. Global media services aim at a global audience with no geographical or national borders and no political, religious, social, cultural, or other differences. The international and global flows of cultural products are helped by the fact that cultural distinctions and political singularities have become less powerful than the free flow of information and that the spread of capitalism is making an impact on all societies.

Global media culture is also making an impact on the nature of broadcasting in all countries. The development of media and broadcasting systems has influenced the development of global technologies involving competition of all information services—broadcast television, cable TV, satellite services, telephone companies, and digitalization.

The global impact on local markets is particularly relevant in this process, because these services have a growing number of outlets to choose from and a growing number of channels that are in need of programming.

The spread of global culture includes nontraditional values and implies common lifestyles of food, fashion, music, entertainment, tourism, and consumption of television programs, which dominate the global flow of information and entertainment. In contrast, more traditional values such as religion, language, and local symbols have remained within the boundaries of local cultures.

The spread of nontraditional values is supported by a large number of influential forces. The shift of policy in favor of deregulation and the transformation into global cultural markets benefits consumers by providing them with lower rates and better service than they would experience under heavily regulated or nonmarket systems. This trend reflects the concerns of the two main actors in policy debates—business corporations, as they seek to position themselves strategically in fast-changing markets, and governments, which are attempting to secure future national wealth by attracting investment. Thus, the growing impact of global culture is supported locally because the diffusion of democracy and capitalism opens up new markets and establishes the globalization of culture and markets.

At the global level of policy, a new form of global culture was established through the diffusion of programming across cultural boundaries and the convergence of cultural policies and technological developments. Such global operations aim at all countries. They capitalize new markets and regard all countries as potential customers of a single global market. Their powers stem from their ability to influence different countries with the same messages and products, operating simultaneously in all markets through global media services. For that reason, the impact of global culture can also be defined as cultural imperialism and media imperialism.

Cultural imperialism is defined as the domination of media cultural products and cultural values delivered across media systems through new media and telecommunications services—creating the globalization of media markets. Media imperialism is transmitted through global media networks, which supply programming to local channels and ignore local institutions by transmitting global television programs.

2. The Diminished Role of Governments and Increased Role of International Organizations. Global culture has changed the traditional role of government as the main provider of information and a key player in protecting local culture and local programming. At the same time, there is a concern that globalization is not necessarily an even playing field. While some cultures will dominate the world, the survival and the accessibility of certain cultures may diminish because of the power, money and access that large global corporations have.

A well-known issue for public debate in different societies is the effect of new technologies on native and local culture. Because commercial television has been developed mainly in the United States, there is a growing recognition that global culture transformed through television has become another tool of American cultural dominance.

American domination of the global television market is a key factor in the rise of global culture and the reason why countries outside the United States feel the need to encourage local television production. In many countries the issue of cultural preservation and domestic content in programming is regarded as the provenance of the national public broadcaster, and the rest of the market is free to provide content as it wishes.

There are three main factors favoring American television companies and leading to American domination of the global television market. These include market size, the dominant status of the English language, and the nature of the American market.

The size of the American market makes it generally cheaper for television channels in other markets to buy programs than make them, because programs are already sold to a vast American audience and can then be sold at far less than it cost to make them outside the United States. Buying already successful programs involves little or no risk and can be done at far less cost than the risky and difficult business of making local programs.

The single (and international) language of American programming—English—is another advantage. American culture and language are relatively familiar to people around the world, and have advantages in diversity of content, popularity, and impact on audiences at both local and global levels. The higher number of viewers for a global production provides possibilities for global distribution of products and global advertising campaigns.

The competitiveness of the American market means that American dominance is self-sustaining in that it ensures the higher availability of skilled and experienced personal. Higher level of competition also makes programs available for purchase around the world. American companies are also more commercially oriented than in other markets and have in place a global distribution system.

In addition to television, with the advent of new technology the Internet is also considered an American technological tool that encourages Western cultural supremacy. Although it gives small communities the opportunity to keep their traditions viable, not all communities and certainly not all economies can afford to have all their members online. Accordingly, many communities perceive the Internet as a dominating technology beyond the reach of the mass, as the vast majority of the users are Western-educated elites whose primary use is to access Western-based information.

According to the International Telecommunications Union, 99 percent of all global Internet traffic is routed through the United States, and a significant proportion of the global traffic is picking up American content. Similar predictions are that even with high-speed Internet access and broadband technology the cultural dominance of foreign content will remain, making the Internet a symbol of American cultural supremacy that forces global culture and influence on less-powered individuals, communities, and governments.[14]

3. The Spread of Global Media Systems and Advanced Technology. The powerful aspects of global culture have been intensified by the rise of new technology, which is readily available and inexpensive to use. The Internet, telephones, fax machines, cellular phones, and e-mail open up new markets with global reach in which information is accessible and convenient to everyone at all times. The important role of availability also refers to people themselves, who can be reached everywhere around the world without relevance to their actual location, the country they live in, or their workplace.

Globalization of television programming has made the world a global village both virtual and real, one that in many ways becomes more unified and more able to find connection with cultures that we may never visit or see or which are distinct from our way of life, and one that draws the world more closely together.

As culture becomes global and technology changes the business, political, and social infrastructure, information and information-based technologies also become global. It is estimated that 66 percent of Internet users and 40 percent of e-commerce revenue will come from outside the United States. In addition, global marketing should concentrate on languages other than English, as almost half of Internet users around the world already come from non-English-speaking countries.[15]

The Internet is changing the way global culture is perceived. It is a global network tied together by a common language, Internet Protocol (IP), which routes packages of data across the network. The economic importance of the Internet is undisputed, as more and more people around the world are now relying on the World Wide Web for information and commerce. Internet companies are becoming increasingly important economic forces, as can be seen by the merger of AOL and Time Warner.

As television and the Internet are converging, rather than competing, companies are seeking a winning combination of old and new media—that is, traditional television services and Internet services. A growing number of broadcasters are offering an enormous amount of information and entertainment services on Web sites and starting to distribute this content through digital television services.

The introduction of multiple interactive services, such as Web browsing, e-commerce, and video-on-demand, will provide new sources of revenue for television broadcasters and will eventually develop into an influential t-commerce industry. According to a study by Forrester Research, the personal computer will dominate 80 percent of the European online e-commerce market, wireless technologies will achieve a market share of 3 percent, and interactive television will maintain 16 percent. According to the research, the strength of television lies in its capabilities as a mass-audience-oriented medium with strong emotional power and easy access, suitable for information delivery and the provision of interactive services. Most people, however, will still use television as a passive entertainment medium, and interactive services will be a second source of income for television broadcasters.[16]

Global Politics

The growing impact of global media has also established the concept of global politics. This concept has become meaningful to the way political institutions operate at the local and global level because with the advent of new technology political developments and global values are being transmitted by international organizations through global media networks. The effects of this process indicate that global political trends have become more powerful than the role of national governments.

The new structure of global politics has been the result of three major developments:

1. *The Triumph of Market Forces and the Global Need for Free Flow of Information.* The most relevant factor that determines the extent of global politics is the free flow of information at the global level of policy. The changed nature of media markets and the addition of a large number of commercial channels have reinforced the influence of commercial forces and forced public broadcasting service organizations into a much more competitive stance.

In the new environment of global politics, multinational companies encourage commercialization and liberalization of media systems and provide television programming that encourages democracy and free speech—making an impact on local political systems. This is also manifest in the fact that reduced public funding of public broadcasters makes them reluctant to invest in advanced technology. In contrast, the interests of policymakers and financial groups, who have separately identified new media and telecommunications as strategic areas, constitute a powerful coalition for policy changes on a global scale.

The role of new technologies has been crucial in the transformation into global policy. Cable and satellite have removed the traditional barriers caused by the scarcity of frequencies and provided a point of entry for new investors and new markets. This was coupled with deregulation policies that expanded the range of delivery services available on the one hand, and diminished the role of governments on the other, by reducing rules that limit market competition and opening the market to new service providers.

According to this analysis, which examines the relative impact of global media on local media markets, policy changes included privatization, commercialization, and globalization of new media markets. The political consequences of globalization have been influenced by the spread of commercialization around the world, and this process followed the growing impact of new media technologies and cultural change.

Local policies have been influenced by technology advancement, as the development of new politics for the broadcast media has been an intensification of the debate about the role of public service principles within a market-led and multichannel media. The further political impact can be measured in the questions that new media technologies have raised about the social and cultural aspects of broadcasting. This assumption can be examined by looking at the extent of adoption of globalization by local media markets. Although the globalization of new media markets differs in response to the combination of global and cultural trends, there have been common results to the impact of global politics. The factors affecting the free flow of information are competition, commercial motivation, and the degree of cultural similarity between the producing and receiving countries.

Following this direction, it can be concluded that when looking at the local and global factors that are shaping the nature of media policy, it is imperative to investigate the impact of new technologies on global media changes. Examination of the overall impact of global media on the globalization of local media markets leads to the conclusion that the transition from a social and cultural perception is proving to be the key aspect in the globalization of politics, because the results of deregulation policies reflect governments' abilities to balance competing interests as part of the global media culture that influences media policy around the world.

2. *The Diminished Role of Governments and Increased Role of International Organizations.* Another important aspect of global politics is the nature of political supervision over the development of local media systems. Whereas in the early period of broadcasting public service broadcasting organizations had a monopoly status within the boundaries of their country and little competition from abroad, today they face national competition from private and commercial channels and international competition from global channels. Thus, the role of governments and the perceptions of local and global concepts are changing with the triumph of global media. Globalization is not a new concept, but its accessibility and the new opportunities offered by global communications networks are enormous. As local and global cultures are being restructured, it is more and more clear that despite national and social differences, the tasks faced by nations in a global world must change accordingly.

The role of governments is changing quickly following the communications revolution. The state as a provider of direct services is diminishing, but its role as an enabler and regulator is increasing. Under the new structure of media policy, the role of governments is to make sure that local societies develop in a global world and local cultures and traditions are maintained.

The responsibilities of governments are also changing, because local institutions have to be responsible to the needs of the community while operating within a global marketplace. Some of the services traditionally provided by governments are becoming the responsibility of local institutions. These services end up being provided by the not-for-profit sector under government regulation or guidance, rather than by the state itself (as was common in most countries during the 20th century).

The communications revolution is also making it difficult for local monopolies to survive. Public service broadcasting and local telecom monopolies cannot dominate (or in some countries even exist) in a global world dominated by new technology, because new technologies provide global service, although their content and services must be tailored to local cultures too.

Accordingly, the triumph of global media and global politics requires a new approach. If a country is to have an advantage in the information age, its people need to have an effective infrastructure— particularly, an effective information technology infrastructure. Such infrastructure involves common technological, economic, political, and cultural issues, because localization develops in line with and within the boundaries of globalization and sometimes involves the crossing of international boundaries into the creation of regional issues and culture. Local and regional networks, as opposed to global media culture, could develop on an ad hoc basis, or they could be deliberately initiated to strengthen economies and cultures operating in a global world.

The scope of new policies has been shaped by the interplay between strategic government departments and a handful of key companies. Local forces are required to deal with new global markets, in which no sole competitor is capable of controlling decision making and the range of competing participants requires local authorities to monitor the demands of all relevant interest groups. International political institutions, such as the United Nations or the European Community, which use global communications networks, have also contributed to the domination of global politics. In the new atmosphere of global media, issues of local politics have global consequences and concerns. Thus, political debates can no longer be considered as restricted to local impact. Rather, they have to be taken into account as part of the larger (and global) political conflict between capitalism and socialism.

In terms of the global media, the conflict between capitalism and socialism can be translated to the debate between commercial and social and cultural media policy. Media services represent different political views while approaching target audiences, and in this way international organizations and global media services can dominate global politics. They also influence local political systems, which are forced to operate within the global scene.

3. The Spread of Global Media Systems and Advanced Technology. On the whole, discussion about globalization is still a topic debated predominantly at the economic and business levels, although the combination of globalization and the increasingly powerful information society offers many opportunities for improved access to information to individuals. This process involves new technology, because the influence of commercialization and global advertising on the nature of programming has increased following the development of new competitive markets with global reach. Technology is particularly relevant to this process, because advancement led to a shift of power in the new competitive environment.

The direct consequence is that new technology changes global politics. It possesses the power to make information, education, and knowledge accessible to local cultures as a global property within which everyone can compete economically.

The transfer of information across global networks has become essential following the information revolution, which is being distributed through a growing number of information networks with global reach. These services include radio and television outlets dedicated to news programming, operating locally or globally, which supply constant and immediate information about political events and current affairs. Other important services are local channels and newspapers, which supply selected relevant information. Advanced technology also offers information that can be distributed globally through the Internet, videoconferences, satellites, telephone, fax, and e-mail services.

The importance of information services to global politics is that global media networks require the exchange of information between societies and the free flow of information. Because of this, global media have prevailed, as media services controlled by governments have lost their ability to provide the information required by the existence of global politics.

This politics requires a new definition of the role of global networking. As mergers between telecommunications providers and media giants continue, the fear of American and European regulators alike is that a handful of companies could dominate the Internet and corner the communications sector. Another concern is that control over global television broadcasting, and as a result over global commerce and global culture, will remain in the hands of few content providers, thus creating global networks of information and entertainment dominated by a small number of single carriers.[17]

6.3 GLOBAL INFORMATION SUPERHIGHWAY

The global structure of media markets is identified by the leading role of market forces and the race to establish new global links. New information technologies are driving global networking forward and fundamentally changing business, society, and politics. Globalization is considered the biggest impact that the new technological revolution is having in terms of media policy.

The advent of new technology has revolutionized the globe, putting power in the hands of individuals and making it harder for governments to control people, technological developments, and global processes. Today technology leaps over borders, currencies, cultures, and politics, and concepts of nationality, customs, and heritage are threatened by new realities of global policy.

Further implications of the triumph of new technology are that digital television will become a medium combining broadcasting and interactivity and the global information superhighway will dominate global media policy. This term was initially brought up by Al Gore in the first Clinton/Gore presidential campaign in 1992 and later was picked up by governments and national telecommunications companies.

The globalization of media policy provides the means for society to enter a new era dominated by information and new technology. The information society, driven by the global information superhighway and the triumph of digital services, is based on the convergence of broadcasting and telecommunications, because interactivity is supplied through computers, satellites, and fiber optics cables. The ability to provide unlimited information at low cost, anytime, anywhere, and in many languages offers the opportunity to combine global and local markets. Global competition requires reaching smaller markets based on groups—ethnic, professional, religious, economic—and other niche markets that are not separated by geographical boundaries. The links that information technology establishes between globalization and localism allow the building of global networks that can be expanded and strengthened through information exchange and the global integration of economic, cultural, and political issues.

This revolution is considered the foremost principle in the development of new technology in the 21st century. For the first time in history globalization has conquered distance and time worldwide and given business, news, and entertainment the ability to arrive at destinations anywhere at any time. National identity and culture mean different things as information, entertainment, and culture move around the world and develop audiences that are no longer of a given country but of a transnational culture.

Knowledge is becoming available to everyone, and this revolution is changing the state of the market economy and world trade. A completely different civilization is being established—knowledge-based societies—and that has created the globalization of communications. The media are increasingly becoming a global phenomenon, and the political climate is changing as global coverage becomes important for the global society. In this vast and unbroken network of communications, information, news, and entertainment, new communities are being created— bound not by geography but by common interests.

The information society has enormous implications for global media culture, which rises to meet the demand of progress. For business, success in the global marketplace is dependent upon strong communications networks and the expertise to use them effectively. For governments, sophisticated telecommunications and electronic systems can spell the difference between economic growth and stagnation. Today one cannot imagine a world without the centrality of communications, and telecommunications is the driving force behind the development of countries.

Nations are also tremendously transformed. If a country has an efficient telecommunications system, it improves economic growth prospects remarkably. But if a country has no decent telecommunications system, it becomes isolated from other advanced countries and from global processes, because traditional systems are not able to provide the new forms of telecommunications that are important for large and sophisticated users. The general economy of those countries suffers because the new technology operations and information essential for global markets cannot be operated competitively with the rest of the world.

The information society is influencing global politics, too. People are now in a situation where they are fully used to seeing events unfolding around the world in real time, as global media services allow direct linkage between viewers and events. Seeing world historical events live, not only through reports but with our own eyes, as they happened, allows the citizens of every country to venture out into a larger community that includes news, music, television, and movies—creating new global markets of common political issues.

The knowledge-based society is similarly based on global culture, which is changing the concept of localism. The cultural aspects of information technology create a new social order in which information can be delivered without geographical boundaries and political direction or control. Because information is available in all countries and to all people, it offers opportunities for equal participation in the cultural flows that make up the new social order. These important changes in the supply of information are making an impact on the way people live, communicate, think, make a living, and purchase essential and cultural products. With the availability of advanced technology, this process offers opportunities to create new global markets with common cultural values in which new actors can become dominant.

The role of the communications revolution in the welfare of countries is tremendous. Global forces and the power of new technology spur global links. European media companies are forming cross-border links, as continental media are building the power of continental politics, and American giants are buying into the action, establishing global links of new technology and media forces. The resulting corporate alliances of European and American technological and economical forces encourage the development of global cultural forces, because commercial channels and advertisers can reach wider mass audiences.

The commercial media world is dominated by a small number of companies that have created global networks. Most of these are American-based corporations, which have become globally oriented and are involved in all media industries worldwide, both globally and locally in different countries.

These companies control all segments of the media and telecom-munications industries, including telephone companies, television sta-tions, cable systems and satellite operations, film production, television shows production, ownership of radio stations, the Internet, book pub-lishing, magazine and newspaper publishing, music production, as well as retail stores, amusement parks, and the like. Their corporate interests are to promote global markets and commercial values, so that their media and commercial products can be distributed to a growing number of countries. On average, whereas by the start of the 1990s media giants generated about 15 percent of their income outside the United States, today the majority of their business is done abroad.[18]

The internationalization of media businesses through global net-works and the integration of broadcast and telecommunications sectors have forced major joint ventures and mergers between media and telecommunications service providers since the start of the last decade.

Consolidation between media and telecommunications compa-nies across national lines is required for several main reasons:

1. To share the heavy costs of new media and telecommunica-tions equipment.
2. To generate the massive increase in programming for new channels and services.
3. To create common markets and be able to compete with other giants.
4. To allow advertisers to centralize their sales and reach global or multinational markets.
5. To achieve common standards for broadcasting, technology, regulatory, economic, and cultural issues.
6. To advance opportunities to become multi-service providers.
7. To get ready for the next generation of digital technology, in which the Internet would be a mainstream media and interac-tive television would dominate.

Some of the major telecommunications and media mergers and joint ventures include deals that involve American telephone operators. Others involve telephone, broadcast, and cable ventures and still others include a combination of old and new media, including the Internet.

The largest mergers in the American telecommunications mar-ket in recent years have involved global deals. Following the merger of the second- and third-largest long-distance companies in America, MCI and Worldcom, the combined corporation asked permission to merge with another major Baby Bell, Sprint Corporation, for $129 billion. Together the companies dominate the American long-distance telephone and fixed wireless markets; American and European regulators denied the merger. Prior to that decision regulators also denied MCI acquisition by British Telecom for $20 billion. Another former European PTT trying to enter the American market is Deutsche Telecom, with the approval of its $50 billion acquisition of American wireless company VoiceStreem (which operates in the European GSM system). Japan's state-controlled NTT (Nippon Telegraph and Telephone) also entered the American market by purchasing the Internet service provider Verio Inc. for $5.5 billion.

In other deals that involve telephone companies, SBC Communications (Southern Bell) acquired the Ameritech Corporation for $72.36 billion and Pacific Telesis (including Pacific Bell) for $16.7 billion, Bell Atlantic merged with GTE Corporation for $71.32 billion and with Nynex for $27.7 billion. In Europe, Vodafone acquired Mannesmann for $226.10 billion (the biggest acquisition ever) and Airtouch for $61.4 billion, to create Europe's largest telecom group with access to 42 million customers in 15 countries. Another competitor in the wireless market is France Telecom, which acquired Orange, UK mobile and international phone company, for $35.4 billion. France Telecom also purchased 25 percent of NTL, United Kingdom's largest cable company.

The broadcast industry is experiencing mergers between content providers and television networks. In America, giant media corporations have purchased two of the largest three networks. The Walt Disney Company acquired Capital Cities/ABC for $19 billion, and Viacom acquired CBS for $36 billion. In Europe, United News and Media and Carlton Communications merged, creating the largest commercial broadcasting group in the United Kingdom, with six ITV franchises covering 65 percent of Britain's homes.

Consolidation of traditional media services and new technologies have become common among all major global media and telecommunications firms. The merger of America On-Line and Time Warner is a mix of traditional and new media. It is driving the next Internet-television revolution, in which the Internet will become a mass-market consumer service that is easy to use and brings the new technology into the familiar television screen. Without cable or other form of broadband delivery, AOL faced the possibility of being left behind as the Internet moved to full video and sound transmission.

The $183 billion merger is the biggest in history. It combines new media and old media to create a company with holdings in a broad range of communications industries: Internet service provider, broadband cable systems, cable channels, movie and television production, publishing, and magazines. It represents the transformation of the Internet into a mass-marketed medium, with Internet access expanding beyond the personal computer through new technologies of telephone, cable, and broadcast television.

Time Warner was formed in 1989 through the merger of Time Inc. and Warner Communications. In 1995 it acquired Turner Broadcasting (including CNN) for $75.7 billion, creating the world's largest entertainment company. Time Warner is a major provider of television broadcasting and cable services. It is the second largest cable operator in the United States, with 13 million customers and control of 22 of the largest 100 markets. Its television channels reach more than 70 million subscribers in the United States. These include CNN, Headline News, CNNfn, CNN-SI, TBS, TNT, Turner Classic Movies, Cartoon Network, and NY1. The premium channels—HBO and Cinemax—reach 39 million subscribers. Some of these channels have local reach as well. It also holds local television stations with a reach of 25 percent of American households.

Time Warner's other media properties include films studios and movie screens around the world, libraries of films, television programs, books, music, cartoons, and magazines. It publishes leading magazines, including *Time, People, Sports Illustrated, Fortune, Life, Money, Parenting, In Style, Entertainment Weekly, Cooking Light, Baby Talk, Coastal Living, Health, Progressive Farmer, Southern Living, The Old House, Teen People,* and *Wallpaper*. It owns the second-largest book publishing business in the world, one of the largest global music businesses in the world, and retail stores of Warner Bros and Turner Retail Group.

America OnLine is the largest Internet service provider in the world, with 30 million subscribers. The merger creates a tremendous global mogul that controls all sectors of the media. It gives the combined company access to Time Warner entertainment and information libraries to be delivered on the Internet, thus offering interactive television applications. On the basis of this merger, all traditional media properties of Time Warner are expected to go into the Internet—including movies, television broadcasting, print, and music.

The deal proves that all parts of media services are no longer exclusive spheres and that Internet services are suited for mainstream audiences, using the advent of broadband, high-speed Internet access through cable television, or telephone lines that bring video, audio, and data services.

The second largest global media firm is Disney. It has holdings in television stations around the world: the American network ABC; local radio and television stations in the United States; American and global cable channels, including the Disney Channel, ESPN, ESPN2 and ESPNews, ESPN International, and holdings in Lifetime, A&E, and the History Channel. It is also involved in film, video and television production studios, magazines, newspaper and book publishing, music labels, parks and resorts (Disneyland, Disney World, and stakes in major theme parks in France and Japan), and Disney retail stores.

The third largest global media firm is News Corporation, which owns global television and publishing interests. The firm is identified with the British pay-TV service British Sky Broadcasting (BskyB). It also has major interests in satellite services reaching Asia, Japan, and Latin America under the Sky Broadcasting label. Sky Global Networks is a corporation established in June 2000. It combines the satellite services operated by Sky, which transmits to 85 million subscribers around the world. The network includes the television operations of BSkyB, SkyPerfecTV, Sky Mexico, Sky Brazil, Stream, Star TV, and other media companies, including *TV Guide*.

Additional television holdings of News Corporation include the American national broadcasting network Fox, and American television stations and cable channels, including Family Channel, Fox News Channel, and Fox Sports Net. News Corporation also has film, television, and video production centers; leading newspapers and magazines around the world, including the *London Times* and *New York Post*; and book publishing interests.

Another European media giant is the German Corporation Bertelsman, which owns several television channels in Europe, including RTL and VOX, and local stations across Europe. Its leading television service is Premiere, Germany's largest pay-TV service. It publishes newspapers, magazines, and books, and owns recording studios and record clubs around the world.

A major global entertainment giant is Viacom, which acquired the American network CBS. It holds interests in various leading television channels with global reach, including MTV, VH1, Nickelodeon, and Showtime. It also owns film, video, and television production companies, including Paramount Pictures; a majority holding in Cinemax International; one of the world's largest theater companies; Blockbuster Video—the world's largest video rental stores—book publishers and theme parks.

Consolidation is increasing in every segment of the Internet too, which picks up new users, transmission capacity, and services. The Internet is a new field dominated by large multinational companies, mostly American-based media corporations, which distribute their media products through global networks and markets, thus creating global competition between carriers of converged services (see Table 6.1).

Table 6.1. The Top 10 American Internet Companies
(Including Content, Services and Software but not Equipment Makers)

	Key business	Market capitalization
1. Microsoft	access, ads, e-commerce	$356 billion
2. America-On-Line	access, ads, e-commerce	$12 billion
3. Yahoo	ads, e-commerce	$74 billion
4. Ariba	business-to-business software	$29 billion
5. VeriSign	e-security, domain names	$34 billion
6. Exodus	Web site hosting	$22 billion
7. Ebay	person-to-person auctions	$13.8 billion
8. Amazon	e-commerce	$12.6 billion
9. Inktomi	Web site services	$12.3 billion
10. CMGI	holding company with stakes in Web portals and ad companies	$11.4 billion

Source: *The Washington Post*, July 27, 2000, page ED1.

SUMMARY

Commercialization and globalization have brought about enormous changes in the nature of media markets, which have become dominated by advanced technology and common cultural characteristics. The main changes have been from social and cultural perceptions to a common structure of global policy with a free market approach and commercial competition of all media and telecommunications services.

The globalization of media markets has been implemented according to the three stages of the development of media policy examined in this book. The main course of transition has been from a social and cultural project to a global media culture. Following the triumph of information technologies, policies of all countries have converged with the dominance of free speech and global competition, leading into the establishment of the global information superhighway in the 21st century.

Global media culture encompasses global economy, global culture, and global politics, and is derived by the growing impact of the global media. Global economy is subject to the development of new technology and global markets; global culture is created through common cultural markets and the transformation of technology and culture; and global politics is implemented through global networks of information and global issues common to all advanced countries.

The global structure has evolved as a result of three major developments: the triumph of market forces and the global need for free flow of information; a diminished role of governments and an increased role of international organizations; and the spread of global media systems and advanced technology. Another aspect of globalization is the formation of communications networks dominated by a small number of companies with global links. These companies are involved in all media industries worldwide, based on the role of digital services and the convergence of broadcasting and telecommunications, as interactivity is supplied through computers, satellites, and fiber optics cables.

The main result of these developments is the establishment of new media markets, because information technology can allow the building of global networks that can be expanded through the integration of economic, cultural, and political issues that are not separated by geographical boundaries. The leading role of market forces and the impact of information technologies are being driven by the formation of the information society and the global information superhighway.

7

Localism of Media Commercialization

When the changeover to digital television started, it was described as one of the most important transitions of the 21st century, which would eventually change the lives of people around the world. The evolving knowledge-based society is changing the concept of localism and creating a new global society in which traditional systems are not able to provide the new technology operations and information that are essential for global operation. The immediate supply of information, which can be delivered without geographical limits and political direction, changes the way people live and establishes the necessity of globalization.

The effects of the commercial changes evident in media policies and local societies can be seen as part of the globalization of the mass media. But the issue being debated in many countries in response to globalization is whether these changes will make the world a truly global village or will the digital age remain out of reach of many societies.

There is certainly no argument that the rapid changes in global media have created a new cultural order of global policy and market rule. There is also no argument that these changes have made their impact on local media policies and markets, although the impact of localism remains significant in all countries.

One question must be asked while examining the impact of globalization on the commercialization of local media systems: are new media becoming global or do they remain local in nature?

This chapter attempts to answer this question by examining differences in local perceptions of commercialization. Media commercialization is defined as the transfer of influence to the free market in all that falls under public policy, programming, and advertising. An important aspect of this analysis is that the commercialization of media policy and markets is a process that all countries are undergoing, although the nature and extent of this course of development differs according to local variations and culture.

Although local cultures have different structures and varying degrees of technological advancement, local markets have absorbed the impact of global communication networks, which consider global consciousness as serving their interests. Local differences are still important, however, and should be considered when examining all aspects of media policy. Global impact can be effective as long as local societies consider global trends to be more important than those of local markets, although key conditions should be made available in local markets, too.

This course of development establishes a new compromise structure of media policy that encompasses all countries. Under this structure, the combination of cultural development of television broadcasting and commercial considerations influenced by global and technological development has had a profound impact on the commercialization of broadcasting systems and the nature of public policy around the world.

The global course of change, from cultural values to commercialization, has created a more or less uniform media policy. This can be identified with certain broad trends that demonstrate the way commercialization in the digital age can be examined. These trends include eight major categories examined in this chapter: the mediating role of media commercialization, commercialization policy, the new public television, new media markets, Americanization, protecting local culture, the social role of advertising, and the linkage between culture and technology.

7.1 THE MEDIATING ROLE OF MEDIA COMMERCIALIZATION

The increased role of commercialization has had a mediating impact, following the addition of new media technologies, which tend to ignore

cultural and political differences and create major changes in local policies. The new structure of media policy is considered today both as a
social process, in which its mediating role refers to the efforts of actors
and institutions in society to determine the nature of the media market,
and as a cultural process, which influences the nature of cultural determinism in the development of national broadcasting systems.

The sources of this mediating role are linked to the impact of
global policy on local cultures. Despite local differences in media policy
among countries, there are obvious implications for the mediating role
of media commercialization, which identify all media systems. The
extent of commercialization of the broadcasting media is the result of
social negotiation, and local public policy is determined according to the
relative impact of global and domestic forces and the consequent extent
of mediation between these forces.[1]

The analysis encompasses three main categories of commercialization common to all media policies and markets: local policy, the quality of programming, and commercialization in the digital age. These categories provide a mechanism to analyze the level of local commercialization policies in response to global policy.[2]

The first category relates to changes in local media systems and
the way they are undergoing a process of change of thinking from public service to commercial perceptions. The mediating role is between
public and commercial broadcasting: the forces that protect the concept
and goals of public broadcasting and those that advocate for a commercial-type and market-led media sector. Mediation between these contrasting prospects and interest groups is achieved through commercialization of public broadcasting systems and the addition of commercial
outlets, including new media services. The outcome of the linkage
between technological advancement and cultural impact determines the
extent of commercialization in each country. In this way, commercialization policy and the extent of mediation between public and commercial
broadcasting can be examined.

In the process of commercialization, this aspect of mediation has
to be examined by taking into account the implications of the use of
mass media as a cultural display. The impact of new media technologies
is associated with the internationalization and globalization of television
broadcasting, which brought in commercial programs not under national control and created the need for deregulation policies and commercialization. New technologies have also created new values and symbols
by imposing cultural changes on nations too weak to resist, with the
result that the cultural flow is being delivered through domination of
production services and distribution of transmissions and media materials. This process has resulted in a debate on the nature of transmissions

to the public, following the impact of commercial programming available through international broadcasting and the imposition of global culture distributed through global communications.

The second category relates to the programming provided by new televised outlets. It examines the impact of transnational channels and transmissions with global reach on the nature of programming at the local level. This category emphasizes the role of domestic social and cultural forces operating within a global media scene, following the shift in public policies, which has identified all media systems. The impact of this process on the nature of media commercialization and the extent of cultural identity results from changes in media policies, because cultural distinctions and political singularities have become less powerful than global trends of media policymaking. The mediating role is aimed at negotiating the contradiction between international broadcasting and global communications. The concept of international broadcasting refers to transmissions that are available in more than one country and in different societies as a result of technological advancement. The concept of global communications refers to transmissions that are intended to create global culture and are available globally.

The programming aspect of commercialization has also evolved as a result of technology changes and the spread of culture across societies. The importance of mediation has increased in the new competitive media environment with the addition of a large number of commercial channels. The underlying goals of maintaining a balance of programming that supports local cultural values have been major concerns in countries that are under pressure from international and global media organizations. In these countries programming generates difficulties because domestic markets for television programming are relatively small and with the addition of new media outlets it is necessary to import foreign programs to meet the increased capacity. This results in heated political debates on the impact of foreign programming on domestic cultural policies and goals and requires mediation among these conflicting perceptions. The outcome of programming policy on the extent of commercialization determines the relative role of the globalization of local media systems. In this way, the nature of local programming and the extent of mediation between local and global trends can be examined.

The third category explores the nature of commercialization in the digital age by examining the perceived social role of advertising and the promotion of open-skies policy. The social aspects are related to the increased influence of advertising on the nature of programming, following the creation of new competitive markets with global reach. The debate between local and global trends involves the impact of cross-cultural transmissions and advertising on local channels, because commercial aspects are demonstrated by the distribution of programs to terrestrial channels in a large number of countries and by the need for advertising to finance these transmissions.

The aspect of mediation in this category is particularly concerned with the debate among local actors on the social role of advertising and the linkage between technology and culture. This debate concerns the extent of commercialization of the broadcasting media in the new global structure, while examining social interests representing local needs and commercial forces representing global trends.

This mediating force means that local cultural and commercial forces debate the extent of global impact. Whereas adoption of global policy objectives is evident in the wider commercialization of the mass media, increased cultural impact means restrictions on commercial operations. Advertising plays a major role in this debate, given the amount of time spent attending to the mass media and the amount of resources invested in mass media production and distribution. This proposes a debate on the social role of advertising, which develops within the overall process of commercialization of the broadcasting media in each country.

The focus of this discussion is on two main policy changes that have manifested the social impact on advertising: commercialization and technological advancement. It is claimed that technology changes have influenced advertising, and that television is benefiting from new media as it is changing in technology and culture. Although the social role of advertising is required to mediate among the forces that influence local media policy, this process has been evidenced in all Western countries, following the impact of global media policy.

The outcome of the social negotiation between local issues and the question of open-skies policy can provide a mechanism to determine commercialization policy in the digital age. In this way, the social role of advertising and the extent of mediation between social and commercial forces can be examined because commercialization combines local and global influence to a degree that varies among countries.

7.2 COMMERCIALIZATION POLICY

Following the triumph of global policy, commercialization has become a major force in the development of broadcasting systems and cultural identities. The new global wave of commercialization is making an impact on all media sectors and societies to the extent that perceptions of free market and widespread competition among all media and telecommunications services dominate current trends.

Examination of the role of media commercialization requires first discussing changes in local policies. These have generally included the commercialization of public broadcasting services and the addition of commercial outlets involving the combination of public and global policy—a process that has had an impact on political and commercial decision making, both globally and domestically.

The importance of this category to understanding local policies depends on the nature of media commercialization and the extent of cultural identity in each country. Globalization and commercialization include a distinct process, in which the most striking structural change has been the introduction of new media technologies. New outlets have provoked questions about the cultural and social influence of different broadcasting media and have intensified the perceived linkage between cultural issues and technological advancement. The outcome of this development is the transfer of influence from the government sector to market forces—a process that identifies the commercialization policy of all countries.

The extent of commercialization is the result of the linkage between two major forces: technological advancement and cultural determinism. The nature of commercialization policy requires mediation between social and commercial forces that represent contrasting conceptions of technological development and cultural identity. Although the new structure of commercialized media systems is considered a global process that applies to all countries, local policies determine the way commercialization policy is being implemented in different countries in response to the global impact.

From the technological outlook, the commercialization of broadcasting systems means privatization and permission for commercial advertising. Technology has extended across national boundaries, following the emergence of global media policy and the globalization of media markets. Accordingly, the technological perspective of media policy involves commercialization of media services and adoption of new media technologies. This is a process that all countries have experienced, although at different speeds.

Local aspects should be examined from contrasting cultural perspectives. Although commercialization has been influenced by global trends, the process has been moderate in some countries, whose main policy objectives were to maintain the public service nature of the broadcast sector and the dominance of local cultures. The cultural aspects are related to the perceived impact of media commercialization, because the increased number of competitors along with the parallel weakening of public broadcasting is forcing public broadcasting services to work with a more commercial outlook in both advertising and programming.

The impact of new technology on local cultures is a key issue in the structure of commercialization policies. A distinctive characteristic of the contrasting technological development and cultural perceptions pertains to the notion of public interest. This notion, which stands at the heart of public broadcasting, is the outcome of a process of democratic debate and decision making, with the result that the idea of public service broadcasting is never fixed but always changing.

The distinction among media policies is evident in the process of commercialization of public broadcasting services, and the social consequences of these institutions differ according to the notion of public interest. In the United States, broadcasting systems were set up by companies that solely intended to make a profit, and were always based on a commercial conception. In contrast, in countries with a strong commitment among broadcasters to public service broadcasting, the media became the site of a permanent war between various social and political interests, and a compromise among conflicting perceptions was an important aspect of the relationship between a society and its media.[3]

Within the broad structure of public broadcasting in countries with strong political influence, policy differences had been related to the role of public service organizations. The impact of commercialization was achieved through changes in the nature of public broadcasting, and a compromise in the way commercialization policy was adopted resulted in mediation between public service and commercial interests. This stage of media policy was required because there has been a shift in the balance between commercial and public broadcasting since the late 1970s, with public broadcasting being under siege from commercial interests and conservative governments.

The transition in public policy resulted in an inevitable decline in the impact of public television. Following the addition of a large number of commercial channels, the concept did not succeed in realizing its potential. It was technological development and the addition of commercial outlets that brought in differing cultural perceptions of the role of public and commercial broadcasting.[4]

The consequent globalization of culture and technology shows that American media policy has been an example for commercialization elsewhere.[5] This process has had three major results involving global impact and local policy changes:

1.   Changes in commercialization policy: in many countries public broadcasting monopolies have been broken with the addition of commercial outlets and the advent of cable and satellite transmissions.

2. Changes in programming policy: the decline in audience shares forced public service organizations to alter their programs to compete for audiences.
3. Changes in advertising policy: with growing difficulties in collecting license fees to finance public channels, which obviously appealed to a shrinking audience, and competition with commercial channels, public broadcasting organizations were forced to rely on advertising in addition to public funding.

In the new structure of media policy, public broadcasting has become a second force to new commercial outlets, with the two services operating under a compromised structure. This new structure of commercialization, which identifies all media systems today, includes both public and commercial broadcasting services and a mediated impact of cultural and commercial transmissions. The nature of mediation that has developed, at the local level in each country but as a global process as a whole, means that public broadcasting has come under the influence of commercial forces, advertisers, and the advertising industry and has practically lost its public service character.

Key players and processes have been involved in changes at the local and global level. At the local level are technological developments, domestic ideological and cultural forces, domestic political and economic forces, and the political nature. At the global level are global market forces, political institutions with global impact (such as the FCC and the EC), the spread of programming across national borders, and the convergence of technologies and policies.

The broad trend of commercialization developed in response to changes on a global scale. This trend is due to the fact that the development of communication technologies and commercialized media systems combines commercial, technological, and cultural aspects with variations in the global impact imposed on local media policies.

The cultural aspects of mediation have become particularly important following the rise of new media. Although the mediating role of the mass media generally refers to the influence of television content, the addition of new media technologies also requires meditation among various forces operating within society while determining the nature of cultural identity. Despite the influence of technological development and global trends, variations in policies of different countries and the extent of commercialization of their broadcasting system are subject to the social and political environment. The prominence of mediation is bound up with the social institutions it serves, because its adoption implies the development of new technologies and transmissions with international and global appeal and reach. The political factor means that negotiation to control the wider social relations is being exercised through media policy. This applies to politicians and governments, broadcasters and advertisers, and experts and authorities of all kinds— and all have to operate according to values of global media and commercial policy.[6]

7.3 THE "NEW" PUBLIC TELEVISION

For public television organizations, the new structure of media policy means transformation from markets dominated by public service broadcasting with limited channel capacity to a digital world of hundreds of channels and a variety of advanced and interactive services.

Perhaps the biggest impact of commercialization has been on public television services, mainly in Europe, where the dominating position of public service broadcasting has been severely challenged by private operators. Since the liberalization of Europe's television markets, private networks have gained growing market share by offering multichannel and pay television services.

Public television traditionally developed as a unique provider of cultural programs along with regular programs that explore science and nature. But with the start of multichannel television through cable and then satellite services, commercial channels have begun offering regular cultural programming, as well as science and nature shows and quality programming for children. Other programs that had previously been only on public broadcasting stations have also been transmitted on commercial channels.

The new commercialized structure of the broadcast media provided changes in public broadcasting systems, and the role of public television is continuing to change in the digital age, forcing national services to adapt to the new competitive environment. Whereas previous plans concentrated on privatizing public broadcasting services, public channels are now being transformed to meet the demands of the new digital marketplace by combining public and commercial service. Although in many European countries national channels are still favored, the growth in new media services is threatening their position and impact. Other important factors advancing the declining market share of public television are pay television services and pan-European and global channels.[7]

Changes are being forced on public service organizations for three main reasons:

1. Commercialization and Multichannel Services Dominate the New Broadcasting Marketplace. The addition of new media has changed the nature of public broadcasting. With new services of cable and satellite providing multichannel television and the triumph of commercial television, the idea behind public broadcasting and the need to pay the license fee have become questionable. Although the majority of public service channels in Europe are partly financed by advertising, the need to reach a wider audience and increase market share forces them to offer a higher proportion of commercial programming, thereby abandoning the original aims of public service broadcasting. The future of the license fee, the traditional main source of income to public services, has also become doubtful as audience share constantly declines.

2. Many of the Founding Missions of Public Television are Now Served by New Media Services. The nature of programming on public broadcasting systems has also changed. In this new commercial environment, the long-standing tradition of public television, which was based on the commitment to a range of program types aimed at diverse interests and publics in contrast to commercial transmitters, has also changed. Today new media technologies of cable, satellite, and terrestrial services offer regular cultural and public interest programming and quality shows, with the result that programs that were previously transmitted exclusively on public channels are now offered by commercial services.

3. New Technology Forces Public Broadcasting Systems to Commercialize Their Programming and Compete for Ratings and Audience Shares. Development of digital television carries with it a challenge for national public service organizations and governments in adapting to the new age of television broadcasting. With the challenges, however, come new opportunities as well—to create a field for national culture and public service while establishing new national media policies that will best meet the demands of the transition to digital TV and the special characteristics of local societies. In response to competition, former national public service broadcasters have expanded their local operations into new activities and joint ventures with telecommunications alliances. The most common response of former local monopolies is to enter the digital TV market by providing a combined telecommunications and broadcasting service with former telecommunications monopolies. Other potential services include content providing and packaging for cable and satellite channels and local pay TV services.[8]

The future holds new opportunities for public broadcasters, as the "new public television" has to operate in a multichannel marketplace and in a commercial environment while providing quality educational and cultural programming. Without the close oversight of governments, public stations are free to present cultural programming and new services and compete in the new digital marketplace.

Although public television is not as influential as in the first years of television, it is still an integral part of the digital age. The most striking element in the transformation of public television is that governments are supporting its new role in the digital age. But the public interest potential of digital television makes it impossible to simply transfer the current analog public interest obligations to digital television broadcasting, and the leading public services are getting ready for digital competition.

The BBC is the world's first public broadcasting service and is considered one of the leaders in the transformation to digital television. The BBC Beyond 2000 sets out the main principles of British public broadcasting for the future: seeking to satisfy all audiences with services that inform, educate, and entertain and that enrich their lives in ways that the market alone will not. Digital technology can benefit public broadcasting viewers, who could catch up on a recently missed episode of a favorite program, watch all news stories of a particular day or week, and receive program material on radio, television, CD-ROM, and online.[9]

Public television is also changing in the United States, where the concept of the New Public Television is rapidly catching on. This concept includes a new outlook for the future, with digital competition and the ability to provide a variety of programming services through different platforms, including free off-air transmissions and multichannel services provided by digital terrestrial, cable, and satellite services.

Both the idea and organization of public television gained new status in the structure of American media policy. The 1998 PBS Annual Report talks about a "new PBS" that has been developed since 1995. The new PBS is more commercially oriented and is making the transition to digital technology alongside commercial operators. To establish this, the Advisory Committee on Public Interest Obligations of Digital Broadcasters was set up to ensure that public television also continues to serve the public needs in a digital environment. Congress approved an increase in funding for the Corporation for Public Broadcasting, from $250 to $300 million, the largest percentage rise since 1967. PBS stations had been required to begin digital broadcasting by 2003, although many local stations already offered high-definition television shows and Internet offerings.[10]

The idea of public television through cable is also catching on in the United States. Congress mandated in the Cable and Television Consumer Protection and Competition Act of 1992 that all cable and DBS providers set aside a portion of their channel capacity for noncommercial, public interest programming. As a result, many of the programs on cable and satellite are simply similar to public channels. While previously public channels provided a commercial-free environment and carried no advertising, making it a real alternative to commercial services, today cable systems offer nonadvertising programs and the need of public channels to compete in a multichannel environment makes it almost impossible to define what makes them commercial-free.[11]

Another response to new media was in creating a regulatory framework for public television in the European Union. The Amsterdam protocol, which became a European Union law on May 1, 1999, recognized that the system of public broadcasting in the Member States is directly related to the democratic, social, and cultural needs of each society and to the need to preserve media pluralism. The main objectives of this policy are to support public broadcasters through an all-European mutual assistance and to maintain the traditional range of independent programming of information, education, culture, and entertainment in each country.[12]

7.4 NEW MEDIA MARKETS

The distribution of global programming has become a major subject for debate in all countries, based on local differences and the dominance of American firms in the global media market. The structure of new media markets is common around the world, with almost the same programming available on all media outlets provided through cable and satellite and in the future through digital terrestrial services.

New media markets include four main fields:

1. Free-to-air channels: these channels are provided as an antenna service and include all the available major national and local channels.
2. Basic channels: these are channels provided to cable and satellite customers for basic service. They are advertiser-supported services that are available with no additional fee to the basic service.
3. Pay TV services: these services include additional channels aimed at cable and satellite customers and provided for an extra cost per channel or per program.
4. Interactive content: these services are available on the more advanced systems. They include services such as interactive content, pay-per-view, near-video-on-demand and video-on-demand.

Based on this analysis, American and European new media markets differ in both structure and the available programming services:

American New Media Markets.   The headline figure for multichannel take-up in the United States stands at around 87 percent of the television households. Sixty-nine percent of the households subscribe to basic cable services, and the penetration of satellite is 18 percent. The very high rate of basic cable take-up is due to the fact that a traditional function of cable TV is as a means of improving reception of local and national television broadcast signals. The basic cable service includes retransmitted broadcast signals, advertiser-supported general and special interest programming, and public, educational, and government channels.

Basic cable service typically provides the following: local affiliates of national networks and local stations; superstations (independent stations that transmit their signals to a satellite for cable or private reception); local community, public, government, educational, and leased access channels; and narrowcasting channels targeted at specific audience groups.

The penetration of premium services is not as impressive, although it is expected to grow when digital services become more common. In Europe, many customers enjoy a wide variety of free television services, and in the United States most households are connected to basic cable as replacement for an off-air antenna. These figures represent "old media habits," because new technology is evidently increasing the rate of premium service penetration. The higher take-up rate in the digital era is related to the greater functionality that digital television offers for new services such as video-on-demand (VOD) and near-video-on-demand (NVOD).

Advanced services offered by American cable networks include digital television, telephony, Internet access, Internet over TV, paging, home security services, near-video-on-demand and video-on-demand. The potential for further growth is enormous, because digital services have only developed (via satellite) since 1994 in the United States and since 1996 in Europe.

Digital satellite services, provided by DirecTV and Echostar (the Dish Network), offer hundreds of television channels and other advanced services. These include cable-type programming, pay-per-view (PPV) movies, subscription sports, and local network affiliates from American biggest markets. Other less commonly subscribed-to channels aimed at alternative locations and audiences include foreign language programming and channels, religious packages, high-definition programming, local affiliates from smaller American cities, and other niche-type services. Local channels normally picked up over-the-air are also available for an extra cost.

European New Media Markets.   There are 240 million television households in the European Union, with an average penetration rate of 97 percent of the households. Terrestrial television channels have a limited reach but generally extend to neighboring countries. Cable and satellite channels considered both as made for specific linguistic communities and pan-European services created for the European market as a whole have not succeeded in developing. Satellite services are prominent in the European broadcast industry, and the major European pay-TV companies operate via satellite. The pan-European satellites are Eutelsat and Astra, which cover most of Europe and parts of the Middle East and North Africa. These satellite operators offer the potential for a wide variety of pay services with digital technology and enjoy an unregulated environment and large capacity.

European programming policy differs from that of the American operators in that they create their own programming with many of the channels distributed through the system. The major satellite television providers are based in the three largest media countries in Europe and are involved in ventures across Europe:

1. Canal Plus is the biggest pay-TV operator in Europe. It was established as a private monopoly for over-the-air pay-TV service in France in 1984 and was a very profitable venture until domestic competition began in 1996. Then Canal Plus established international activity by acquiring the European activities of the South African-backed pay-TV operator Nethold, which operated in Italy, the Benelux, and the Nordic countries. Since the merger Canal Plus has extended its operations into 10 countries: France, Spain, Italy, Belgium, The Netherlands, and Scandinavia (Denmark, Sweden, Norway, and Finland).

2. The second largest European pay-TV operator is British Sky Broadcasting (BSkyB) in the United Kingdom. The service started in November 1989 and transmits from Luxembourg via Astra satellite. Initially the service was aimed at the pan-European market but it soon closed its European offices and concentrated on the British market. In October 1998 BskyB started a 200-channel digital service for the British market.

3. In Germany there are two big players. Premier is the largest analog pay-TV and Digitales Fernsehen 1 is a digital pay-TV service. Together these parties hold all of the important German-language pay-TV programming rights.[13]

Although Europe remains a checkerboard of small markets divided by culture and language, industry consolidation means that broadcasters have bigger and more efficient organizations to help them offer national programming within a European market. The result is dozens of private and commercial channels that operate throughout Europe, locally or as pan-European services. The combination of new technology and global economy is forcing relatively small players to join forces to cover the costs of switching to digital technology and of marketing integrated bundles of television, telephone, and Internet services.

The future looks bright for European programming in the competition with American dominance. The breakdown of national monopolies and the convergence of media and telecommunications services are contributing to cross-border deals across Europe. The European television industry must cope with American imperialism in both cultural and technological fields. The unification of Europe has created the potential for a common market for broadcasting. The issues that had prevented the creation of a common European market have been resolved through common European laws and common policy issued by the European Community, and European companies now have the opportunity to challenge America's supremacy in television programming.[14]

7.5 AMERICANIZATION

Despite the evolving global structure of new media services, American and European broadcasting markets have evolved differently. The United States is generally regarded as the most developed television market, representing the most significant indicator for the future of television and the adoption of new technologies and services. This conclusion is based on the analysis examined earlier, according to which the development of the broadcast media in Europe and in other parts of the world lags a decade or more behind the United States.

There are three main reasons for the different structure of American and European media markets:

1. Language: whereas in the United States the English language is dominant and thus a huge market for programming can be created, Europe has a diversity of lifestyles and cultures and no single language.
2. Global programming: American dominance of global programming is the result of the diversity of media policies in different countries and differences in the adoption of new technologies. Similarly, no pan-European pay-TV services has developed,

because of language and cultural differences, copyright issues, and different policies of governments and key media organizations that control access to consumers in different countries.

3. New technology: the dominance of American firms is related to the cost of new technology, as well. The cost of new digital systems is daunting to European corporations that make their revenues from relatively smaller national markets in comparison with America.

The result of the dominance of American firms in global media markets is the development of economic, cultural, and technological imperialism, or as called in other parts of world outside of the United States, American dominance or "Americanization."

1. Economic imperialism is created because large international concerns have annual sales that are greater than the national products of many countries. The commercial forces that lead the technological revolution of the television industry are enormous in terms of size, global reach, and the commercial applications of new technologies. These concerns, most of them American-based, are multinational companies with enormous power to make investment decisions based on tax and wage levels in individual countries. They no longer have ties to localities and are able to make decisions that profoundly affect communities and individuals without having to live with the consequences of those decisions.

2. Cultural imperialism is the dominance of American producers in the television market. Global programming means that programming is supplied to commercial stations to fill access slots and transmissions are delivered around the world without any reference to local cultures, thereby intensifying the impact of global media culture and cultural convergence following the concern about the integrity of national sovereignty that emerged with the aggressive proliferation of technology and culture.

3. Technological imperialism is the dominance of American firms over the crucial technology that will run the television industry of the future. The spread of culture across societies has been the driving force behind the development of commercial programming policies. Technology made the vast flow of information and entertainment available through a complex structure of competition of broadcast, new media, and telecommunications services, with digital television and interactive services on offer through all technologies.

The globalization of media markets has been the result of the influx of American television programming. Cultural interests have long dominated European broadcasting and are now being challenged by increasingly powerful commercial interests. The impact of corporate alliances is related to the initiation of global culture, because commercial forces are providing a gateway for advertisers to reach wider mass audiences. They also provide an opportunity for Europe to challenge American supremacy in television programming.

With the global flow of information and entertainment, the inability of public policy to control the nature of programming has become a critical impetus for the globalization of media policy and markets. The challenge for media organizations is to establish a structure that could mediate between the two opposing trends of technology and culture. In practice, this means that they have to operate profitable broadcasting networks but avoid cultural discontent. Their main problem is the ability to maintain the distinctiveness of national services, and this is becoming increasingly problematic in a marketplace where American producers have the double advantage of offering programming at low prices (as they have already covered their initial investment by national sales) and of being attractive to the general public.

There is an analogy between American success in selling movies and television programs around the world and what seems to be the imposition of global culture in delivering its basic model of development at the local and global level. These links are direct, because American investment has also become a major factor in the development of new media around the world. American companies have been investing in Europe and Asia as part of the new global media development, which also means that the same programs are distributed in all countries. This has created cultural convergence, according to which selling programs to local stations and to foreign markets after a successful network run in the United States is where the real money is made in broadcasting.

The extent of global and local programming is an obvious outcome of the new attitudes in broadcasting, which reinforces the influence of commercial forces operating within the broadcasting media in each country, as they have a growing number of outlets to choose from and a growing number of services that are in need of programming.

The key for success in the global market is to change traditional business models by providing better programming and adding tiering and premium services. Narrowcasting allows advertisers to beam their message to a more specific group of customers without having to pay for sending their message to millions of people who are unlikely to buy the particular product. With the growth in the number of channels and the need for programming, the demand and price for content have grown tremendously. Most popular are films and global events such as sports and entertainment.[15]

7.6 PROTECTING LOCAL PRODUCTION

The local aspects of the relationship between media policy and society have been an issue for debate in all countries. The conflict between new technology and local interests demonstrates that the historical development of the broadcast media is related to larger social questions of national identity and democracy and the shifting structure of the media sector.

Following the adoption of commercialization policy and the free market approach in America and in Europe, technological convergence and globalization have influenced media policies around the world. Within this course of development, new media policies have dominated changes in the broadcast sector, as the influence of commercialization stimulated increases in the number of the channels available and created global media markets.

The conclusion that can be drawn from this development is that the impact of commercialization and globalization on the overall advancement of the media is related to the development of new media technologies. Transnational transmissions have eroded the decision-making capacity of national governments and diminished the impact of local authorities in response to the global media.

A concern has been expressed at the local level in many countries in the context of problems that relate to the cultural impact of advanced information and telecommunications technologies. Despite the compromise, structure negotiated between public and commercial broadcasting at the local level in each country and at the global level in general, media policy continued to change following the diffusion of programming across media markets and boundaries. The increased impact of new technology and global forces that distribute cross-cultural transmissions and media products means that mediation between local forces did not suffice to determine the nature of media policy and the extent of commercialization of the media sector.

The rapid changes in the structure of public broadcasting services were intensified by two major developments: a new global communication order and a new cultural order, which goes beyond the impact of local policies. Deregulation has helped the United States to become a leader in the development of global media markets, and a similar impact was evident following liberalization in other parts of the world. The role of cross-cultural transmissions is important in this process because the global spread of culture has made its impact beyond commercialization, thus expanding the limits and effects of culture from a local level into a process in which cultural experiences and meanings can be seen as global.

The relevance of programming policy is related to larger social issues of the quality of programming—the relative impact of local culture and local programming within the entire scope of the broadcast media. The essence of this issue is the result of cross-cultural transmissions and the response of local cultures to this imperative influence. This can be considered both as a global process influenced by common programming policy, and as a local process that is subject to the way local cultures adopt policy changes.

These trends have resulted from technological advancement and policy changes in favor of market forces. They have influenced local media policies in a way that puts the issue of the quality of the programming into a commercial rather than public perspective. This course of change in perception is particularly relevant to the role of public broadcasting organizations. In the early stages of media policy, the quality of programming was one of the main aspects of public broadcasting policy, but the commercialization of broadcasting services and the addition of new media outlets changed the ability of public authorities to maintain strict public supervision over the quality and nature of programming.

Local authorities find it difficult to combat global communications, which provides commercial transmissions and increases advertising on public channels. The overall impact is apparent, and as a result subject to constant debate on the definition of the essence of local programming. When taking into consideration the cultural aspect, global flow of information is related to the transnational proliferation of mass-market advertising. The distinction here is not only between technological and cultural impact, but also between local transmissions, which due to technological advancement are also available to other cultures, and global transmissions, which are aimed to create and appeal to a global culture.

The international and global flow of cultural media products means that cultural distinctions and political singularities have become less powerful than the free flow of information and the spread of commercial programming. In all that relates to global impact on programming, the new cultural order has been established with the diffusion of programming across political and cultural boundaries and the convergence of cultural policies and technological developments. This structure is making an impact on the nature of broadcasting in all countries, to the extent that the same transmissions are available and make an impact on different societies.

The issue of protecting and encouraging local production has been largely debated in Europe, as a function of different national culture. The policy of the European Community on Domestic Content was determined in the 1989 Television Without Frontiers directive. It defines local production as anything that is not "news, sports events, games, advertising and teleshopping." Article 4 states that "Member states shall ensure . . . that broadcasters reserve for European work" . . . "a majority proportion of their transmission time, excluding the time appointed to news, sports events, games, advertising, and teletext services." Article 5 states further that "broadcasters reserve at least 10 percent of their transmission time . . . or alternatively at the discretion of the member state, at least 10 percent of their programming budget, for European work created by producers who are independent of broadcasters." Additional sections deal with defining the position of international coproduction and setting minimal standards for advertising and content. The EC also provided assistance by allocating money to support training people in the industry, grants for production projects, and assistance in distribution.

The scope for European integration in the field of television is, however, extremely limited, despite the common policy determined by the EC, and member states are free to make own legislation regarding language content. Because it is difficult (and to some extent even impossible) to generate programming for the whole region, given the vast cultural and linguistic differences, different member states have widely differing approaches to developing their national industries. Whereas French protection of its national culture is taken for granted (France is trying to get 50 percent quotas in European broadcasting), Britain and Germany allow broadcasters to compete without external barriers.

There are three main methods for encouraging local production in Europe:

1. Social responsibility in broadcasting: According to the social responsibility approach, the requirements for creating and using local drama productions are put into effect by a process of monitoring the companies involved in local broadcasting and putting public pressure on them to conform to these requirements. The assumption is that these companies will seek to fulfill public expectations out of their desire to serve society according to their role of preserving local culture and social needs.

2. Quotas: The quota approach is the alternative to the social responsibility system, because it imposes clear limits and requirements based on local broadcasting licenses. These requirements—regional, national, or pan-European—are determined by specific laws and regulations and may involve

direct interventions to achieve the goals set. The nature of the requirements is based on the objectives that are stressed—the integration of minorities, language, programming aimed to serve certain groups, community, educational, public or governmental programming, or according to different types of production.

3. Direct financial assistance: The system of positive measures to encourage high standards in programming content or to develop local television industries is the result of public pressure, because neither of the previous two systems works in a multichannel environment unless direct intervention by regulators is provided. The system exists all over Europe, although it varies among countries, from simply providing tax reductions to more strict regulations that actually benefit local production industries or broadcasters.[16]

7.7 THE SOCIAL ROLE OF ADVERTISING

Television broadcasting is changing in the digital age with the expansion of media services and the growing debate on the social role of advertising. Although in its simplest form advertising seeks to boost the sale of goods and services, because of the cultural and commercial conflicts involved it has always been surrounded by controversy. The social role of advertising is not just a means to advance commercial products. It is also an integral part of modern culture that has an impact on the nature of cultural determinism and media policy at the local and global level. In this form the social role of advertising has become a site of conflicting perceptions.

Such conflicts are only going to accelerate in the future. The market for television advertising and the total expenditure will grow in the digital age because of the new advertising opportunities made available with the increased number of channels. The nature of television advertising will change, too, as the growing number of channels will force advertisers to address smaller but more focused groups. Despite the separation of targeted audiences, the conception of many niche channels will provide opportunities to earn advertising revenues from new sources.

The new structure of commercial media systems advocates new social issues. Although the commercialization of broadcasting is generally regarded as a means to achieve economic benefits, in many countries cultural aspects of new media technologies have provoked political debates about the social consequences of new technologies and the profound changes they have facilitated. This debate reflects the two contradictory trends at work in the relations between cultural and commercial aspects of the mass media—social influence and technological advancement.

The impact of advertising can be evaluated as having a mediating role between cultural considerations and commercial impact. The social role of advertising deals in this context with the way that technological development should keep pace with the major policy changes taking place in international economic, political, and cultural realities.

This approach considers the social role of advertising as a mediator between cultural and commercial forces. From the commercial outlook, advertising touches the center of cultural and economic life by shifting the weight to commercial considerations. From the cultural perspective, critics of advertising claim that it is a tool to manipulate and control consumers and that the advertising and the ratings industries are determining the actual relationship between broadcasters and advertisers.

The argument made here is that advertising has become a vehicle of social change and a form of media policy. In this social context, advertising influences social institutions and cultural identities in all countries. It has created broad economic changes and provoked social and cultural debate that seeks to understand the significance of these major changes in the media sector. This impact is consistent with all types of society, in response to global trends of media commercialization.

The social role of advertising provides the arena for both cultural and commercial forces in the debate on who should control and run the media. The process of transferring influence from the government sector to market forces has had different results in response to global developments and commercialization of broadcasting systems. But it has also demonstrated that differences between those who defend the concept of cultural aspects in broadcasting and those who campaign for a free market approach can be resolved through the social role of advertising.

Advertising has had a profound impact on the transformation of broadcasting systems into a mass media business in which a mix of both cultural and commercial considerations influence technological development and programming outlook. These developments have created the rules under which advertiser-supported channels can operate within the new cultural order of media commercialization. According to this analysis, the social impact of commercialization in each media system is determined according to the rules for advertising on local channels, and the nature of the advertising policy can be seen as a compromise reached between commercial and cultural perceptions.

In addition to common cultural aspects of globalization, the social role of advertising explores the extent of commercialization of the media sector in each country—in response to global influence. In this process, it is possible to ascertain the main aspects of advertising policy common to all countries, as they determine the way that local media markets are adopting commercialization. They also consider the rules of advertising on public and commercial outlets as beneficial to both governments and the public sector as part of a technological and cultural development that influences all countries.

The adoption of common cultural aspects requires mediation on the nature of commercialization. Commercial channels are financed via advertisements and sponsorship or through subscription fees, thus emphasizing the role of commercialization at the global level. This means that countries are being forced to permit commercial-free broadcasting media, although full compliance with this requirement means that global policy has prevailed. The social role of advertising can be seen as a way that the cultural aspects of media commercialization can be exploited while operating within a global media environment that tends to ignore local advertising restrictions.

Another dimension of mediation is between global forces representing commercial interests and domestic sources representing cultural objectives. This is necessary because the structure of media policies explores social and cultural aspects on the one hand, and economic influence of groups and institutions with particular services on the other. The social topics that are raised aim to endorse the cultural aspects unique to each country, whereas commercial broadcasters aim to reach as large an audience as possible, thus ignoring political and cultural differences and relying on international and global advertising to finance their transmissions.

The cultural aspects that identify media policies and markets, both domestically and globally, emphasize the role of advertising policy in the process of commercialization. At the local level of policy, the coalition of interests that determines the social role of advertising in each media system is certainly in need of a mediating process. This compromise is required on the extent of commercialization and the relevant impact of advertising at the local level. In terms of global policymaking and the impact of new media technologies on the evolution of new cultural definitions and common cultural aspects, global media has provided audiences with a much greater potential choice of programming, entirely outside the control of local broadcasters. This applies to the impact on local media systems and requires mediation concerning the way that local media systems adopt the impact of global and commercial flows.

When considering the interplay between society and culture, the impact of advertising on broadcasting is explained in the dependence of the commercial media on advertising and the cultural impact of this process. The relationship between cultural and commercial aspects is also explained in the increasing connection between broadcasting services and giant corporations, which operate according to economic considerations and ignore local and cultural considerations. Their aim is to distribute common perceptions of commercial operation, whereas local forces try to minimize this impact.

As part of this process, which in practice determines the nature of media policy as a compromise structure between the powerful coalition of interests of policymakers and financial groups, mediation becomes a key element. The consequent mediated structure of media policy means that all the involved parties have realized that commercialization is suitable with their view of media development. Another significant result is that once a compromise has been found between conflicting interests, they have all helped to maintain policy changes in favor of new channels financed by commercial rather than public means. The mediating factor has not changed with the impact of new technologies, but the range of possible solutions has been extended following the new context of global competition. The end result is that advertising organizes the broadcasting media so that they are not truly independent, because they have to take into account the demands of dominant economic institutions and cultural forces. In this structure, the role of mediation determines the extent of media commercialization.

The overall television advertising market will continue to grow, as new opportunities to earn advertising revenue from new sources are created, forming a direct connection to special interest groups and highly focused audiences. This will create a distinction between traditional mass-market channels and the new established specialist channels with small audience shares.[17]

7.8 THE LINKAGE BETWEEN TECHNOLOGY AND CULTURE

The sources of commercialization described thus far have been examined according to technological and cultural changes at the local and global level. The combination of these factors has emerged as a result of the complex interaction of an array of forces of a technological, ideological, political, economic, and domestic political nature in each country in response to global influence.

The imposition of digital technology is raising issues involving the role of local cultures in the globalization of media policy and markets. Advances in technology have had an impact on the social role of information technologies too, because the transition in media markets that followed the adoption of open-skies policy is providing the means for further technological advancement with global impact.

This process constitutes the main trends of media systems and can reflect future developments in the broadcasting, new media, and telecommunications sectors. Whereas traditionally media systems were characterized by a high degree of regulation in the interest of public service criteria, deregulation policies have now become dominant around the world, leading to free market competition common to all countries.

Examination of the global impact on changes in local media polices is based on the assumption that media commercialization can be designated as having a mediating role between cultural perceptions and technological trends. The increased role of mediation developed as a result of the globalization of media policy and the prominence of new technologies in the transfer of influence to the free market. It comprises the growing dispute between cultural and technological policies, which generally results in changes in advertising and content.

The combination of cultural and technological development has had a profound impact on the commercialization of broadcasting systems and the nature of public policy. This structure has been of a global nature, although its specifics have differed among countries, according to domestic aspects that maintain the type of mediation of media commercialization.

In the new structure of media policy, similar developments can be attributed to all advanced countries, as a general local nature of commercialization evolves within the global communications network. This nature can be described within the framework of ten major conclusions that stimulate the way localism is employed within a global market:

1. New media developments have gone through the same basic trends of development, although at different speeds. The main course of development has been a shift in the nature of policy from a perception of cultural values into a definition of new media as a market-led industry dominated by commercial and competitive forces. Within this course of development, initial national differences in the social and political development of new media technologies diminished following the swift development of American cable and European regulatory responses to these changes.

2. Each of the major experiences in exploring the local and interactive capabilities of new technology—either initiated by public authorities, as in France and Germany, or commercially oriented, as in Britain and America—demonstrated attempts to advance the concept of an information society. Based on this analysis, it is argued that local and interactive perceptions

have not failed, but the specific technology (cable) was unable to implement these ideas. Now that a new atmosphere exists, with digital technology and deregulation policies, the social advantages of an information society and telecommunications networks have started to flourish once again. The development of new technologies comprises the same ideas of interactivity experienced in the 20th century, although the means to achieve these goals—through new technology and new policy—make the difference in the 21st century.

3. The overall result of media policies in the United States and the large media countries of Europe is that new media technologies and services are of a commercial type, with programming as the main attraction to consumers. The competition among technologies has given the consumer access to a wide range of new media services, with the forces of commercial and technological developments prevailing over social, cultural, and political perceptions.

4. The linkage between technological and cultural developments has been a major issue for public debate in all countries, as it has influenced the development of information technology and the larger issue of the social role of the information society. The transition in media policies and markets is providing the means for further technological advancement with global impact.

5. The linkage between global and local impact has intensified the mediating role of media commercialization while developing as an integral part of the globalization of media policy and markets. The argument made here is that the most important aspect of commercialization is the role of mediating policy, which allows the co-existence of global and local policy trends. As a result of this compromise structure, the role of media commercialization has proved to have an important capacity in the development of the new cultural order in broadcasting.

6. In this process, although new policy tends to clash with local aspects of public policy involving culture and technological development, the role of mediating policy has been crucial in the assessment of changes as a compromising force between cultural and global demands. This is because despite the evident global impact, domestic specifics have differed in each country. Local aspects depend on the extent of the changes imposed by the combination of cultural and technological aspects, thus determining the mediating role of media commercialization.

7. The global trends examined in this chapter demonstrate the changes in media policy in the last few decades and in the

decades ahead. Past experience shows that advanced technology and global media clashed with cultural policy because of different perceptions of commercial determinism. Competition from new media technologies offering digital transmissions has further accelerated the global impact of new media policies by promoting multiple channels and reducing the impact of national governments. For many years, a central characteristic of media policy has been that local markets differed according to national and regional characteristics and political issues had an impact on media policies. But in the current state of commercialization, global developments make new technology available and affordable for smaller markets and cost effective for huge companies with global appeal. In this way, commercial services are delivering an increasing number of channels and services, and global services are becoming a reality, not a theory.[18]

8. The wave of the future is digital services that will provide access to local programming while offering global services and diminishing differences between local media policies and markets. Media commercialization is implemented in all media systems, and the overall process of commercialization in the digital age can be considered as a general process that all countries should adopt and operate within its limits.[19]

9. Global culture is influencing yet is also dependent upon local agents and on the way globalization is perceived locally. Although globalization is influencing all countries and despite the development of global and international service providers, communications also remains a local business process that is dictated by local cultures. The combination of global and local culture is such that cultural products and television programs are global in their nature, but they can be distributed through local agents, which understand the culture and how to do business in their areas.

10. The linkage of culture and technology in the digital age requires joint ventures of global forces with local groups. New technology creates common media policies and global markets, but localism remains a dominant element in all countries. The direction of global media players is to form partnerships with groups. This is the way of reaching new market segments of non-English speakers. This is also the way commercialization is heading in the 21st century: global networks with local affiliates.[20]

SUMMARY

Global and local are two contrasting elements in media policy, although new technology and the commercialization of media systems have blurred the boundaries between cultural values and commercialization and created a more-or-less uniform media policy, which can be identified as commercialization in the digital age.

Digital technology is predicted to establish a new global society in the 21st century, but the effects of the new information age on the development of local societies are still unclear. Although it is already evident that globalization and technological advancement are changing the concept of localism and creating a new global society, dominated by a new cultural order of global policy and market rule, the impact of globalization on local media systems has to be examined according to differences in local perceptions of commercialization.

Media commercialization is defined in this chapter as the transfer of influence to the free market in all that falls under public policy, programming, and advertising, and the extent of these processes differs according to local variations and cultural determinism.

Commercialization in the digital age is examined according to eight major categories: the mediating role of media commercialization, commercialization policy, the new public television, new media markets, Americanization, protecting local culture, the social role of advertising, and the linkage between culture and technology.

These categories establish a compromise policy structure, which combines cultural and commercial development in each society. Commercialization of media systems has been an issue for debate around the world, following the main transition in media policy—from a regulated to a competitive media system. The compromise model of localism of media commercialization has developed as part of the new structure of global media policy that is linked directly to technological advancement of global media networks.

Digital technology is raising further the conflict between local cultures and the globalization of media policy and markets. Advances in technology can reflect on future developments in the broadcasting, new media, and telecommunications sectors, demonstrating the major changes in media policy and creating free market competition common to all countries. In this situation, although the counter relations between global and local developments in media policy are determined differently in each country, commercialization has changed the way commercial competition and cultural aspects are perceived.

Conclusion

Media policy in the third millennium has been a major issue for public debate both at the global level and domestically around the world. The growing reliance on the media for information and entertainment has intensified the argument on key issues involving media policy. The most important aspects include the extent of public regulation, the question of free speech and open-skies policy, the global expansion of pluralism, and the counterimpact of cultural and commercial perceptions. Technological development of new media and telecommunications services has raised additional questions on the role of new technologies in society and the impact of the process of globalization of media policy and markets.

The effects of the changes have been tremendous in all countries, as the process of globalization is making an impact on local media systems. All advanced countries have witnessed the adoption of commercial perceptions and have become vastly dependent upon global changes in media and telecommunications policies. The main course of development common to all media systems and services is evident with the triumph of technological advancement and policy changes. All countries are heading in the same direction of the same global media policy.

In the simplest definition of the realization of global policy changes in broadcast, new media, and telecommunications services, it can be said that policies and markets are going global. The process of change in media policy has been decisive, illustrating a common transformation in public policies leading to deregulation and privatization of national media and telecommunications systems and a global process of open-skies policy. These developments are leading to convergence of media and telecommunications policies and universal competition of all services available to the public.

In practice, however, the future structure of media systems is unclear and dependent upon the consumption of the new services by different societies. The future expansion of digital technology is also unclear, because the major changes to the structure, ownership, and regulation of media and telecommunications systems have encouraged growing competition of all media and telecommunications services and intensified the debate on the nature of policy for the 21st century.

The main conclusion in this book is that a general model of policymaking is broadly applicable to all advanced democratic countries with local aspects that influence particular outcomes. This structure is predicted to dominate media policy in the future, too. The discussion in the concluding chapter concentrates on the main changes predicted in media policy: establishment of global and uniform structure, new markets identified by multiple competition, secondary markets identified by local aspects, and the continual public debate and competition to determine the technologies that will dominate this century.

This chapter provides conclusive approaches to the main issues of media policy and presents an analysis of the new structure. The description of future tendencies illustrates the way that social, cultural, political, technological, economic, and commercial changes will continue to increase with the growing transition into digital technology and the policy changes that are expected to follow this direction.

The future analysis offers explanations for the outcome of policy-making processes that shape the development of new media. One major symptom of the new structure is that all countries are faced with the same fundamental imperatives that are pushing the broadcasting and telecommunications sectors into becoming global industries. According to this view, deregulation, privatization, and convergence processes are logical results of the rise of a technologically driven service economy and the development of competitive markets. But despite the global impact, future forecasts must evaluate competing approaches to the policy-making process that relate to local developments.

The account of the process of media policy for the 21st century put forward draws on and elaborates underlying themes that establish a new structure under which integration of media and telecommunications policy is evident. The role of regulators has been reduced to encouraging competition and maintaining public interest in new services. These developments have changed the traditional concepts of international and global fields and have influenced the natural adaptation of the globalization of media policy and markets. The impact of these policy changes on local media markets can be examined according to opportunities posed by new competitive markets and the formation of the information society.

CONCLUSION ONE: A GLOBAL STRUCTURE OF MEDIA POLICY

The new structure of media policy, which dominates developments at the global level, is making an impact worldwide. The research in this book examines the course of change by advocating that the development of public policies has gone through three distinctive stages leading to the development of a uniform structure. This course of change has taken place in all countries, which have witnessed the restructuring of the media and broadcasting sectors away from public service obligations, and approaches greater dependence on market forces.

The process of the changing structure of media policy encompasses major developments, starting from initial limited development of new media, followed by new media policies, and moving in the direction of global policy. Globalization has followed American and European major deregulatory moves, which spread to other parts of the world. This trend is common to all advanced countries, with pending deregulation across all regions predicted in the years ahead. The new global structure certainly increases commercial domination and international investments in new media and telecommunications operations.

Deregulation policies have been a major factor in accounting for the convergence and globalization of new media policy around the world and the establishment of a competitive environment in which direct competition of all media and telecommunications services dominate policy processes. The global challenge to national policies has elevated the media and telecommunications sectors to the level of global policy, with the two major policy developments being convergence of policy and technologies and competition of all media technologies and information services. These developments identify the current stage of policy and have created a new global structure that makes an impact everywhere.

Globalization of media markets and policy means one large market for the distribution of television programming and services and policy objectives that create uniform policy structure. Deregulation policies have combined technological, political, commercial, and cultural forces, leading to ideological changes in media policy and to the convergence and globalization of media markets. It is evident in this process that convergence of policy and technologies has become prominent, creating a global process of change.

Although new technologies are taking the world by storm while creating new international and global markets, examination of the development of media policy requires relating to differences in international and global fields. Whereas the definition of global is transparent, the limits of international fields are subject to different perceptions according to geographical location and policy preferences.

Globalization and localism have many definitions and differ in various parts of the world. Around the United States the common definition of globalization refers to all parts of the world outside of North America. In Europe domestic operations are considered as those that are taking place across the continent, and all other operations are international. Even in Europe there are different areas and different policy structures with regard to the media sector and the extent of development of media markets. Additional emerging areas of new media developments are Latin America, Asia, the Middle East, Australia, and Africa. These are considered developing markets in terms of technological advancement, and global developments are particularly influential in those areas. Competition is growing rapidly with the adoption of new technologies, and new program providers generally concentrate on direct-to-home services in certain countries within these regions.

As this research demonstrates, policy changes indicate that the success of new media technologies depends on programming rather than on the physical infrastructure by which programming is being delivered or the social and cultural perspectives of new media policies. Whereas the technologies of cable and satellite had been interlinked, they are now in direct competition, together with other technologies, creating global media policy and markets. The result of the new social order that has developed as part of an international and a global media market is that convergence has become evident, involving competition between all information services—broadcast television, cable TV, satellite services, telephone companies, wireless communications, and the Internet—guided by commercial considerations.

Globalization has resulted from the combination of cultural and political considerations together with technological and commercial domination. This process included the displacement of social and cultural policy objectives, which dominated early development, in favor of commercialization and globalization.

The new environment of global media culture means that programming is distributed among a variety of media markets, creating a global flow of programming and competition in which geographical and political boundaries have become meaningless. Entertainment is America's largest export, and American programming is available globally. Europe has long been the most lucrative and constant area for the distribution of programming, but the advent of new markets is also promising. Asia is the fastest growing market for media services, representing almost two-thirds of the world's population, and Latin America is effectively a two-language region.

The policy dynamics outlined in the book underline the role of technological developments and market forces in the development of media policy and markets. The similarities and the differences in the policies pursued in different countries demonstrate that despite differences in approach, media markets have proliferated following the adoption of new technology and commercial policy. The development of new media policies represents a similarity in the development of broadcasting systems around the world as the domination of open-skies policy becomes worldwide. This process demonstrates that opportunities posed by global media markets are in fact implemented within the limits of global media policy while establishing a global structure.

Following the adoption of new media technologies of cable and satellite, the nature of cultural characteristics and social intercourse has changed also. The research advocates that the early perceptions of cable as part of a social and cultural policy thinking agenda can be seen as indications for later and more comprehensive changes in media policy. The unsuccessful outcome of these attempts was the trigger for policy changes, with Europe following the American experience of deregulation and market-led policy for cable and satellite. These technologies can now be considered as a commercial and technological initiative, with the entire media sector following the same trend.

Despite substantial differences among countries, it is nevertheless argued that implementation changes policy aims to some degree and that policy has become global and dominated by commercial perceptions. The conflict between new media and cultural identity became significant following the globalization of media policy and markets with the notion of national sovereignty being under siege as a result of developments in new media and telecommunications services.

According to this analysis it is clear that the United States, Britain, France, and Germany are at the forefront of media policy. They have determined the course of media policy in terms of historical development, regulation of the media, and the cultural context and structure within which the media operate. As this book confirms, the development of global media policy offers an ideal arena in which the interplay of the competing factors of politics, sociological welfare, and cultural identity—national as well as global—can be examined.

The future forecast regarding the nature of international and global media markets offers a distinct course of development that is illustrated by deregulation and globalization. Whereas in the early phases, public service perceptions dominated broadcasting systems, the American experience of deregulation and market-led policy for cable and satellite was the trigger for policy changes in the three largest media countries of Europe. This course spread later on a global scale. This leads to the conclusion that the emergence of international and global media markets have resulted from changes in the four countries examined in this book and have led to further technological development and internationalization and globalization of media policies and markets around the world.

Conclusion and Forecast

In examining future tendencies in media policy, changes in local policies should be considered as part of a global process. The global impact is evident because the globalization of broadcasting led to a growing recognition of the need for wider regulatory changes, which created new markets for broadcasting, new media, and telecommunications services. The combination of technological development and policy changes emerged as a result of the complex interaction of an array of forces of a technological, ideological, global, political, economic, and domestic political nature. American free market and open-skies policy, the directives issued by the European Council, and the increased competitiveness of American and European broadcasting, new media, and telecommunications industries have all provided for global competition of all information services, with market rather than government domination.

The transition into global media policy includes political, technological and social implications, which are in effect in all advanced countries and create a global process of change:

1. Political Implications. The new structure is influenced by deregulation policies, convergence of new media policies, and the start of new competitive markets for media and telecommunications services. This process has had global consequences, representing new frontiers for television. Although policies in all countries have confronted similar problems of social, cultural, and political issues that delayed new media developments, the American experience of free market has prevailed in

Europe as well. The provisions for cable operators to carry satellite transmissions have diminished the impact of public broadcasting, and policy differences have been reduced due to changing political attitudes, which created increasingly international networks of finance, ownership, and programming.

The transition into digital technology has tremendous political effects of both a local and global nature, because the relative advancement of countries will be examined though their adoption of digital technology. If leading countries like the United States and Britain convert their broadcasting systems into fully digital networks, other countries will be forced to do the same, simply because the supply of programming and transnational transmissions will be available only in a digital form.

2. Technological Implications. The technological transition evident today is from the analog method of signal transmission into a digital method of storing and converting data in the form of binary digits. Digital transmissions and services can be delivered to the home through a range of advanced and competitive technologies: digital terrestrial television, digital satellite, and digital cable services. Digital terrestrial stations, like new media services of satellite and cable, now have the capacity to broadcast hundreds of channels. Digital satellite has been one of the fastest growing industries in American history and is spreading across Europe and in other parts of the world. The more advanced cable networks are also making room for new channels while upgrading the analog networks into digital service. Other providers also seek to compete in the new market. These are telephone companies, wireless communications—Local Multipoint Distribution Services (LMDS) and Multichannel Multipoint Distribution Services (MMDS)—and Internet Service Providers.

3. Social Implications. Following the liberalization of new media and telecommunications policy in America and Europe, the wider processes of globalization have placed new demands on multinational companies and national governments. This course of development has changed the relationship between giant companies and political institutions. The efficiency of global operations is increasingly dependent on fast and secure international communications, using new media and information services, and they are less and less supportive of the relevance of national boundaries and jurisdictions.

The end result of this process is evident—public organizations, which have traditionally provided satellite and telephone services exclusively, are also being privatized and competing with the services provided by cable, DBS, and broadcast television. The implementation of a new competitive environment will open up new market developments and offer new opportunities for both public and private operators.

Technology services are becoming global, creating a global society, also known as the information society.

Privatization and commercialization are radically changing the social implications of new technology. For example, the privatizing of multinational satellite services should enable these organizations to become more competitive by creating joint ventures and offering direct access to consumers. Other examples include the privatization of telephone companies and the permission for them to supply television and wireless services (including third generation wireless technology). The result is enormous social change, following the growing competition to determine which industry will be the primary deliverer of advanced information and entertainment services.

CONCLUSION TWO: COMPETITION AS ALTERNATIVE TO REGULATION

New technologies, new programming options, and favorable regulatory conditions are stimulating the growth of media and telecommunications services in the international and global fields. In the new structure of media policy, commercial opportunities prevail in broadcasting and intense competition is matched by telecommunications.

The direction of media policy illustrates the three-stage model, which included early perceptions of public service broadcasting in the first stage, new media policies in the second stage, and is now dominated by global media policy in the third and current stage. This course of change demonstrates that in the early stage of media policy the old structure of broadcasting dominated public policies and prominence was given to terrestrial broadcasting. The development of new media policy in America has been promoted since the 1970s, and Europe followed suit in the 1980s, both moving toward deregulation. In the course of this transformation, public authorities have launched plans to develop new media technologies as a secondary force, but the current stage is characterized by a deregulatory stance that is more hospitable to commercial services. This trend was intensified in the 1990s and continues in the 21st century, as new media technologies have become subject to major policy initiatives. Although the new policy aim has been achieved through deregulatory moves, international institutions such as the FCC and the European Community have assumed prominence.

The substantial changes that have characterized public policy have made an impact on the role of public authorities. In the new era of global and commercial competition involving all new media and telecommunications services, the efficiency of regulation has become questionable due to the deliberately diminished role of governments and public authorities in media policy. The globalization of policy and markets, which results from the move closer to global media policy, is evident in that commercially driven new media services are expanding swiftly around the world. These outlets offer services, programs, and events that had previously been available to viewers for the price of a license fee, whereas today new services financed through advertising, pay-per-view, and subscription are consistently taking a leading role in the new media scene.

The new structure of global broadcasting poses challenges to the legitimacy of national broadcasting systems, and policy convergence has essentially become the new platform for public policy, identifying the operation of new media and telecommunications services in the new global order. The consequent formation of global media policy has proved that although each country faces similar problems of maintaining their cultural identities all are also faced with the same fundamental global impact of convergence and deregulation.

In examining the development of media policy in past, present, and future directions, it is evident that the contrasting experiences of the countries discussed in this book and the different ways that new media policies have subsequently developed can be attributed to the interplay of a series of factors. These include differences in social and political perceptions of cable and satellite, the political culture, the regulatory environment, and the relative power of central and local governments. It is claimed that despite these distinctions, the marketplace for television around the world has been remarkably transformed, as technological developments and market changes have accelerated new media policies. This conclusion is illustrated by the trend of events that led to the growing global convergence of media policies.

Following policy changes in America, European regulations have been in flux, as the emphasis has shifted from a culturally based to a market-led policy. Britain has had the most liberal policy, France has concentrated on the cultural aspects of broadcasting, and Germany has been in between—not as market-dominated as in Britain, but opposed to the way media policy had been practiced in France.

Analysis of the role of national governments explains the main trends of policy dynamics. Although it is evident that there are differences in the policies of the countries examined in this book, it can be concluded that all three largest media countries of Europe have gone through the same distinct stages of development in regard to the role of governments. Whereas in the first stage governments did not permit cable developments, since the 1980s European cable developments have been encouraged by national governments that had initially seen public policies and social and cultural aspects as more important than commercial initiatives. In the third stage, market forces mainly determine the pace of development of new media. Although the end result of this transition is that policies have become common, the role of regulators is still important.

The transition in new media policies has also included technological development and market change and provided the driving force behind the global revolution. The ability of new technologies to provide transmissions with wider geographical coverage has resulted in global distribution of programming and the formation of global media markets. The increased globalization of media markets and the advent of commercial competition have further changed the political and commercial role of new media and made it relatively easy to transmit a variety of channels.

The current phase of global policy, which dominates in all advanced countries, has raised the complex distinction between advanced technology and free flow of information. These issues are being raised because the boundaries between the old structure of terrestrial broadcasting and new media and telecommunications services are diminishing, following the triumph of commercialization and globalization and the emergence of the information society. Further changes in the global television landscape can be predicted, because the ties that bind national policies have been broken with the emergence of new competitive markets.

In these markets, advanced technology and competition of all broadcast, new media, and telecommunications services have provided the means for new technological and policy trends to dominate. As a result, traditional distinctions between the various sectors of telecommunications and media industries are becoming increasingly blurred while creating an umbrella industry in which voice, data, and entertainment are carried on single networks.

The biggest challenge facing new media markets is the advent of competition. The main initial advantage for digital direct-to-home satellite services has been their ability to provide multiple channels and programming services, and today other technologies are following with new products and marketing strategies. Getting ready for the entrance of new competitors into what have been monopoly or highly concentrated markets, cable operators are also adopting digital technology in order to take away the advantage of satellite services. Capital spending in cable systems has increased dramatically to build infrastructure to multiply the number of channels and to upgrade systems in two-way capacity to bring signals back out of the home. In addition to new media services of cable and satellite, digital terrestrial television is starting, and telephone companies are making plans to supply video services. Similar competition is developing in other markets, such as telephone services and wireless technology.

The inevitable course of development has been that commercial perceptions have prevailed over social and cultural objectives. The role of governments has been reduced to maintaining competition, with different technologies available to the public. Although in the course of the transformation in media policy, public authorities, at different points in time, moved to promote technological development to meet broader public interest objectives, the current stage is characterized by a deregulatory stance that is more hospitable to commercial services.

Conclusion and Forecast

Competition is now the alternative of regulation. The role of regulators in the new competitive environment is crucial to the transformation from a regulated media system dominated by monopolies to a free and competitive market. In this policy structure, the role of public authorities is limited to maintaining free competition, as part of a new commercial policy thinking. Although it is commonly agreed that vigorous competition is the best way to provide the most efficient and advanced media and telecommunications services, regulators have generally seen it necessary to guarantee that the change of media policy would enable the formation of open-market and competitive media systems.

In forecasting the future role of regulators in a deregulated global media market, some conclusions on the changing structure of national media systems can be reached:

1. *Changes in Public Policy.* The commercial impact on the development of the broadcasting sector explores the changing role of media policies and the shift in the balance between public service and commercial policies. Digital technology can provide hundred of channels and a variety of advanced services, and in this way pose additional challenge to terrestrial broadcasters, both public and commercial, which struggle to maintain a leading role in broadcasting.

2. *Changes in New Media Policy.* The globalization of media markets means that despite important policy differences, the main course of development for new media technologies has been a shift from the social and cultural perception to a definition of them as a market-led industry dominated by commercial and competitive forces. Initial national differences diminished as a result of commercialization and globalization, as market forces took center stage, displacing cultural policies initiated by governments and political institutions.

3. Changes in Global Policy.   The role of regulators is changing with the triumph of new technology. With technologies such as DBS, the Internet, and digital television there are no effective ways of regulating global services. The lesson that can be learned from this analysis is that the triumph of deregulation policies and free market approach has become a global trend shaped by the combination of technological advancement and market forces. Within this global process, the extent of commercialization in local markets is determined according to their response to global trends. The global and interactive capabilities of the new services make an impact on local regulatory authorities, because their ability to control the spread of technological advancement and cultural rational becomes questionable.

4. Changes in Competition Policy.   Today free market approach and open competition to all services and technologies are widely accepted as the cornerstone of media policy. The debate that identifies media policies and systems in the new competitive age is not about the question of whether competition should be introduced or not, but about its terms and conditions. In the new competitive markets, governments are encouraging the involvement of commercial operators, because in addition to attempts to gain national economic benefits in the global market, the changes are typically beyond the budgets and technical expertise of governments. Another difficulty for governments moving from a monopoly to a competitive environment is the need to react faster than before to consumer demand in order to keep market shares.

CONCLUSION THREE: CHANGES IN LOCAL MARKETS

The opportunities offered by new competitive markets and advanced technologies have changed the way local societies consider the options posed by television programming. In the global process of media policy, advancement of broadcasting systems differs from country to country in response to the challenges imposed by new media technologies, but the main elements are similar to all countries. Commercialization has highlighted the dispute between commercial competition and cultural aspects on the structure of media policy and the relative impact of local and global culture.

In the impending process of global revolution in media policy, the pattern of changes in local markets and policies has had some common characteristics. According to this structure, commercialization is examined in this book as a general process that should apply to all countries, even though the terms vary according to local policy differences. Under this general process of development, technological advancement and policy changes have determined the nature of commercialization at the global level, and local specifics have been determined according to mediation between social and commercial forces in each country.

In this context, both global trends and domestic debates on the nature of national broadcasting systems influence programming and advertising. The impact of commercialization on broadcasting policy is explained in the social mediation between cultural and commercial aspects and the extent to which it organizes the broadcasting media. The development of new technology has provided the overall impetus for global changes in policy, as the terms of commercialization policy establish a new structure that mediates among the main forces that operate in each country.

The initial most significant change was the shift in balance between public service and commercial broadcasting. The experiences in the first two stages of media policy contain lessons about success and failure in public service broadcasting, and the current structure can be applied to the larger question of public service and commercial broadcasting.

Perhaps the most important lesson is that it was not until the early experiences proved unsuccessful that commercial competition and market policy were adopted across Europe and then around the world. Examination of the way commercialization policy has developed in different parts of the world is beneficial in providing a format according to which the extent of changes can be evaluated. It offers an established structure to evaluate commercialization at the global level and as a local process. Although it is not easy to give a general definition of the essence of commercialization, the cultural experiences of this development can be seen as an ongoing process that profiles the main aspects of media policies adopted by different countries.

Another conclusion that emerges when evaluating the global process is that the driving force behind the telecommunications revolution has been provided by the combination of technological developments and market change. The regulatory changes that affected European broadcast media, following the American experience, and the growing global enthusiasm for privatization, advocate a new deregulated market model for broadcasting and telecommunications services. Throughout this process it has become evident that despite public attempts to promote cable development to meet broader public interest objectives, such as community transmissions and interactive cable systems, the role and impact of governments has diminished, and deregulation and convergence of global markets now characterize new media policies.

These conclusions bring up the impact of globalization on local policies. Commercialization of media systems has been an issue for debate in many countries, as they have experienced the main course of change from a regulated to a competitive media system. As the research corroborates, media policy has become a global issue, influenced by global transmissions that ignore local issues and cultural differences. This process demonstrates that commercialization is an obvious result of the new era of global media policy and is linked directly to technological advancement and global media networks.

The general course of media commercialization examined in this book has developed along with the growing impact of new media technologies, and accordingly has to be perceived as part of the globalization of new media policy and markets. This perspective is based on the assumption that the development of cultural aspects in broadcasting has been evidenced in all Western countries, although within this common structure, local versions of commercialization policy have differed in response to the combination of global and cultural impact.

The role of media commercialization also demonstrates that although the end result is that globalization has prevailed, the effects of commercialization differ according to the local adoption of global and commercial trends. This general course demonstrates the relevance of differences in local policies, which can evaluated within the general course of development of media policy—a course that all national media systems are heading toward.

The argument made here is that changes in local markets have gone through a distinct course with general characteristics common to all countries. The addition of new broadcasting services has been a major force in the commercialization of public broadcasting systems, because the legitimacy of governments to regulate broadcasting became questionable with the availability of commercial transmissions.

Mediation has been an important factor in the transition of new media policies from cultural values to globalization and commercialization. Common to all three largest European media countries is that following initial unsuccessful attempts to implement cable policies that highlighted public policy and cultural values, attitudes changed and new approaches for new media development were adopted. The new services can now be considered as commercial initiatives, with the entire media sector following the same trend of competition.

The course of development of cable policies can reflect on the overall transition of the broadcast media into a market-led industry in which commercial considerations have prevailed over social, cultural, and public service perceptions. The impact of new technology on the evolution of commercialized media systems has been the result of the globalization of media policy and markets. The new structure followed changes in the nature of public broadcasting services, which have become the sites of mediation between the defenders of cultural aspects in broadcasting and those who campaign for commercial and competitive transmissions. This course followed the adoption of new technologies in America and Europe and then became a global trend in effect in all advanced countries.

Conclusion and Forecast

The development of public policy for the broadcast media has involved the decisive role played by cultural aspects, which clashed with technological advancement and global policy. This ultimate characterization has influenced all countries, because the advent of new technology has changed public policies and forced new attitudes that are dominated by commercialization and globalization. According to this analysis, technological development and policy changes in favor of free market domination have formed a new structure of media commercialization that requires mediation between local forces and global media policy.

In determining future trends in media policy, the implications of mediation of local policies define the extent of cultural determinism in each country, according to the following principles:

1. A Prominent Process of Change.   The structural changes that have occurred in the process of commercialization have followed the three-stage development course of media policy. The commercialization of media systems started with structural changes in the nature of public broadcasting services and the addition of private commercial channels. This process was evident in the second stage of media policy, after commercialization was generally restricted in the first stage. In the third stage, the combination of global and local developments in technology and culture results in the defacto process of media commercialization.

2. Globalization.   The general impact of new technology leads to the conclusion that the resulting process of media commercialization is common to all countries operating within the new system of global media policy. Changes in local markets have resulted from the global impact and should be examined within this perspective. With the mediating role of commercialization, globalization of media policy and markets has become the ultimate direction in which all countries are heading. This goal is secured by the role of mediating policy in each country, which balances the contradictions between global and local policy trends.

3. The Counter Impact of Local Forces. Although the model of media policy has to be considered as part of a global process that affects all countries, policy processes at the local level need to be understood as the outcome of the power plays of key interest groups in each country. Internal policymaking is likely to be influenced by experiences elsewhere, especially in the countries that are perceived as being at the forefront of relevant developments. This is particularly likely to be so in areas where the country in question has prior experience with media policy and developments in the sector in question resonate with wider shifts in policy ideologies. Local policy outcomes must therefore be understood as the product of a complex intersection of lessons from abroad that being mediated through the forces generated by the specificity of a country's history and by the special characteristics of its social, cultural, and political system.

CONCLUSION FOUR: THE TECHNOLOGY OF THE FUTURE

The future structure of media policy may be unknown, but forecasts can be made based on the way global media policy has developed. The analysis in this book is based on the global course that has dominated developments in the broadcasting and telecommunications sectors in the last decades. This generalization of developments in past and present perspectives is similarly important to evaluation of future analysis of media policy research. It demonstrates that current tendencies are likely to be effective in the decades ahead and that the current stage of media policy is also likely to lead policymakers in drawing future plans.

New media services are growing rapidly with massive investment around the world. Developments over the next few years will take media and telecommunications services to new fields of even greater appeal and diversity. The demand for a wider choice of television programming and advanced services is increasing rapidly along with advances in technology and market changes. The main aspect of these developments is competition. Policy changes in all countries are designed to create an open and competitive market in order to significantly increase consumer choice.

In examining the prospects for digital television, it is evident that its development is surrounded by social, cultural, regulatory, technical, and commercial obstacles, reflecting uncertainty about its potential market. New opportunities to serve the interests of social groups depend on the links among different forms of broadcasting and telecommunications services and on public demand for nontelevision services.

Unlike previous experiences with new technologies, the role of public authorities in endorsing technological and policy changes will be decisive with regard to the adoption of digital technology, because the impact of technological changes is global. Because new technology and global policy changes are driving convergence, they are encouraged by government moves to deregulate monopoly markets.

The current phase of development is based on commercial competition and digital service. This is clearly demonstrated by the fact that previously the development of new media technologies combined the services of cable and satellites, whereas after the development of digital technology these services operated in a competitive environment, together with other advanced technologies.

However, the future structure of digital expansion is unclear and dependent upon the consumption of new services by different societies. Some argue that convergence will dominate, allowing competition among a variety of platforms—terrestrial solutions of broadcast networks, broadband cable services, direct-to-home digital satellites, digital subscriber line (DSL), wireless communications provided by telecom companies, and the Internet. Others predict that the personal computer will be the leading home terminal for advanced services and that Internet services will also dominate the television broadcasting market. The telecommunications industry forecasts that telecom services will dominate not only traditional telephone services but also new areas such as television broadcasting, advanced interactive services, and Internet access.

The prospects for interactive television and Internet access to become mass media are also unclear. The competitive environment requires all operators to rethink their traditional business strategies and compete with other service providers. In the convergence with the Internet, the advantages of interactive television in providing data broadcasting are better video quality and availability in every home. The direct possible linkage between a television show and interactive services of commerce and data allows viewers to take television as far as they wish in the comfort of the living room, and the relatively low cost of data broadcasting should make interactivity attractive to both programmers and viewers.

The advantages of interactive television are tremendous in terms of the social activities that can be attached to television viewing. These include, for example, the ability of individual viewers to control the program, to watch related events and previous shows and collect professional information, or to purchase merchandise and items presented on television. Other options are the availability of purchasing premium services such as virtual VCRs, video-on-demand, and high-speed access to interactive information and transaction content.

These advantages exploit the social functions of interactive television and demonstrate the main difference between Internet and television. Television viewing is a social activity, whereas the Internet is a solitary activity for professionals. Interactive television can develop as part of television programming, whereas Internet content is developed for PC users. In order for Interactive television to succeed, programs have to be driven by the ability to provide entertainment for the mass; retransmitting Internet content on television without any direct link to the entertainment aspect or to television programs cannot be attractive enough to capture a mass audience.

The competitive environment is changing the way traditional services operate. Media and telecommunications have traditionally been considered stable industries, because information and entertainment are always in demand, even during difficult economic conditions, because customers then tend to remain at home more often for their entertainment. But in the new structure of media markets, as national telecom companies move from monopoly to competition, although new unprecedented opportunities to expand the ability of digital services exist, the stakes for broadcasters are high. Media companies are becoming telecommunications providers, offering customers multiservice applications. Since the deregulation of telecom services around the world, advanced cable systems are a threat to traditional telecom operators because cable can offer telephony and Internet services.

The central aspects of the technological revolution are digitalization and interactivity—the ability to compress video information in digital form through normal phone lines and the development of switching technology that allows two-way communications through the television set. New media policy deals with the convergence of technologies, but the distinction between television and telecommunications services has become so blurred that the separation between media and telecommunications companies cannot be maintained.

It remains to be seen if interactivity will develop on television and if interactive television will take over the entertainment market. It also remains to be seen how broadband will develop as part of global communications and which new services and special channels will develop as interactive video-based technology that will become readily available in every home.

The actual implementation of the idea of digital democracy is dependent on the diffusion and popularity of interactive services, and it remains to be seen if new applications of television broadcasting will indeed prevail. As demonstrated in the history of television, the experience gained thus far with advanced capabilities of media and telecommunications technologies and services has proved that the medium is by far the prime source of entertainment and information in the home. The future adoption of advanced services, in addition to or in replacement of the traditional structure of programming services, is dependent primarily on the social adoption of information technology.

Based on this analysis, it can be predicted that the impact of the Internet as an entertainment medium for the mass will diminish. The Internet will become a service for professionals, regulators, and academics, whereas the main applications of television broadcasting and interactive services will be through interactive television and broadband technology.

Conclusion and Forecast

Several new technologies have appeared in the last decades, many of them providing the opportunity for interactive communication. The new technologies allow two-way services, in which users are part of the process and can determine the time and nature of the system. Users can "talk back" through the system and operate it at the time and location convenient to them. The most prominent development is digital technology, which allows voice, sound, text, data, and images to be stored and transmitted using the same basic technologies. The social implications of the digital age are important, because technological advancement permits different channels of information and an open marketplace of ideas. Global understanding of the importance of information is therefore one of the key issues that new technology and the marketplace of ideas need to facilitate the information society.

Uncertainty is dominating the structure, technologies, and the services that will eventually dominate future developments in information technology. On the one hand, the enormous advantages to the public provide optimistic forecasts for the adoption of new services. In contrast, the still low penetration rate of advanced services gives no indication of the way they will be finally adopted by the public.

Forecasts are based on contrasting assumptions about the technology that will dominate the digital age and the way different societies will adopt these technologies:

1. *Enormous advantages to the Public.*   Accessibility to new services is a major benefit of the digital revolution. The ability to enter the broadcasting media has become extensive because of advances in technology and digitalization, which offer a greater variety of channels and services at lower costs. Purchasing a satellite transponder and acquiring programming at a reasonable cost have become a reality in the new global television market, and will make narrowcast television and specialized services that appeal to small niche audiences a viable idea again.

The possibility of starting an Internet business by operating a portal or even becoming an Internet Service Provider is also widely available.

These services, which can appeal to the tastes of particular markets in each country, can also benefit from new tendencies that identify media policy around the world—that is, having no regulatory restraints and generally almost no content restrictions while using advertising and subscriptions to finance transmissions. In considering international markets and the relative ease of transmitting cross-cultural channels, new services such as specialized channels can gather a massive global audience.

2. Optimistic Forecasts. Further advancement in new media and telecommunications fields will become evident with the growing penetration of digital services. With hundreds of new channels and value-added services, viewing habits and patterns will also undergo major changes. If current optimism proves correct, international markets will certainly grow. The changes will include an increase in the number and variety of the programming and data outlets and in advertising revenues. This optimism is based on the fact that entertainment pay TV and information services are becoming common and that the adoption of digital services will also be rapid due to the much greater variety on offer. How and when digital services will prevail around the world are the two related questions that remain to be answered. Optimistic forecasts are that by the year 2010 digital services will dominate the market worldwide, after leading countries adopt digitalization.

3. The Future Remains Unclear. The digital revolution is going to change the way people live around the world, although predictions are always problematic. In light of the immense impact of digital broadcasting, there are concerns about the potential revenues and the number of services provided and how they would be perceived. The still low penetration rate of advanced services is another problem broadcasters and regulators are faced with. Despite comprehensive efforts, the public reaction is one of hesitation. Most people around the world will still have analog transmissions and view television as a passive experience, as they watch what is on the screen at a given time. When television will become truly digital people will move into an era of interactive television, and they will be able to interact with their television like they already interact with their computer. Interactive data services will bring the information society closer to the mass of the population in all advanced countries. The question remains whether interactive services will become a mass media and dominate the future structure of media policy or remain a secondary service to traditional broadcasting and telecommunications industries.

CONCLUSION FIVE: THE VISUAL DEVELOPMENT
OF MEDIA POLICY

This conclusion is meant to provide an analysis and forecast for the new structure of global media policy. The following analysis is constructed in a way that demonstrates the different stages media policy has developed through and the way leading to the current structure.

The comparative information in this conclusion summarizes the main aspects of the discussion in this book. It should help the reader understand different policies and the state of their globalization advancement, including the possible implications in different countries and the policy changes that should be expected in the future.

Another main goal is to provide a comprehensive outlook for the future by drawing a future structure of expansion and demonstrating the way the new structure will be forced worldwide. This structure has to be seen as a global process that is making an impact on all countries, including countries that lag in the adoption of new media and global media policy.

Characteristic	First Stage of Media Policy: The 'Old Structure' of Broadcasting	Second Stage of Media Policy: New Media Policies	Third Stage of Media Policy: Global Media Policy	The Digital Age
Policy Trend	Early perceptions of broadcasting were dominated by social and cultural values, as part of a national structure for broadcasting and telecommunications services aimed at endorsing public service objectives and monitoring the development of new technologies.	A new approach started to dominate in the United States and the largest media countries in Europe, with national media policies based on the adoption of new technologies and the addition of commercial television outlets.	A global course of change. New media policy has been adopted around the world, based on three main principles: deregulation and privatization, policy convergence, and competition of all media and telecommunications services.	Transformation into digital technology is progressing, with a new global policy for new technology, television services, and programming. The new structure is changing the way local societies use media and telecommunications services in the 21st century.
Timetable	Since the early 1940s until the early 1970s in the United States and until the early 1980s in Europe.	Since the early 1970s in the U.S. and the early 1980s in Europe, until the late 1980s in both continents.	Since the early 1990s in the U.S. and Europe, spreading around the world in the 21st century.	The digital age is going to dominate media policy for the 21st century.
Structure	A local structure. Dominance of public service principles, encouraging the social and cultural role of broadcasting.	A mixed structure. Deregulation of media systems and development of cable systems with new services delivered through satellites.	A global structure. Media policies have become global and commercial. Multi-channel services led to adoption of free-market competition.	The 21st century is dominated by transformation into digital technology and competition of all media and telecommunications technologies.

Characteristic	First Stage of Media Policy: The 'Old Structure' of Broadcasting	Second Stage of Media Policy: New Media Policies	Third Stage of Media Policy: Global Media Policy	The Digital Age
Techonology	Off-air television transmissions with limited channel capacity dominated broadcasting markets. Media policy gave prominence to the quality of programming, which only national organizations could guarantee, and the development of other technologies was not permitted.	Initial changes in media policy were made possible with the advent of new technologies. Technological advancement was adopted through competition between old media of off-air broadcasting and new media technologies of cable and satellite.	New technology is spreading globally, with competition of all media and telecommunications services. A new competitive environment influenced by deregulation, privatization, and convergence policies leads technological advancement.	The transition into digital technology combines a variation of advanced services: digital terrestrial television, digital satellite, broadband cable, telephone companies, wireless communications, the Internet and interactive applications.
New Media	New media was restricted in the U.S. and generally prohibited in Europe. New technologies were defined by policy-makers as having a secondary role to broadcast television. Their main role was to enhance the quality of local and national transmissions.	Permission was given for new technologies to operate alongside the old structure of terrestrial broadcasting. Multichannel services by cable and satellite provided the most important development in media policy in the last century.	Uniform and global policy thinking with new media and telecommunications services spreading around the world. Market forces have taken center stage, displacing social and cultural policies initiated by governments and creating new policy objectives common to all nations.	The transition into digital technology is spreading globally. All new media and telecommunications systems are capable of carrying a variety of sophisticaled services, with a significant increase in the number and quality of the channels and the services offered.

Characteristic	First Stage of Media Policy: The 'Old Structure' of Broadcasting	Second Stage of Media Policy: New Media Policies	Third Stage of Media Policy: Global Media Policy	The Digital Age
Cable and Satellite	Multichannel services were not permitted. Cable systems were available only in remote areas. They developed as Community Antenna Television systems (CATV). Satellite services were unavailable. They were restricted by government control and not permitted for private or commercial use.	Cooperation of the two technologies. Cable systems developed with programming that was produced and packaged for distribution solely to their subscribers. New services delivered through low-powered satellites provided transmissions directly to cable systems.	New services provided through Direct Broadcast Satellites gave new opportunities for the establishment of market-oriented principles and global operation. Cable and satellite have transformed the broadcasting sector by offering additional programming to the services available through terrestrial transmissions.	Cable and satellite operate in a digital, global, and highly competitive environment. Policy differences have diminished with the rise of commercialization, globalization, and adoption of digital technology. Free market competition, advanced technology and new services dominate future cable and satellite developments.
Commercialization	Restrictive policy dominated, aimed at encouraging public broadcasting and cultural perceptions. In Europe almost all commercial operation was prohibited. In the U.S. the policy was designed to create a non-commercial alternative to the commercial television system—in the form of public television (PBS—Public Broadcasting Service).	Market-oriented policies allowed for technological development, deregulation and adoption of independent and competitive television services of new media technologies. Media policy became commercial, dominated by domestic and global financial interest groups rather than by public authorities.	A new structure of commercial media policy is evolving, with deregulation and privatization (policy changes at the local level) and globalization (adoption of open-skies policy), policy convergence and competition of all media and telecommunications services. Global media policy has become dominated by new technology and global competition.	Commercialization and multiservice competition have become the core elements of media policy for the 21st century. Telecom companies are becoming Internet and telephony providers, cable companies are moving away from traditional cable services, and satellite operators and Internet service providers are moving to make all services available.

Characteristic	First Stage of Media Policy: The 'Old Structure' of Broadcasting	Second Stage of Media Policy: New Media Policies	Third Stage of Media Policy: Global Media Policy	The Digital Age
Public Policy	The role of public authorities was decisive in developing national broadcasting systems and ignoring new technology and multichannel services. In Europe public broadcasting dominated, aimed at exploring the social and cultural aspects rather than the commercial capabilities of broadcasting. In the U.S. media policy favored broadcast television, and local multichannel services were limited because of restrictive public policies.	Transformation of the role of governments—from a regulated media system with public goals into a deregulated industry with commercial perceptions. Policy shifted tremendously with the adoption of a market model. The role of governments was particularly substantial in the development of new media policy and technologies and permission for commercial television and new technologies.	Competition is the alternative to regulation. Political decisions have changed the course of media policy by diminishing the role of governments, converging media and telecommunications policies, and enhancing competition within the broadcast media. A global structure has been developed, in which all technologies participate in the competition for the provision of advanced services on a global scale.	Market forces and global regulatory authorities dominate today's policies. Regulatory moves concentrate on enhancing competition among all services, removing competitive restrictions and integrating all technologies. Media policy is a global process that applies to all countries, with deregulation, privatization and convergence policies dominating the development of the media and telecommunications sectors.

Notes

INTRODUCTION

1. Source: Saul Hansell, "TV's monoliths learn that the Web is a fragmented world," in: *The New York Times*, August 14, 2000, Technology Section.
2. Source: National Cable Television Association (NCTA), 2002.
3. For additional information on the development of cable and satellite in Europe, see for example: www.SkyReport.com
4. Source: National Satellite Convention, 2002.
5. Source: www.skyreport.com, May 21, 2002.

CHAPTER 1: THE THREE-STAGE DEVELOPMENT COURSE OF MEDIA POLICY

1. On the First Amendment, see: Healy, 1986; Papas, 1987; Sandman, Rubin and Sachsman, 1982; Salvaggio, 1983; Saylor, 1986.

2. On the development of public television in the United States, see for example: Bittner, 1983; Black and Whitney, 1983; Dunham, Lowdermilk and Broderick, 1958; Frank and Greenberg, 1980; Gibson, 1977; Gordon, 1965; O'Brien, 1979; Marcus, 1986; Pember, 1983; Sterling and Haight, 1978; Summers, Summers and Pennybacker, 1978.

3. For additional information on the development of American cable policy in the first stage, see for example: Hollins, 1984; Kaatz, 1982; Mosco, 1979; Rogers, 1986; Singleton, 1986; Wadlow and Wellstein, 1986.

4. On the model of the "old structure" of broadcasting in Europe, see for example: MacDonald, 1988; McQuail, 1990, 1995; Tunstall and Palmer, 1991.

5. On the development of new media technologies in Europe in this period, see for example: Dutton and Vedel, 1992; Dutton, Blumler and Kraemer, 1987; Ferguson, 1986; Negrine, 1989, 1990.

6. Further discussion on the role of governments in Europe in the development of cable can be found in Chapter 2.

7. The mixed model in Europe is described in McQuail, 1995.

8. On the change of policy for noncommercial television in the United States, see: Baughman, 1992.

9. A transponder is a component in a satellite that receives and transmits television or date signals (Dizard, 1994).

10. More information on the nature and impact of the deregulation of cable in the United States in the 1970s and 1980s can be found in: Berman, 1986; Cantor and Cantor, in Ferguson, 1986; Corn-Revere, 1993; Dizard, 1994; Grow, 1985; Howard and Carroll, 1993; Laudon, in Dutton, Blumler, and Kraemer, 1987; Rogers, 1986; Singleton, 1986; Willis, 1994.

11. Following the deregulation of the media sector, the role of federal authorities is considered as checks and balances, in which the main concern is the provision of free competition. For example, see: Herman and McChesney, 1997. On the development of cable, see: Singleton, 1986; Corn-Revere, 1993; National Cable TV Association (NCTA), 2000.

12. On the development of new media and broadcasting in Europe in the 1980s, see for example: Dutton and Vedel, 1992; McQuail, de Mateo and Tapper, 1993; Negrine and Papathanasspoulos, 1990; Siune and McQuail, 1993.

13. For further discussion on the definition and outcome of deregulation of new media, see for example: Dyson and Humphreys, 1989.

14. More information on the process of deregulation can be found in: Mosco, 1988, 1990. The impact of deregulation on new media policy in Europe is also discussed in Chapters 2 and 3.

15. For more information on the definition and mechanisms of privatization discussed in this section, see: Murdock, 1990.

16. The European Union was set up in 1993. Today there are 15 member states. The organization gathers 375 million people and is the world's largest economic power. In 2004, 10 new members of the former eastern block will join the EU.

17. For additional information and further discussion on the impact of digital technology on convergence policy, see for example: Global Struggle for Communication, Media Literacy Online Project, College of Education, University of Oregon, www.interact.uoregon.edu/medialit.

18. On the development of digital services in the United States, see Chapter 4. Further information on the Telecommunications Act can be found in section 2.4.

19. On the development of digital services in Europe, see Chapter 4. Further information on the Broadcasting Act can be found in section 2.4.

20. European regulatory policy is discussed in section 2.4.

21. It can be assumed that new laws by national governments would also guarantee more deregulatory movement and increased competition with global impact in the future.

CHAPTER 2: THE DIMINISHING ROLE OF GOVERNMENTS IN MEDIA POLICY

1. On the policy of the FCC during this stage, see for example: Kaatz, 1982; Mosco, 1979.

2. More information on the development of European cable policy in this stage can be found in: Dutton, Blumler and Kraemer, 1987; Head, 1985; Negrine, 1985.

3. Open-skies policy is discussed in Chapters 1 and 4. More information on the growth of American cable and public policy in this stage can be found in: Hollins, 1984; Singleton, 1986.

4. On the role of local authorities in regulating cable in the United States, see for example: Berman, 1986; Grow, 1985; Krug, 1985; Lloyd and Kerry, 1987; McGreger, 1987; Ross and Brick, 1987; Wadlow and Wellstein, 1986.

5. The Cable Act is discussed in Chapter 1.

6. The courts also played a major role in the deregulation course of cable in the United States. In 1977 the District of Colombia Circuit Court of Appeals vacated the FCC Pay TV rules and authorized satellite-supported services and cable operators to carry all pro-

gramming on cable pay TV channels. In 1985, in Quincy Cable TV Inc. v. the FCC, and Turner Broadcasting System v. the FCC, the District of Colombia Circuit Court of Appeals found that the FCC Must Carry rules violated the First Amendment right of cable operators and programmers (Fidde and Hslung, 1987). The court in the Quincy case found that by imposing mandatory carriage of local broadcast signals, the FCC rules infringed the editorial discretion of cable operators and restricted the opportunities of cable programmers to sell their services (Greene, 1986).

7. Integrated Services Digital Network (ISDN) is a plan for the establishment of telecommunications systems with digital technology, permitting the integrated transmission of any combination of voice, video, graphics, and data over a common system (Dizard, 1994).

8. For additional information on the development of European cable in the second stage, see for example: Cappe de Baillon, 1987; Dutton, Blumler and Kraemer, 1987; Dyson and Humphreys, 1988; Dyson and Humphreys, 1989; Ferguson, 1986; Head, 1985; Hollins, 1984; McQuail and Siune, 1986; Muller, 1987; Murphy, 1983; Negrine, 1985, 1989; Tydeman and Kelm, 1986.

9. On the development of the national cable policies in the three European countries, see for example: Dyson and Humphreys, 1989, 1991; McQuail, 1995; McQuail, de Mateo. and Tapper, 1993; Negrine and Papathanassopoulos, 1990; Ostergaard, 1992.

10. As of March 31, 1999, there was no regulation of higher tiers of service, such as "expended basic service," premium or pay-per-view service.

11. Former FCC Chairman, William E. Kennard, in an interview in *USA Today*, February 8, 2000, page 17A: "Telecom's Future: More Competition, Cheaper Prices."

12. The plan is entitled "A New FCC for the 21st Century." Published on August 12, 1999 by FCC Chairman William E. Kennard.

13. Jean Frannois Pons, Deputy Director General, Directorate General for Competition (DGIV), European Commission, in a speech at the International Bar Association, September 14, 1998.

14. On the state of European telecom privatization, see section 4.4.

15. On the programming aspects of European broadcasting, see Chapter 7.

16. Source: *Satellite Communication*, September 1998, page 24.

17. On European competition policy, see:
— The European Commission (EC), www.europa.eu.int/comm.
— The application of competition and antitrust policy in media and telecommunications in the European Union, a speech by the Deputy Director General for competition, The European Commission, September 14, 1998, in: http://europa.eu.tin/

comm/dg04/speech/eight/en/sp98041.html.

— The European Digital Convergence Paradigm: From Structural Pluralism to Behavioral Competition Law, www.elj.warwick.ac. uk.

— A Study to estimate the Economic Impact of Government Policies towards Digital Television, by: NERA, Phillipa Marks, Mark Viehiff, Ivan Viehoff, Smith Systern Engineering, and Richard Wornsley, January 1998, London, in: www.twinpentiuen.lep.l inst.ac.uk/library/nera2.htm.

— The European Digital Convergence Paradigm: From Structural Pluralism to Behavioral Competition Law, www.elj.warwick. ac.uk.

— Media Laws in Europe, www.liss.it/medialaw/lex/eurolex-uk.htm.

— IJCLP *International Journal of Communications Law and Policy*, www.digital-law.net.

CHAPTER 3: THE GLOBALIZATION OF MEDIA POLICY

1. On the development of American and European media policy in these stages, see Chapters 1 and 2.

2. For further information on differences in the social and political perceptions of new media policy in the three largest media countries of Europe during this period of media policy, see for example: Dutton, Blumler and Kraemer, 1987; Dutton and Vedel, 1992; Dyson and Humphreys, 1989.

3. This section discusses differences in political culture that have affected the main policy objectives in the three largest media countries of Europe. The related issue of the role of governments is discussed in Chapter 2.

4. These claims were made mainly by the TDF, which was responsible for cable head-ends and faced no cooperation from local authorities.

5. Changes in media policy have been distinct, combining technological development and policy and market responses to these advances. The convergence and globalization of new media policies has been the result of the competition between the new media technologies of cable and satellite. This competition was made possible because a new generation of high-powered Direct Broadcast Satellites (DBS) is providing unmediated reception by relatively small domestic dishes, with cost-effective services and a wider geographical coverage. Following the development of satellite ser-

vices, which offer a wide geographical coverage, cable and satellite are now considered as rival technologies. For further information on the development of new media, see previous chapters.

6. Permission for the supply of telecommunications services was later granted in the United States. See Chapter 1.
7. American and European regulatory processes leading to open-skies policies are discussed in Chapters 1 and 4.
8. Television Without Frontiers directive is discussed in Chapters 1 and 2. The document can be found at: www.europa. eu.int/comm/dg10/avpolicy/index–en.html.
9. Source: *Satellite Communications*, April 2000.
10. Source: www.HorwithAssociates.com.
11. Source: *The Washington Post*, June 7, 2000, page ED1 and SkyReport, January 24, 2003.
12. Source: Cable Satellite International, February 2002.
13. A number of senators in a letter to FCC Chairman Michael Powell and Attorney General John Ashcroft, www.skyreport.com, May 28, 2002.
14. In a presentation to the FCC, May 20, 2002.
15. On British broadcasting, see for example: ITC—Digital Terrestrial Television Background, www.isu.com/products/5–6g.html.
16. Source: www.ntl.co.uk.
17. Source: www.mediacentral.com, August 22, 2000, "Telewest Digital Delay UPS Merger Pressure."
18. Source: ITC, November 1998.
19. Source: ITC and the Broadcasting Act.
20. According to a research from Strategy Analytics, in: www.SkyReport.com, January 22, 2002.
21. ITC. www.itc.org.uk
22. See, e.g., P. Gumbel, "France, Succumbing to Multimedia Fever, is Racing to Catch Up with Competitors," in: *The Wall Street Journal Europe*, February 28, 1994, page 6.
23. Information on the French media market can be found in The Inside Cable and Television/Europe Datafiles, www.inside-cable.co.uk.
24. Information about the German media market can be found in The Inside Cable and Television/Europe Datafiles, www.inside-cable.co.uk.
25. Source: *Access Europe Broadband*, May/June 2002.

CHAPTER 4: THE NEW STRUCTURE OF MEDIA POLICY

1. The International Telecommunications Union defines high-defini-

tion as follows: "system designed to allow viewing at about three times the picture height, such as the system is virtually, or nearly, transparent to the quality of portrayal that would have been perceived in the original scene or performance by a viewer with normal visual activity. Such factors include improved motion portrayal and improved perception of depth."

2. The main interest of SDTV is multichannel television. Interactive services can also be on offer, although they are provided as added-value services.

3. On Digital Video Broadcasting, see for example: www.dvh.org. /dvb_dtv.html and www.dvh.org/dvb_news/dvb_ pr038.html.

4. See Chapter 6.

5. Cooperation between governments and broadcasters is required to implement the transition to digital technology. Despite the different approaches and technical systems, digitalization has been widely accepted around the world as the technology of the 21st century. In the summer of 1997 the International Telecommunications Union (ITU) formally adopted a new universal digital TV standard that combines features from separate digital HDTV standards that America's Advanced Television Standards Committee (ATSC) and Europe's Digital Video Broadcasting (DVB) Group have already adopted. The result is a single compatible system for digital television sets and a boost for digital services.

6. On the role of governments in the transition to digital television, see Chapter 2.

7. Programming is discussed in Chapters 6 and 7.

8. On digital TV timetable and formats in America, see for example: www.digitaltelevsion.com, www. atsc.org and www.ineract.uoregon.edu/medicalit/familiarticllefolder/global.html.

9. See wireless communications in section 2.5.

10. A single HDTV broadcast has three links: video, audio, and data channels, and the data channel is going to be the future of HDTV (a high-definition channel can send up to 19.3 MB of data per second. Sometime that data space is unused when the background of the picture does not change, and the data channel sends raw digital data over the unused section).

11. In a speech in the National Cable and Telecommunications Association's Convention, May 8, 2002.

12. Source: www.cscinte.co.uk, April 2002.

13. On the transformation to digital television in Europe, see for example: *The European Digital Convergence Paradigm: From Structural Pluralism to Behavioral Competition Law*, www.elj.warwick.ac.uk.

14. The leading interactive services are Video-On-Demand, interactive shopping and interactive video games. VOD allows viewers to

access and view movies and television shows from an information bank. Interactive shopping allows viewers to choose the type of goods they wish to be presented through virtual shopping malls and stores and select the items they wish to purchase. Interactive video games offer the ability to participate in games of choice and compete through the television set with other participants.

In VOD a large number of programs are stored in a central video library and any viewer can purchase the desired program directly from the television set. The program can be controlled by each viewer—stopped, repeated, or wound forward or backward in the same way as a videotape. A less technically complicated version is Near-Video-On-Demand (NVOD), in which a particular program is broadcast with certain intervals on some channels, so a new version is started every time. For example: the program is broadcast on six channels staring every ten minutes, so that the viewers can start, stop and then rejoin the program as they choose.

15. See section 6.3.
16. According to the Cable Television Year-End Review of 1998.
17. Source: Gartner Group. Inc., in tele.com, November 13, 2000, page 32.
18. The FCC, the National Cable Television Association, and the Consumer Electronics Association voluntarily agreed on technical specifications that will allow future consumer digital television sets and digital cable systems to work together.
19. Primarily Bell Atlantic Corporation—the largest local phone carrier in the United States.
20. Statistics on U.S. multi-channel market can be found in section 6.3
21. On mergers in cable and satellite industries, see section 3.3.
22. On the future of American cable, see for example:
— National Cable Television Association, ncta.com.
— FCC—www.fcc.gov.
— The Future of Cable: Cable's Public Affairs Efforts in Programming and Technology, published by FIOC, Public Affairs by the Cable TV Industry, www.ntca.cyberserv.com/qs/user–pages/floc.cfn.
— White Papers, Cable Television Technology Development, www.nap.edu/readingroom/books/wpui3/ch-33.html.
— Green, R. Richard, "Cable Television Technology Deployment", *White Papers*, www.nap.edu/readingroom/books/wpni3/ch-33.btml.
23. Eutelsat predicts that by 2004 there will be more digital television households than analog (*Satellite Communications*, January 2000, page 28).
24. According to Euroconsult. For more information on European satellite services, see for example: *Via Satellite*, September 2000, pages 18-28.

25. Satellite information can be found in: www.21st-satellite.com and
     www.dbsdish.com
26. Source: www.skyreport.com, April 25-26, 2002.
27. Source: IC—*International Cable*, July 2000, pages 22-25.
28. Source: 1999 VSAT Report, *The Comsys Broadband Report*, July 1999.
29. Source: *The Satellite Industry Guide*, published by the Fulron
     Corporation and the Satellite Industry Association, December 1999.
30. Source: Regulatory Access/FCCfiling.com.
31. Source: Telecommunications Industry Association, in tele.com,
     October 2, 2000, page 27.
32. Source: Cable and Satellite Interational, July/August 2001 and
     December 2001/January, 2002.
33. In Japan there are hardly any DSL customers, and wireless com-
     munications is leading the high-speed Internet access market. For
     more information see section 2.5 on wireless communications.
34. According to a Federal Communications Commission report, man-
     dated by Congress to examine the digital divide in the United
     States, published August 3, 2000.
35. Source: John Markoff, "Internet in Japan is Riding a Wireless Wave,"
     in: *The New York Times*, New Economy section, August 14, 2000.
36. Source: The Yankee Group, in Tele.com, October 2, 2000, page 82.
37. Source: The Forrester Research, August 1, 2000.
38. For information on the new opportunities for telephone companies,
     see for example: *Global Telephony*, September 2000, pages 54-60.
39. Matt Flanigan, president of the Telecommunications Industries
     Associations (TIA), says in the race to deliver voice, video, and
     data to customers there are three main competitors—cable, DSL,
     and wireless technologies. He predicts that wireless will win in the
     long term, but not in the short term. However, according to this
     view, cable and DSL are wired technologies, and wireless technolo-
     gies include fixed wireless, satellite, and digital broadcast trans-
     missions (in: *The Last Mile—Cover Story* by Jim Barthold,
     CableWorld, the on-line news magazine for video, voice, and data,
     August 13, 2000, www. cableworld.com).
40. Long-distance telephone operators are using MMDS as a response
     to interactive cable offerings and local incumbents' DSL services.
     One of their main advantages is that in the United States, cable
     companies are barred from buying MMDS licenses.
41. Source: *Communications Technology*, June 2000.
42. Source: Allied Business Intelligence, *Communications Technology*,
     June 2000, pages 227-229.
43. See: www.individual.com, August 14, 2000 ("WorldCom Focuses
     on Fixed-Wireless"), and www.infoworld.com, August 14, 2000
     ("WorldCom Files for Fixed Wireless Permission").

44. On the success of the WAP in Europe, see for example: "WAP, Europe's Wireless Dud?," in the *Washington Post*, September 15, 2000, page ED1. On common standards for second generation, see for example: David Lake, "Wireless Net: Not Yet," in *The Standard*, www.thestandard.com, August 24, 2000, and Carl Weinschenk, "Plenty of pain in AT&T's gain," in tele.com, July 31, 2000, page 18.
45. According to Gerald R. Faulhaber, FCC's chief economist, in: www.CNETNews.com, August 23, 2000 ("US Wireless Industry is Laggard, FCC Economist Says").
46. Source: , *Financial Times 3G—Country Information*. www.FT.com.
47. Simon Romero, "Cellular Phone Carriers Untangle a Wireless Web," in: *The New York Times*, July 10, 2000, Technology Section.
48. Source: The Pew Research Center For The People & The Press, www.people-press.com.
49. A memorandum issued on October 13, 2000 by President Clinton.
50. Source: Stephen Labaton, "President Orders Review of Wireless Spectrum," in: *The New York Times*, October 13, 2000, Technology section.
51. Source: The FCC, April 9, 2000, and *The New York Times*, March 13, 2000, Technology section.
52. According to FCC chief economist, by then 4G technology may be the way to go, and Europeans may be taking a risk by committing themselves to a specific platform.
53. Source: *The Washington Post*, August 1, 2000, page ED1.
54. Source: John Markoff, "Internet in Japan is Riding a Wireless Wave," in: *The New York Times*, New Economy section, August 14, 2000.
55. Source: WWW.FT.com (*Financial Times*), August 13, 2000.
56. See: Saul Hansell, "Wireless Web has Big Promise but a Few Kinks," in: *The New York Times*, July 10, 2000 Technology Section.
57. According to the ABC Group of London, August 2000.
58. Source: Brough Turner, "A Prolonged Transition", in: *Global Telephony*, September 2000, page 46.
59. Sources: Allied Business Intelligence, *Communications Technology*, June 2000, pages 227-229.
60. *Global Telephony*, June 2000, and www.wirelessreview.com.
61. According to a report by SRI Consulting's Business Intelligence Center: "High-Growth Mobile-Data Applications: 2000-2005," in: *RF Globalnet—Digital Marketplace for the Wireless, Microwave and RF Industry*, www.rfglobalnet.com, August 15, 2000.
62. Source: *Satellite Communications*, June 2000, page 26.
63. See for example:Alan Cowell, British Telecom Ordered to Open Network to Rivals, in: *The New York Times*, Technology section, July 7, 1999.

64. Forecasts may be somewhat confusing, however. Over 40 percent of U.S. households own a computer, but only about 5 percent of them use high-speed Internet services over broadband pipes. These services are provided by some competitive technologies, although the major providers are local telephone companies and cable TV systems—each serves about 1.5 million customers (*The Economist* lead article: "The Failure of New Media," August 21, 2000).

65. Source: tele.com, November 27, 2000, page 35.

66. The merger was subject to the approval of American and European regulatory authorities. American regulators are the Federal Trade Commission and the Federal Communication Commission, and the European Union antitrust committee includes a special merger task force. Decisions of all relevant authorities was seen as important to approve the deal, because a close degree of cooperation exists between anti-trust authorities in both continents. For more details, see: "EU Puts a Big 'if' on AOL Merger", in: the *Washington Post*, September 29, 2000, page A01.

67. Denise Caruso, "Convergence Raises Concerns About Access," in: *The New York Times*, Digital Commerce section, January 31, 2000.

68. *The Washington Post*, August 1, 2000, page ED1.

69. Source: Carl Weinschenk, "Plenty of Pain in AT&T Gain", in: tele.com, July 31, 2000, page 18.

70. *The Washington Post*, July 27, 2000, page ED1.

71. In a public hearing discussing the merger. Source: www.SkyReport.com, July 28, 2000.

72. Source: www.SkyReport.com, October 12, 2000.

73. Source: "FCC to open debate on Internet cable access," *Mediacentral*, September 13, 2000 .

74. Source: Alec Klein, "FCC Approves AOL-Time Warner Merger," in: *Washington Post*, January 11, 2001.

75. For additional information on future TV applications and formats, see for example: www.fsr/pub/info2000-uk/chalo.html and www.sinfonia.net.

76. Source: Jennifer Whalen, "Open Access a Reality," in: *Communications Technology*, April 2000, page 46.

77. Recommended Internet sites for current information on interactive developments:

     Sky Report, www.SkyReport.com
     CIT Publications, www.telecoms-data.com
     Netcenter, www.technews.netscape.com
     TVBEurope, www.tvbeurope.com
     Individual, www.individual.com
     Infoworld, www.infoworld.com

The Standard, Intelligence for the Internet Economy, www.the
  standard.com
Mediacentral, www.mediacentral.com
The Daily Deal, www.thedailydeal.com
CNET, www.news.cnet.com
CableWorld—The On-Line News magazine for Video, Voice
  and Data, www.cableworld.com
EETimes.com—The technology site for engineering and techni-
  cal management, www.eetimes.com
UpsideToday—The tech insider— www.upside.com

CHAPTER 5: THE SOCIAL ADOPTION OF INFORMATION TECHNOLOGY

1. The Starr Report (August 1998) was the first to be made available
    first and wholly through the Internet, making the concept of digital
    democracy a reality at the global level. The investigation was of the
    relationship between President Bill Clinton and Monica Lewinsky,
    which led to the impeachment inquiry by Congress. The entire
    process became a global affair with vast information provided
    globally through the Internet.
2. Although Federal regulations make no requirement for public
    access channels, some cities require local cable companies to make
    public access channels available and to transmit other local chan-
    nels. There are three main categories of public access channels:
    public, government and education, and leased access. For example,
    see: Grow, 1985; Papas, 1987; Saylor, 1986.
3. On the American Must Carry Rules, see, for example: Kaatz, 1979;
    Mosco, 1988; Rogers, 1986. On American policy with local and
    community television, see, for example, Head, 1985; Hollins, 1984;
    Negrine, 1985; Singleton, 1986.
4. On the European experience with community transmissions, see
    for example: Bertand, in Negrine, 1985; Dyson and Humphreys,
    1988; Hollins, 1984; Hutchison, 1984; Lewis, 1978; Muller, 1987;
    Negrine, 1985; Steinfield, in Dutton, Blumler and Kraemer, 1987.
5. For more information on the European pilot projects, see: Bertrand,
    in Negrine, 1985; Dyson, in Dyson and Humphreys, 1988; Gerin
    and Tavernost, in Dutton, Blumler and Kraemer, 1987; Negrine,
    1985; Smith, in Dutton, Blumler and Kraemer, 1987; Steinfield, in
    Dutton, Blumler and Kraemer, 1987; Vedel, in Dutton, Blumler and
    Kraemer, 1987.

6. This was evident in the 1970s and 1980s. Commercial operators in Europe initiated interactive services in the 1990s on a trail basis.

7. The experiments included the Rediffusion Inc. pilot project, which included 200 participants; the Sterling Communications television polling system, with terminals in four buildings; and the Telecable Corporation's provision of educational applications, which included audio and visual communication to some institutional users. Later in the 1970s the National Science Foundation sponsored interactive cable experiments in Reading, Pennsylvania; Spartanburg, South Carolina; and Rockford, Illinois.

8. For more information, see: Becker, in Dutton, Blumler and Kraemer, 1987; Laudon, in Dutton, Blumler and Kraemer, 1987; Rice, 1984; Willis 1994.

9. Statistics on the American multichannel market can be found in section 3.3.

10. Source: National Cable Television Association, August 2000, and *Communications Technology*, July 2000, page 70.

11. The report was released in September 2000 and reflects the state of British digital expansion at the start of the 21st century.

12. Datamonitor, "Digital TV Markets in Europe, 1999-2004," by Alexander Rainer, 2000.

13. The Forrester Research, August 1, 2000.

14. Source: www.mediacentral.com, August 22, 2000.

15. *The Washington Post*, July 27, 2000, page ED1.

16. This report was released prior to BskyB's aggressive campaign to switch into digital technology.

17. According to a report by the American Consumer Electronic Association, *The New York Times*, August 7, 2000, Technology Section.

18. According to a Federal Communications Commission report, mandated by Congress to examine the digital divide in the U.S., published August 3, 2000.

19. Source: August 22, 2000.

20. The Associated Press, December 9, 1999.

21. *The Washington Post*, February 3, 2000.

22. The Associated Press, December 9, 1999.

23. The State of the Union was transmitted live on all major channels on January 27, 2000.

24. *The New York Times*, February 10, 2000.

25. In a memorandum issued on October 13, 2000, by President Clinton to review spectrum for third generation wireless communications technology.

26. In a speech on April 27, 2000.

27. In an interview for *The Washington Post*, August 4, 2000, page ED3.
28. Stacy Lawrence, "Bridging the Worldwide Digital Divide", in: *The Standard*, www.thestandard.com, August 14, 2000.

CHAPTER 6: THE GLOBALIZATION OF MEDIA MARKETS

1. According to Hamelink (1994), global communication can be effective as long as local societies consider global consciousness as serving their interests. To reach this, key conditions are necessary. These include awareness that local events have global consequences, understanding of the political roots of global problems, sensitivity to the need of global solidarity, and acceptance and mutual recognition of sociocultural differences while sharing the perception that the needs of the global community are more important than those of the local community.

2. On the course of development of cable systems in these countries in the 1970s and in the 1980s, see Chapters 1 and 2. The role of European governments in cable policy is discussed in Chapters 2 and 5. Further information on the European experience with community transmissions can be found in: Cappe De Baillon, 1987; Dyson and Humphreys, 1988; Lewis, 1978; Negrine, 1985.

3. The requirement for Must Carry channels can be considered as part of the policy that dominated European cable's development until the 1980s, which is discussed in Chapters 1, 2, and 3. Further information on these rules can be found in: Compaine, 1985; Coustel, 1986; McQuail and Siune, 1986; Muller, 1987 Neuman and Wieland, 1986.

4. For further information on the European pilot projects, see for example: Dutton, Blumler and Kraemer, 1987.

5. Negrine and Papathanassopoulos (1990) argue that internationalization of television takes place when the same television signal becomes available simultaneously in at least three countries.

6. According to Forrester Research Inc., in: *The Washington Post*, April 5, 2000, page G01, "Net Firms Get Down to Business."

7. According to Gartner Group Inc., in: *The Washington Post*, April 5, 2000, page G01. "Net Firms Get Down to Business."

8. Source: The Standard, September 6, 2000. According to Forrester Research Inc., in: *The Washington Post*, April 5, 2000, page 601, "Net Firms Get Down to Business."—"Study: US Keeps E-Commerce Lead Over Europe".

9. Source: ActivMedia Research LLC's "Real Number Behind Net Profits 2000", in: *Global Telephony*, September 2000.

10. Source: Duncan Brown, John Davison and Ann Walsh, "Mobil E-commerce Market Strategies,"www.duum.com.
11. According to Chase H&Q, in tele.com, June 31, 2000, page 32.
12. The Forrester Research, July 9, 2000.
13. See for example: "A New Politics Born of Globalization", by Steve Pearlstein, *The Washington Post*, October 1, 2000, page H01, and "Dividing the nature of business," *The New York Times*, Technology Section, October 2, 2000.
14. *Cable and Satellite Communications International*, March 2000, page 12.
15. Source: Global Reach: International Online Marketing & Website Promotion, www.globalreach.com.
16. Source: World Broadcast Engineering, June 2000, page 33.
17. Further discussion on global media policy is discussed in: "Global Struggle for Communication, Media Literacy Online Project, College of Education, University of Oregon, http://interact.uoregon.edu/medialit/familiarticllefolder/global.html; The Global Media Giants, www.fair.or/extra/9711/gng.html; The Future of Television in Europe, www.standard.edu/-cjacoby/eutotv.html.
18. Source: The Global Media Giants, www.fair.org..

CHAPTER 7: LOCAL ASPECTS OF COMMERCIALIZATION

1. Within this process, there are distinct aspects of mediation, which can be perceived as parallel to the three categories of media commercialization. Mediation between public and commercial broadcasting is required to determine commercialization policy; mediation between international broadcasting and global communication is required to determine the quality of programming; and mediation between social and commercial forces is required to determine the social role of advertising.
2. These categories determine the impact of new technologies and new media policies on local media policies and systems. Each has a role in the new media scene, and the combination of the three categories is required to deal with new technological and cultural development.
3. There are obvious differences in the adoption of new technology among countries. But despite differences in social and cultural aspects, it was not until local requirements were lifted that new technology had the chance to develop commercially in Europe, following the American experience of deregulation of new media policies.

4. On the decline in the impact of public broadcasting, see for example: Etzioni-Halevi, 1987; McQuail, 1990; Murdock and Golding, 1989; Siune and McQuail, 1993.

5. The availability of satellite transmissions enforced policy changes and created a more-or-less common process of change in local markets. New technologies have become global, creating tremendous changes in technology and culture worldwide.

6. The main aspects of mediation can apply to the implementation of the model of media commercialization at the local level. While considering the global impact on local media systems within the new structure of media policy, future forecasts of the development of competitive markets support a general course of development of media policy. This structure includes a global model of policy-making with particular local aspects that influence the policy structure in each country—which should continue to add to the development of media and telecommunications policies, markets, and services.

7. On the new public television in Europe, see for example: Rolf Brandarud, Digital TV and Public Service in the Nordic Countries—www.nrk.no/interaktiv/artikler/dtv-pbs.html.

8. On the commercialization of public television in the United States, see for example:
    — "New Study: Public TV More Corporate, Less Public Than Ever", News release by FAIR Fairness & Accuracy in Reporting, 130 W. 25th Street, New York, NY 10001, www.fair.org/press-releases/phs.
    — "The Heritage Foundation: After Privatization: Public Television in the Cultural Marketplace," www.heritage.org.
    — "The Cost of Survival" Political Discourse and the New PBS," by William Hoynes, www.fair.org/reports.pub-study-1999.html and www.thridworldtraveler.

9. Source: "The BBC Beyond 2000," published by the British Broadcasting Corporation Broadcasting House, London, 1998.

10. In the United States, contrary to Europe, PBS is controlled at the local level and not nationally.

11. In the United States, too, local franchising authorities may require cable operators to set aside a portion of their channels for public, educational, and governmental access programming. Systems with 36 or more activated channels must designate a portion of their channel capacity for commercial leased access by unaffiliated third parties. The rates, terms, and conditions for leased access channels are set according to FCC regulations.
    On cable programming and public affairs, see for example:

— The Future of Cable: Cable's Public Affairs Efforts in Programming and Technology, published by FIOC, Public Affairs by the Cable TV Industry.
— "How is the Cable Television Industry Regulated ?" www.ciilvermore.ca.us/cfr/CFR-regulations.btm#fedregs.
12. Source: TVB Europe, February 2000, page 8.
13. Differences between American and other markets are evident, although the development of media policy is discussed in this book as part of a global process that all countries are heading toward.
14. Digital television, which brings the global information superhighway to homes, combines broadcasting and interactivity. See for example: "Television's Internet Future: Pressure on Broadcasters to Exploit Interactive TV," TVBEurope, February 1999, pages 10-12.
15. In a digital world competition for quality programming will become even more important as a way to attract subscribers.
16. Different countries have different rules. See for example: Dutton, Blumler and Kraemer, 1987; and Ostergaard and Kleinsteuber, 1994.
17. For additional information about subscription fees and advertising, see for example: "European Broadcast Media Executive Summary," www.bestpractice.baynet.com, and "The Freedom Forum," www.freedomforum.org.
18. Competition started with the deregulation of American media and telecommunications markets and is intensifying globally. The result of massive deregulation of local and long-distance telephone services as well as cable, video, and broadcast services in the Telecommunications Act of 1996 are dramatic, according to fomer FCC Chairman William Kennard. The major changes are the rise of the Internet and wireless services and digital television. The 1999 satellite law cleared the way for direct-to-home satellite TV broadcasters to beam local programming to more than 50 million households in the 20 top TV markets. The law gave satellite services a competitive opportunity equal to cable TV operators in the supply of multichannel video programming and boosted the interactive TV market. The 1997 European Commission Green Paper on the Regulatory Implications of Convergence is considered a platform for defining the policy response to the evolving communications and media environment. Following the liberalization of telecoms in 1998, media policy in Europe aims to bring together legislation on the provision of infrastructure, services, content, and on conditions for access to that content via all services—television, computer, and telephone.

19. Following the growing competition for the supply of television programming and data services, it can be expected that the distinction between television receivers and personal computers will disappear as the Internet gradually becomes a viable home entertainment medium.

20. The assumption that can be made from the commercialization and globalization trends that dominate all countries is that the development of each media system has to be examined differently. Adoption of commercialization means that the policy examined has adopted the terms and conditions of global media policy. Any partial adoption of commercialization means that the media policy examined has not been fully integrated into the level of global policy, and influential local aspects are still dominating the development course of the particular system.

References

Baker, E., (2002). *Media, Markets, and Democracy*. Cambridge: Cambridge University Press.

Balnaves, M., Donald, J., and Donald, S.H. (2001). *The Penguin Atlas of Media and Information*. New York: Penguin Putnam.

Baughman, J.L. (1992). *The Republic of Mass Culture*. Baltimore, Maryland: Johns Hopkins University Press.

Bauntlett, D., and Hill, A. (1999). *TV Living*. London and New York: Routledge.

Bennet, C.J. (1988). Different Processes, One Result: The Convergence of Data Production Policy in Europe and the United States. *Governance: An International Journal of Policy and Administration*, Vol. 4.

Berman, D. R. (1986). The End of Government Regulation of the Rates Cable Television Services Charge Their Subscribers. *Cardozo Arts & Entertainment Law Journal*, Vol. 5, Part 1.

Bernet, M. Y. (1986). Quincy Cable and its Effects on the Access Provisions of the Cable Act. *Notre Dame Law Journal*.

Black, J. and Whitney, F. (1983). *Mass Communication*. Dubuque, Iowa: Wm. C. Brown Company Publications.

Bittner, R. J. (1983). *Mass Communication*. Englewood Cliffs, New Jersey: Prentice-Hall.

Brants, K., and Siune, K. (1994). *Public Broadcasting in a State of Flux*. In K. Siune and W. Truetzschler (Eds.), *Dynamics of Media Politics*. Euromedia Research Group, Chapter 7.

Cappe De Baillon, J. (1987). The Legal Framework of French Television. *Journal of Law and Practice* (January).

Cimatoribus, M., De Tommaso, A., and Neri, P. (1998). Impacts of the 1996 Telecommunications Act on U.S. Model of Telecommunications Policy. *Telecommunications Policy*, Vol. 22, No. 6, pages 493-517.

Collins, R., Garnham, N., and Locksley, G. (1988). *The Economics of Television*. London: Sage.

Collins, R. (1990). *Satellite Television in Western Europe*. Montouge, France: John Libbey.

Compaine, M. B. (1985). New Competition and New Media. *Rundfunk and Fernsehen*, Vol. 33.

Corn-Revere, R. (1993). Economics of Media Regulation. In A. Alexander, J. Owers, and R. Carveth (Eds.), *Media Economics, Theory and Practice*. Hillsdale, New Jersey: Lawrence Erlbaum Associates.

Coustel, J.P. (1986). Telecommunications in France: The Regulated Monopoly and the Challenge of Competition. *Telecommunications Policy* (September).

Cuilenburg, J., and Slaa, P. (1993). From Media Policy Towards a National Communications Policy: Broadening the Scope. *European Journal of Communications*, Vol. 8.

Curran, J., and Part, M. Y-J. (2000). *De-Westernizing Media Studies*. London: Sage.

Danczak, J. (1989). *Cable and Satellite: The Potential for the Information Market*. Electronic Publishing Services, British Library Research Paper 59.

Davis. L.J. (1988). *The Billionaire Shall Game: How Cable Baron John Malone and Assorted Corporate Titans Invented a Future Nobody Wanted*. New York: Doubleday.

Dizard, W. (1994). *Old Media New Media*. New York: Longman.

Downing, J. (1996). *International Media Theory*. London: Sage.

Doyle, G. (2002). *Media Ownership*. London: Sage.

Dunham, Lowdermilk and Broderick (1958). *Television in Education*. Washington DC: U.S. Department of Health, Education and Welfare.

Dutton, H.W., Blumler, G.J., and Kraemer, K. (Eds.) (1987). *Wired Cities: Shaping the Future of Communications*. London: Cassell.

Dutton, H.W., and Vedel, T. (1992). The Dynamics of Cable Television in the United States, Britain and France. In J. Blumler, (Ed.), *Comparatively Speaking*. London: Sage.

Dyer, G. (1989). *Advertising as Communication*. London and New York: Routledge.

Dyson, K., and Humphreys, P. (1988). *Broadcasting and New Media Policies in Western Europe*. London and New York: Routledge.

Dyson, K., and Humphreys, P. (1989). Deregulating Broadcasting: The West European Experience. *European Journal of Political Research*, Vol. 17.

Dyson, K., and Humphreys, P. (1991). *The Political Economy of Communications*. London: Routledge.

Etzioni-Halevi, E. (1987). *National Broadcasting Under Siege*. London: The Macmillan Press.

Featherstone, M. (1995). *Global Culture*. London: Sage.

Ferguson, M. (1986). *New Communication Technologies and the Public Interest*. Beverly Hills, California: Sage.

Fidde, P.J., and Hslung, T.C. (1987). Pay Television: A Historical Review of the Siphoning Issue. *Communications and the Law* (April).

Fletcher, J. (1993). The Syndication Marketplace. In A. Alexander, j. Owers and R. Carveth (Eds.). *Media Economics*. Hillsdale, New Jersey: Lawrence Erlbaum Associates.

Fowles, J. (1996). *Advertising and Popular Culture*. London: Sage.

Fortner, S. R. (1993). *International Communication*. Belmont, California: Wadsworth.

Frank and Greenberg (1980). *The Publics of Television*. Beverly Hills, California: Sage.

Frederich, H.H. (1993). *Global and International Relations*. Belmont, California: Wadsworth Publishing Company.

Friedland, L.H. (1996). Electronic Democracy and the New Citizenship. *Media, Culture & Society*, Vol. 10, No. 2 (April).

Gibson, H. G. (1977). *Public Broadcasting*. New York: Praeger.

Gripsrud, J., (1999). *Television and Common Knowledge*. London and New York: Routledge.

Gordon, N. G. (1965). *Educational Television*. New York: The Center for Applied Research in Education.

Greene, A.K. (1986). Quincy Cable Television Inc. v. Federal Communication Commission: Should the FCC Review Cable Television's Must Carry Requirements? *Loyola of Los Angeles Law Review* (June).

Grow, J.C. (1985). Cable Television: Local Government Regulation in Perspective. *Pace Law Review* (Fall).

Gudykunst, W.B., and Mody, B. (2002). *Handbook of Intercultural Communication*. London: Sage.

Gunther, R. (2000). *Democracy and the Media*. Cambridge: Cambridge University Press.

Gurevitch, M. (1991). The Globalization of Electronic Journalism. In J. Curran and M. Gurevitch (Eds.), *Mass Media and Society*. London, New York, Melbourne, Auckland: Edward Arnold.

Hamelink, C.J. (1993) Globalism and National Sovereignty. In K. Nordenstreng and H. Schiller (Eds.), *Beyond National Sovereignty: International Communication in the 1990's*. Norwood, New Jersey: Ablex.

Hamelink, C.J. (1994). *The Politics of World Communication*. London: Sage.

Head, W. S. (1985). *World Broadcasting Systems*. Belmont, California: Wadsworth.

Healy, B. R. (1986). Preferred Communications Inc. v. City of Los Angeles: Impact of the First Amendment on Access Rights of Cable Television Companies. *Catholic University Law Review* (Spring).

Herman, E.S. (1993). The Externalities Effects of Commercial and Public Broadcasting. In K. Nordenstreng and H. Schiller (Eds.), *Beyond National Sovereignty: International Communication in the 1990's*. Norwood, New Jersey: Ablex.

Herman, S. E., and McChesney, W. R. (1997). *The Global Media*. London and Washington: Cassell.

Hollins, T. (1984). *Beyond Broadcasting: Into the Cable Age*. London: BFI Publishing.

Holzhias, D. T. (1986). Access to Cable: Natural Monopoly and the First Amendment. *Columbia Law Review* (December).

Howard, H. H., and Carroll, L. S. (1993). Economics of the Cable Industry. In A. Alexander, J. Owers, and R. Carveth (Eds.), *Media Economics: Theory and Practice*. Hillsdale, New Jersey: Lawrence Erlbaum Associates.

Hutchinson, R. (1984). *Cable DBS and the Arts*. London: Policy Studies Institute.

Jacobs, R.M. (2000). *Race, Media and Civil Society*. Cambridge: Cambridge University Press.

Jhally, S. (1990). *The Codes of Advertising*. London and New York: Routledge,

Kaatz, B. R. (1982). *Cable: An Advertiser's Guide to the New Electronic Media*. Chicago, Illinois: Crain Books.

Keren, M. (Ed.) (1996). The Concentration of Media Ownership and Freedom of the Press. Proceedings of an International Conference Entitled "Media Ownership, Freedom of the Press and the Future of Democracy," held at Tel Aviv University, 29-31 October 1995, 1996 by Ramot Publishing, Tel Aviv.

Kleinsteuber, H. J. (1994). The Global Village Stays Local. In K. Siune and W. Truetzschler (Eds.), *Dynamics of Media Politics*. Euromedia Research Group, Chapter 10.

Krasnow, E., Longley, L., and Terry, H. (1994). The Politics of Broadcast Regulation. In D. Graber (Ed.), *Media Power in Politics*. Washington, DC: Congressional Quarterly..

Krug, D. (1985). Cable Television Franchise Fees for General Revenues: The 1984 Cable Act, Wisconsin Law and the First Amendment. *Wisconsin Law Review*.

Leiss, W., Kline, S., and Jhally, S. (1990). *Social Communication in Advertising*. Nelson Canada.

Levinson, P. (1999). *Digital Mcluhan*. London: Routledge.

Lewis, M. P. (1978). *Community Television and Cable in Britain*. London: British Film Institute.

Litman, R. B. (1993). The Changing Role of the Television Network. In A. Alexander, J. Owers, and R. Carveth (Eds.), *Media Economics: Theory and Practice*. Hillsdale, New Jersey: Lawrence Erlbaum Associates.

Lloyd, F. W., and Kerry, C. F. (1987). Franchise Fees Enforcement Under the Cable Act: An FCC Responsibility. *Federal Communication Law Review* (May).

MacDonald, B. (1988). *Broadcasting in the United Kingdom, a Guide to Information Sources*. London and New York: Manswell Publishing.

Marcus, N. (1986). *Broadcasting and Cable Management*. Englewood Cliffs, New Jersey: Prentice-Hall.

McAllister, M. P. (1996). *The Commercialization of American Culture*. London: Sage.

McAuliffe, E. R. (1987). *Advertising, Competition and Public Policy*. Lexington, Massachusetts: D.C. Heath and Company.

McGreger, M.F. (1987). Will the Real Cable TV Industry Please Stand Up? The Divergent Regulatory Treatment of the Cable TV Industry Prior to the Cable Communication Policy Act of 1984. *Communication/Entertainment* (Fall).

McQuail, D. (1990). *Mass Communication Theory: An Introduction* (Second Edition). London: Sage.

McQuail, D. (1992). *Media Performance*. London: Sage.

McQuail, D. (1995). Western European Media: The Mixed Model Under Threat. In J. Downing, A. Mohammadi, and A. Sreberny-Mohammadi (Eds.), *Questioning the Media*. London: Sage.

McQuail, D., de Mateo, R., and Tapper, H. (1993). A Framework for Analysis of Media Change in Europe in the 1990's. In K. Siune and W. Truetzschler (Eds.), *Dynamics of Media Politics*. The Euromedia Research Group.

McQuail, D., and Siune, K. (1986). *New Media Politics: Comparative Perspectives in Western Europe.* London: Sage.

McQuail, D., and Siune, K. (1998). Euromedia Research Group.

Medge, T. (1989). *Beyond the BBC: Broadcasting and the Public in the 1980's.* London: The MacMillan Press.

Melody, H. W. (1990). Communication Policy in the Global Information Economy: Whither the Public Interest. In M. Ferguson (Ed.), *Public Communication—The New Imperatives.* London: Sage.

Meyrowitz, J. (1995). Mediating Communication. In J. Downing, A. Mohammadi and A. Sreberny-Mohammadi (Eds.), *Questioning the Media.* London: Sage.

Mohammadi, A. (1997). *International Communication and Globalization.* London: Sage.

Mosco, V. (1979). *Broadcasting in the United States.* Norwood, New Jersey: Ablex.

Mosco, V. (1988). Toward a Theory of the State and Telecommunications Policy. *Journal of Communication*, Vol. 38.

Mosco, V. (1990). The Mythology of Telecommunications Deregulation. *Journal of Communication*, Vol. 40.

Mowlana, H. (1996). *Global Communications in Transition.* London: Sage.

Mowlana, H. (1997). *Global Information and World Communication.* London: Sage.

Muller, J. (1987). Cable Policy in Europe. *Telecommunications Policy* (September).

Murdock, G. (1990). Redrawing the Map of the Communications Industries: Concentration and Ownership in the Era of Privatization. In M. Ferguson (Ed.), *Public Communication: The New Imperatives.* London: Sage.

Murdock, G., and Golding, P. (1989). The Information Poverty and Political Inequality: Citizenship in the Age of Privatized Communications. *Journal of Communication*, Vol. 39.

Murphy, B. (1983). *The World Wired Up: Understanding the New Communications Puzzle.* London: Cmedia Publishing Group.

Negrine, M. R. (Ed.). (1985). *Cable Television and the Future of Broadcasting.* London: Croom Helm.

Negrine, M. R. (Ed.). (1988). *Satellite Broadcasting: The Politics and Implications of the New Media.* London and New York: Routledge.

Negrine, M. R. (1989). *Politics and Mass Media in Britain.* London and New York: Routledge.

Negrine, M. R., and Papathanassopoulos, S. (1990). *The Internationalisation of Television.* London: Pinter Publications.

Nueman, B., and Wieland, B. (1986). Competitive and Social Objectives: The Case of the German Telecommunications. *Telecommunications Policy* (June).

O'Brien, C. (1979). In B. Logan and K. Moody, K. (Eds.), *Television Awareness Training*. New York: The Media Action Research Center.

Ostergaard, B. S. (Ed.). (1992). *The Media in Western Europe*. London: The Euromedia Research Group, Sage.

Ostergaard, B.S., and Kleinsteuber, H.S. (1994). The Technology Factor. In K. Siune and W. Truetzschler (Eds.), *Dynamics of Media Politics*. Euromedia Research Group, Chapter 5.

Papas, N.J. (1987). In Defense of Monopoly Cable TV Franchising. *Rutgers Computer and Technology Law Journal*.

Parks, L., and Kumor, S. (Eds.). (2003). *Planet TV—A Global Television Reader*. London and New York: New York University Press.

Pember, R. R. (1983). *Mass Media in America*. Chicago, Illinois: Science Research Association.

Perth, A. (1999). *Rethinking the Media Audience*. London: Sage.

Peterson and Bens (1994). Models of Local Media Development. In K. Siune and W. Truetzschler (Eds.), *Dynamics of Media Politics*. Euromedia Research Group, Chapter 11.

Poster, M. (1995). *The Second Media Age*. New York: Polity Press.

Rice, E. D. (1984). *The New Media*. Beverly Hills, California: Sage.

Rogers, M. E. (1986). *Communication Technology—The New Media in Society*. New York: The Free Press.

Ross, S.K., and Brick, B.L. (1987)). The Cable Act of 1984—How Did We Get There and Where Are We Going? *Federal Communications Law Journal* (May).

Salvaggio, L. J. (1983). *Telecommunications*. New York and London: Longman.

Sandman, P.M., Rubin, D.M., and Sachsman, D.B. (1982). *Media*. Englewood Cliffs, New Jersey: Prentice-Hill.

Saylor, J. D. (1986). Municipal Rip-off: The Unconstitutionality of Cable Television Franchise Fees and Access Support Payments. *Catholic University Law Review* (Spring).

Scannell, P. (1995). For a Phenomenology of Radio and Television. *Journal of Communication*, Vol. 45.

Schneider, C., Miles, T. and Vedel, T. (1991). The Dynamics of Videotext Development in Britain, France and Germany: A Cross-national Comparison. *European Journal of Communication*, Vol. 6.

Seymour-Ure, C. (1987). Media Policy in Britain: Now You See It, Now You Don't. *European Journal of Communication*, Vol. 2.

Singleton, A. L. (1986). *Telecommunication in the Information Age*. Cambridge, Massachusetts: Balinger.

Siune, K., and McQuail, D. (1993). Wake Up, Europe!. In K. Siune and W. Truetzschler (Eds.), *Dynamics of Media Politics*. Euromedia Research Group.

Siune, K., and Truetzschler, W. (Eds.). *Dynamics of Media Politics.* Euromedia Research Group,

Sorlin, P. (1994). *Mass Media.* London and New York: Routledge.

Sterling, C.H., and Haight, T.R. (1978). *The Mass Media—Aspen Institute Guide to Communication Industry Trends.* Westport, Connecticut: Praeger.

Stevenson, N. (2002). *Understanding Media Culture.* London: Sage.

Sreberny-Mohammadi, A., Winseck, D., McKenna, J., and Boyd-Barrett, O. (Eds.). (1997). *Media in a Global Context.* London: Edward Arnold.

Summers, B. H., Summers, E. R., and Pennybacker, H. J. (1978). *Broadcasting and the Public.* Belmont, California: Wadworth.

Tunstall, J., and Palmer, M. (1991). *Media Moguls.* New York: Routledge.

Tydeman, J., and Kelm, E.J. (1986). *New Media in Europe.* London: McGraw-Hill.

Turow, J. (1992). *Media Systems in Society.* New York & London: Longman.

Vedel, T., and Dutton, H. W. (1990). New Media Politics: Shaping Cable Television Policy in France. *Media, Culture & Society*, Vol. 12.

Vestergaard, T., and Schroder, K. (1992). *The Language of Advertising.* Cambridge, Massachusetts: Blackwell.

Volker, I. (1999). *News in the Global Sphere.* Luton, UK: University of Luton Press.

Wadlow, R.C. and Wellstien, L.M. (1986). The Changing Regulatory Terrain of Cable TV. *Catholic University Law Review* (Spring).

Wells, W., Burnett, J., and Moriarty, S. (1989). *Advertising—Principles and Practice.* Englewood Cliffs, New Jersey: Prentice-Hall.

Willis, J. (1994). *The Age of Multimedia and Turbonews.* Westport, Connecticut: Praeger.

Winston, B. (1998). *Media Technology and Society.* London and New York: Routledge.

Yspilanti, D., and Xavier, P. (1988). Towards Next Generation Regulation. *Telecommunications Policy*, Vol. 222.

Author Index

Subject Index

The following terms appear throughout the text and have not been specified in this section: cable, satellite, digital terrestrial television, new media, United States, Europe, Britain, France and Germany.

Printed in the United States
42269LVS00003B/133-141

9 781572 735194